FROM RAQQA

JORDAN RITTER CONN

BALLANTINE BOOKS

NEW YORK

Published in the United States by Ballantine Books, an imprint of Random House, a division of Penguin Random House LLC, New York.

BALLANTINE and the HOUSE colophon are registered trademarks of Penguin Random House LLC.

See My Raqqa is an online project to reintroduce the city of Raqqa in Syria to the world and preserve the cultural heritage of the city after it was destroyed during the battle to defeat the so-called Islamic State (ISIS) in 2017. The online project was launched in 2017 to include the voices of the residents of Raqqa in the future of the city, and it ultimately aims to support the revival of daily life and cultural events there. **See My Raqqa** gathers hundreds of pictures from different social media platforms of Raqqa before its destruction, in collaboration with local and foreign photographers.

seemyraqqa.com • Facebook.com/SeeMyRaqqa • Instagram.com/seemyraqqa

Hardback ISBN 978-1-984-81718-1
Ebook ISBN 978-0-525-48271-0

Printed in Canada on acid-free paper

randomhousebooks.com

9 8 7 6 5 4 3 2 1

First Edition

Book design by Jen Valero

AUTHOR'S NOTE

I first met Riyad Alkasem one afternoon in January 2016, when I pulled up to a restaurant in a Tennessee strip mall, tucked down the street from gun shops and bait shops, near stores bearing the word "Dixie" and trucks adorned with Confederate flags. Above the restaurant, there stood a sign that said CAFÉ RAKKA. This, I'd been told, was where I'd find the best Arabic translator in Middle Tennessee.

For my then job at ESPN, I'd recently returned from one trip to the Syria-Turkey border, and I was gearing up for another. I was reporting on a soccer team aligned with the Syrian rebel forces, a team that hoped to harness the power of sport for the purpose of revolution. Before I returned to the border for my second trip, I needed someone near my home in Nashville to help me place phone calls to an Arabic-speaking source. A friend at the Islamic Center pointed me toward Riyad.

I walked inside and introduced myself. His eyes were dark, his hair curly. He spoke with the ease of a man who had settled into his place in the world and the accent of someone who had journeyed a long way to find that place. Together, we called my source, and I watched Riyad fight back tears as the three of us spoke about the war tearing apart his homeland, about the men and women who believed they were fighting to build a better Syria than the one Riyad had years earlier left behind.

Afterward, he took me to a table. We sat. He summoned two cups of pomegranate tea and mountainous plates of shawarma and baba ghanoush. Finally I asked the only question on my mind: What was a restaurant named after Raqqa, Syria—a city then known as the home of the world's deadliest terrorist organization—doing here in Tennessee?

His answer unspooled over many hours that day and for several years afterward. Much of it centered on his relationship with his younger brother Bashar. Both of them, Riyad explained, loved their hometown, Raqqa. But Riyad had chosen to leave it decades ago, pulled by the promise of America. Now Bashar was being forced to do the same, pushed by the brutalities of terror and war.

I returned to the Syria-Turkey border the next month to continue reporting on the soccer players affected by their country's war, but even there, I couldn't get Riyad and Bashar's story out of my mind. Together, they represented two faces of immigration—those who leave home for a brighter future and those who leave because their original home has become unrecognizable.

This book is their story. It is nonfiction. It is based primarily on their own accounts of their lives, though dates, times, locations, and additional facts have been confirmed with other sources. The dialogue is reconstructed based on the memories of Riyad, Bashar, and others who appear in the book. Some names have been changed to protect safety and privacy. Details of some characters' lives—for example, the Alkasems' mother and sister—have been omitted for the same purposes.

This is by no means a full account of the Syrian civil war, the rise of the Islamic State, or the story of immigration in America. It is simply a telling of the story that grabbed me so fiercely that afternoon in that restaurant, a story about family bonds that endure through war and terror, about a search for home that stretches across decades and oceans.

This is the story of Riyad and Bashar.

THE ROAD FROM RAQQA

PROLOGUE

They used to tell a story in the desert about an eighteenth-century warrior named Ibrahim, who led an Arab army across the Levant—known long before as Mesopotamia—fighting on horseback and on camel for the Ottoman Empire. Ibrahim was loyal to the Ottomans and ruthless to their enemies, and so the empire's leaders rewarded him with a gift. It wasn't much, just a swath of land in the desert, tucked inside the elbow of the Euphrates River, some of the land bare and desolate, some of it green and alive.

Only Ibrahim didn't care much for land. He was a warrior, not a settler. So he left the land untouched and continued to roam the Levant and to wage battle, uninterested in anyplace where he could not find a fight. Ibrahim had a son named Issa and a grandson named Hamed, also nomadic warriors, and Hamed had a son named Taha. When they would tell this story centuries later, the boys and girls of the desert would speculate that Taha did not like to fight like his father, grandfather, and great-grandfather, because if he liked to fight, then he would have continued roaming in search of violence, but instead he came to the land that had now been passed down to him, and he wondered if perhaps he should stay there, if perhaps he should build a life.

Taha found a spot that he liked. Dangerous tribes inhabited the land's western and eastern edges, but here in the center was a river and an ancient wall, long ago abandoned, and the river and wall together formed something of a cocoon, and Taha decided that here he would be safe. Here he would stay.

He put up a tent and decided to make coffee. He took a stone rod and used it like a mortar and pestle to smash the beans. When they were fully ground, he mixed them with water he boiled on a fire. He waited.

A breeze wafted in from the Euphrates, carrying the smell of coffee across the desert to small and scattered tribes. They took the smell of the coffee as an invitation. One by one, members of each tribe came to Taha and joined him. Together, they sipped.

Taha asked them to stay. Settle here, he said, and let's work together, share our resources to build a community. To convince them, he offered pieces of his land. Some said yes, and more tribes came. As the years passed, Taha gave away more pieces of his land until there were twelve subtribes in total, and together they decided that the sliver of land just north of their settlement would be the community land, to be divided among every male descendant of every original founder for as long as their city stood.

A *city*. Yes. That's what it was now, with homes and markets and mosques and a school. They called it Raqqa. It would stand for centuries, here on this plot of land passed down from Ibrahim to Issa to Hamed to Taha, and its people would remain close-knit, cloistered as they were and uninterested in the outside world. Yet they would always greet visitors with extravagant welcome, providing warm beds and hearty meals and fresh coffee, just as Taha had once done.

TAHA HAD A SON named Jurf, and Jurf had a son named Hammoud, who had a son named Kasem, who had a son named Muhammad, who had a son named Abdul-Rahman, who had several sons, the oldest two of whom he named Riyad and Bashar. And Riyad and Bashar grew up learning the stories of their ancestors and of their city, and they saw themselves as carrying on the traditions passed down from Taha on the land passed down from Ibrahim.

And then one day new warriors arrived, and the people of the city looked overhead to see them, in airplanes sent by leaders in Damascus or Moscow or Washington, D.C. And those warriors dropped bombs, and those bombs pounded the city until it was barely anything more than what Taha had found on his journey through the Levant so many years ago. And Riyad and Bashar wondered what makes a city when its people have fled or died, what makes a home when a house has become rubble, what makes a family when brothers and sisters are sent to scatter across the world.

CHAPTER

1

The war zone spread out beneath him, a sheet of darkness pocked with light. Riyad Alkasem was tired. His black hair was matted, the curls greasy and flat. He'd been in transit for nearly twenty-four hours, unable to sleep for several days. Now he stared out the window, feeling the plane make its final descent, and he took comfort from the fact that up here all appeared calm. Just below the plane lay Gaziantep, Turkey, a city once known for its baklava, now known as the final stop on the way into Syria's civil war. It was March 2013. Just south of Gaziantep there stretched a border, about five hundred miles long, running from the Mediterranean Sea and snaking across the Tigris and the Euphrates, following stretches of the Baghdad Railway and the Orontes River. On one side, Turkey. On the other, Syria. And somewhere south of that border, where the war had now been raging for two years, was Riyad's destination.

Raqqa. Home, or something like it.

He didn't know why he was going, not really. Sure, he had an answer when people asked. His family was in danger. They needed his help. It sounded simple when phrased in those terms, as if the pull across continents were no more than obligation, a dutiful son and brother looking out for his own. There was something else, though, some tug he'd felt ever since the war began. Sometimes he would lie awake in his quiet home in his quiet Tennessee town, next to his southern-belle wife and just rooms away from his two American sons, and he would wonder if it had been worth it to remain here, if America's promise had delivered all he had hoped that it would. He couldn't imagine life without his wife or his boys, but sometimes he imagined them all living out a different story, back in the city he still called "my soul."

For nearly a month, he'd heard that rebels were closing in on Raqqa. He called his brother Bashar multiple times each week. Every day at the restaurant Riyad owned in Tennessee, he took breaks from running the kitchen to scroll through Facebook, reading news from friends and family and from anonymous pages run by citizen-journalists. For Bashar and the rest of the Alkasems, the war lived at their doorstep. It lived in their streets and in their schools, in their children's voices and their own bodies. Yet Riyad's war raged in his mind and in his pocket, haunting him but eluding his grasp. It was a fight he experienced, mostly, by staring at his phone.

But not anymore. Because eventually Bashar quit answering. And eventually the Facebook updates stopped. And one day Riyad found a video online from the main square in the center of the city, just footsteps from his family home. On his screen, he saw the familiar palm trees, the same vast sky, the drab government buildings that had been the backdrop to so much of his childhood. And there in the middle, he saw the same statue that he'd walked by so many times in his life, the one of former president Hafez al-Assad, wearing a suit and a flat smile. As a teenager, Riyad had hated that statue, hated that *man*. Now he hated the former president's son and successor, Bashar al-Assad, the architect of Syria's war. So he held a mix of awe and terror as he stared at the video on his phone and watched thousands of revolutionaries filling the square, arms aloft and screaming. A few took axes to the statue's foundation. They wore blue jeans and windbreakers, hair gel and gaping smiles. Some carried machine guns. All watched as Assad's stone body came unmoored, as he toppled, dumbly, straight forward to the ground. They shouted *Allahu Akbar* ("God is great") and *Suriyah! Hurriye!* ("Syria! Free!"). Some removed their shoes and used them to slap Assad's body. Others swung axes and chipped away at his head. A few celebrated by firing bullets into the sky.

This was historic. For the first time since the Assad regime took power in 1971, it no longer ruled Raqqa. Rebels had taken the city. Riyad's home had wrested free of the dictatorship he'd so long despised. But as he watched, sitting awake one night six thousand miles away, he found himself unable to revel in the regime's failures, incapable of connecting to the tears of ecstasy he saw from men on the screen who looked like younger versions of himself.

He thought only of his family, of the order that had now been lost and the violence that would surely grow. Raqqa was free, yes, but now it was more dangerous than ever. Riyad called. Still no answer. He checked Facebook. Still no updates. His portals into the life of his city had been closed. With the government ousted, Raqqa had gone dark.

His wife, Linda, watched him plodding through the rhythms of daily life. At home and at the restaurant, he seemed vacant, a husk. Gone was the energy of the man who'd built a life from nothing here in America. His eyes had gone red, his face pale. Often in conversation, his gaze drifted away. This was still the man she'd married, yes, but right now, she knew he belonged somewhere else.

"Go," she said.

Three days later, Riyad boarded a plane.

THE FLIGHT FROM ISTANBUL carried diplomats and journalists, politicians and spies. Even here, ten thousand feet in the sky, the air crackled with a strange and hypnotic energy. Every passenger seemed stitched together by shared purpose. Some would stop in Gaziantep, while others would cross the border and head for their homes, and still others would make their way to the battlefield. Each had a destination with its own proximity to the awaiting violence. But for now, they traveled as one, all headed toward the fight.

Riyad didn't know what he'd find when he arrived. His family didn't know he was coming. His phone calls had never gone through, and he hadn't been able to find a way to deliver a message, so now he was on his way to his childhood home, completely unannounced. He carried some sense that he could help, but the particulars remained unclear. Maybe he'd pay to smuggle his family out of Raqqa. Maybe he'd tend to any of them who had been wounded or, God forbid, make funeral arrangements if someone was killed. Or maybe, if they were in danger, he would fight. He was a Syrian, after all. In military camps as a kid, he'd learned his way around weapons.

The plane approached the runway. Sometime before it touched down, Riyad wondered if he should buy himself a gun.

LATER THAT NIGHT, he settled into a motel room in the town of Karkamış, yards away from the border, surrounded by police and their dogs. Karkamış was a nothing town, a barely there place, home to three thousand residents and a refugee tent camp, little more than a way station on the path to the war. On a hard mattress under a thick blanket, he slept.

The flags stood high the next morning, flapping at each other across an imaginary line. Just above Riyad, there was Turkey's white star and crescent, bathed in red. Yards away, on the Syrian side, he saw the green and black flag of Syria's rebels. Elsewhere he knew he'd find the flags of Kurdish nationalists and of hard-line Islamist brigades, along with the one he'd grown up under, that of the Assad regime. All these flags marked their own swaths of land, all across his country. Syria was a puzzle, its pieces melting into one another all the time.

The sky was clear, the air cool. The land around Riyad was bathed in morning sunlight, giving the brown dirt a reddish tint. He walked toward the border, passed by Peugeots spewing exhaust and carrying foodstuffs. Near the gate, he saw a group of children, mostly boys. They were aged twelve or maybe fourteen, and they huddled together smoking cigarettes and laughing, teasing one another in Arabic. Syrians, he realized. Refugees. Riyad approached. He said hello, and the boys said nothing. He asked how they were, and they said nothing still. They wore T-shirts and jeans, flip-flops and vacant stares. They carried homemade shanks crafted from toothbrushes and blades and twine.

He asked about their lives in the camp, and they shrugged. He asked if they went to school, and they laughed. One boy mentioned that sometimes a teacher came to give them lessons, but they usually chose not to attend. "We're going to be men soon," he said. "We don't need school."

The boys felt familiar and foreign all at once. Their accents sounded much like his own. They were just a few years younger than his own sons, Kasem and Sammy, both in school back home in Tennessee. Kasem was eighteen, about to head off to college at East Tennessee State. Sammy was sixteen, a sophomore at the local Catholic school, already learning to work in the kitchen like his dad. They carried Syrian blood but lived American lives. They looked to Riyad so much like the boys who stood before him right now.

But these boys held a detached anger that felt foreign to Riyad. When he first moved to America, during his years living in Los Angeles, he'd grown accustomed to the rage of the young and dispossessed, the stares from kids that made him lock his windows and clutch his wallet or scan his surroundings for a way out. He'd never felt that in Syria, though. As a kid he'd seen violence, but it was always tribal, ordered. These boys carried the promise of something different, a rage that held no place in Riyad's version of his country. Any one of them, he thought, looked like they would kill him for a dollar.

"You shouldn't smoke," he told the oldest boy, and the boy laughed.

"You can't tell me what to do."

THE LINE AT THE CROSSING was short. Riyad had both his American passport and his Syrian state ID in his bag, each to be used at its appropriate time. On this side of the border, it felt expedient to identify as American. The Turkish were tiring of the endless flood of refugees into their country. By showing himself as a citizen of the United States, Riyad proved he was different from most Syrians these guards encountered every day.

The guard took Riyad's passport and flipped through its pages, looking up here and there to inspect Riyad's face. Seconds passed in silence. Finally, he placed it on the table before him, peered upward, and asked Riyad, "Where are you going?"

"Raqqa."

"What is your business in Raqqa?"

"I'm going to see my mother."

The guard exhaled and shook his head. He paused for a moment, not yet willing to stamp Riyad's passport. "People are fleeing your country every day," he said. "You know that?" His eyes narrowed. "They are leaving because if they don't leave, they will die."

Riyad nodded. "I know," he said. "I know. That is why I have to go see my mother."

"Don't you think your mother wants you to be safe?"

Riyad said nothing, and now the guard's voice went soft. "Tell me the truth. Is someone pressuring you to go there? Are you in danger?"

Riyad smiled and shook his head. In truth, Riyad was the only person on earth who believed this journey was a good idea. The guard stamped his passport, but then left his booth to follow Riyad all the way to the gate. He pointed southeast, through the craggy and flat desert, toward the place where the Euphrates grew fat and poured its way deeper into the Syrian plains.

"There is a road," the guard explained, "that runs along the river to the tomb of Suleyman Shah." Shah was the grandfather of

Osman I, founder of the Ottoman Empire, and though he was buried in Syria, his tomb remained Turkish property. The guard told Riyad that as long as he stayed on that road between the border and the tomb, Turkish police had authority to enter Syria on his behalf. The moment he went beyond the tomb, though, Riyad was on his own. The guard gave him a phone number to call if he needed help.

"Why are you doing this for me?" Riyad asked.

"Because," the guard said, "you're an American."

Riyad crossed the border. He reached into his bag for his Syrian-government-issued ID and placed it in his wallet. Then he took his American passport and tucked it in a pouch that he hung around his neck, buried underneath his clothing, against his skin. On this side of the border, it could only bring him danger.

Riyad wanted to shout. He wanted to hug and kiss strangers. He had done it. He'd returned to Syria. More than that: He had returned to witness *the revolution*. He imagined this was no longer the country he'd left as a young man, nor even the one he'd visited just seven years before. As he wandered into the town of Jarabulus, he believed he was walking on the soil of a new Syria, of the country as he'd always dreamed it might be.

Here inside the border, though, he saw no immediate signs of the fight. He saw unmarked cars and vans and scattered drivers, and he saw other men like himself, waiting for someone, anyone, to transport them through the war. The moment he crossed, drivers swarmed him. Some wore T-shirts and jeans, others white Bedouin robes. A few dangled cigarettes from their mouths. All said they could take him wherever he needed to go.

He joined a group of travelers in a van headed for the city of Manbij. As he rode, he saw evidence of war all around him. The new

Syria appeared even darker and more desolate than he imagined. He looked out the window to see bombed-out buildings and black smoke hovering over villages. His fellow passengers seemed not to share his revolutionary excitement. He rode alongside them, amid silence and distant stares.

They stopped at checkpoints manned by members of various brigades. Some were angry, others indifferent. All asked for IDs, some for bribes. His American passport still pressed to his chest under his clothes, Riyad handed them his Syrian-state-issued ID. A few saw that he was from Raqqa and laughed, calling him *sha'awi*, a playful slur similar to "redneck." It didn't matter where Riyad had traveled, the people he'd met, or the life he'd built. Here in Syria, he was just another middle-aged man from the "forgotten territories." He didn't mind. Better they think of him as a *sha'awi* than as an American.

When the van reached Manbij, he got out to change money and buy traditional Bedouin clothes. Then he found another van, this one headed east toward Raqqa. He was close. He looked toward the backseat of the van, where a man rested against the window. His frame was frail but his brown eyes were strong, his face lined with the crevices of sun and age.

"Can I sit next to you?" Riyad asked.

The old man looked up and smiled. "Yes."

Riyad climbed inside, carrying two Samsonite suitcases, both filled with clothes and gifts for his family. The old man eyed the bags, then Riyad, curious.

"Where are you coming from?"

"Turkey."

The man chuckled, knowingly. "What about *before* you were in Turkey?"

Riyad went cold. Was he that obvious?

"That's none of your business," he said.

The old man seemed to consider this for a second. In some ways, it didn't matter. Whether he'd been in the United States or Saudi Arabia, in the jihadist camps in the countryside or the regime-controlled neighborhoods of Aleppo—right now, in Syria, everyone was coming from or going to someplace that could get them killed.

The old man asked, "Do you have anything illegal in those suitcases?"

Riyad shook his head.

Now the old man shrugged and reached for Riyad's luggage. He put the expensive suitcases underneath the seat, tucked under the cover of his robe, out of the way.

"Don't let anyone see these. If they do, they're going to know you're not coming from *Turkey*."

Riyad nodded and sat.

The old man smiled. "Cigarette?"

Riyad declined.

The old man lit up his own, then winked. "Don't worry, my son," he said.

The van moved. More hills, more desert, more black smoke rising from distant towns. Every thirty minutes the old man lit up a new cigarette, offered one to Riyad, and seemed surprised when Riyad declined. And every so often they hit still more checkpoints, with more small talk and more bribes, Riyad passing his Syrian ID to the window at every turn.

After three hours on the road, Riyad could see Raqqa in the distance. As they neared the final checkpoint, the old man sat up straight and rushed to put out his cigarette, its smoke hanging thick in the air. He turned to Riyad, eyes big, grinning, and he nudged him and nodded toward the checkpoint.

"Here come the crazies!"

The van slowed down. The checkpoint looked the same as all the others: a flag, a few chairs, just some men sitting by the side of the road. Only here, instead of one or two men, there were four. They did not look bored. They did not look friendly. In fact, with their faces covered by black masks, they didn't look like anything at all. Riyad knew them only by the flag of Jabhat al-Nusra that flew overhead, representing the Syrian branch of Al Qaeda.

Riyad turned to the old man and whispered, "Are they really crazy?"

Another grin. "You'll see."

When the van came to a full stop, one of the masked men approached the front window and demanded their IDs. He pulled one passenger from the van, roughly, and fixed his Kalashnikov on the man's skull. He invited another to join him, warmly, and they kissed each other on the cheek. Both were taken out deep into the desert. The first seemed frightened, the second thrilled. Riyad suspected he'd never see either again.

Now they scanned the remaining passengers. The old man and his ID looked good, apparently. So did the others who remained in the car. But when they came to Riyad, the guards studied his ID carefully, then studied his face and his clothing, then his ID once again.

"Where are you going?"

"Raqqa."

"Why?"

"It's my home."

"Where were you?"

"Turkey."

"Why?"

"I needed to buy medicine," Riyad lied.

Now the guards paused a few moments longer, talking to one another about something Riyad could not hear. When the interrogator returned, Riyad tracked his eyes. Riyad's body was covered in the traditional Syrian clothing he'd bought in Manbij—everything except for his shoes. He'd forgotten to buy slippers, had instead kept his sneakers, bright blue and orange and yellow. Now he tracked the guard's eyes down to his own feet, where they lingered.

Shit, Riyad thought.

The guard reached out his hand. "Show me the medicine," he said.

Riyad grew flustered. "I couldn't find the medicine I wanted," he replied. "I will have to go back to look again tomorrow."

Now the guards returned to their private conversation, glancing in Riyad's direction as they spoke. He dreaded the thought of them searching him, discovering the American passport. He watched as they whispered and pointed, and he wondered where, out in the desert, they kept their makeshift jails.

Finally, a voice from the van interrupted their conference. "Hey!"

They turned around. It was the old man.

"It's getting late," he said. "We need to get home. What do you want from him? He already answered your questions."

The guard held up his hand. "Give us a minute."

"Come on," the old man replied. "I've known this guy his whole life. He just wants to go home."

The guards returned Riyad's ID and closed the door. The van revved up and pulled away.

The old man turned to Riyad and winked. "See?"

Crazies.

The van approached Raqqa from the west, riding through farmland that had long belonged to Riyad's tribe. There they'd grown cherries and peaches, apples and apricots, a land of plenty bridging the gap between the Euphrates and the desert. He'd ridden out here so many Fridays for picnics as a child, carrying a basket of pitas and grilled meats, picking berries and sitting by the lake, whiling away afternoons. But now the crops were neglected. The land looked unruly, overgrown, and filled with craters from stray bombs. Riyad saw a number of encampments scattered throughout the old farmsteads, all set up by nearby militias.

The old man watched Riyad staring out the window at the camps. "*Zua-rann,*" he said. Thugs.

These militias had pillaged nearby villages, robbing homes, slaughtering able-bodied men, and raping women and girls. They were loyal to no one, driven by no country or ideology. In a war rife with fatalism, these groups were perhaps the most nihilist of all. And now here they were, looking at the city from their camps. Riyad thought back to a movie his sons had often watched as young boys, *The Lion King*. He remembered the scene where hyenas gather around a group of defenseless cubs, waiting for their moment to attack. *These men are the hyenas,* Riyad thought. *When their moment comes, they will fill Raqqa with blood.*

Now, though, the van rolled into the city through its western gate, then stopped. Riyad got out and hailed a cab. Bombs had been falling all afternoon, the driver said, but tonight all was quiet. Riding through familiar streets, now disfigured by war's ruin, Riyad saw children running and families walking through the destruction, risking the threat of an evening bombing for the chance to breathe fresh air. But Riyad still saw little of the revolutionary energy that he'd expected upon his return. He studied people's faces, and a thought struck him: *Everyone looks like they're already dead.*

THEY WOUND THEIR WAY into the Old City, where the Alkasem family home had stood for centuries, one of the first ever built in Raqqa. They pulled up to his street, and Riyad asked the driver to turn right.

"I can't," the driver said.

Riyad was confused. "What do you mean, you can't? Just turn right." The driver shrank into himself a little, as if embarrassed, and made the turn.

Seconds later they encountered a man in all black, carrying an AK-47, standing in the middle of the road. He stopped the car. The window rolled down, and the gun peeked inside. The man studied them, passenger and driver both.

"Where are you going?" he asked.

"My house," Riyad said. "I live right down there."

The edges of the guard's face sharpened. "Your house?"

"Yeah."

"How long have you been away from home?"

"Just today," Riyad said.

"Then you should know," the guard said, "that this has been a one-way street for at least five years. You can't drive this way."

Riyad's face turned hot. "Yes," he stammered. "Of course. I just thought that maybe, after you guys took over the city, maybe you changed it back to the way it was."

The guard considered this for a second. His focus eased, replaced by an air of detachment, until he shrugged and said, "Turn around. Find another way home."

The driver rolled up the window and turned the car around. Riyad thought of another landmark where the driver could drop him off and let him walk. He pointed straight ahead. "Just take me to the *jenaiyah*," he said, referring to a law-enforcement precinct building. "Right up there."

Now the driver shook his head. "What are you talking about? That building moved outside the city at least eight years ago."

"I don't care!" Riyad said. "Just drive me to where it used to be."

They rode in silence until they reached the old building.

As Riyad paid the driver, the driver gripped his hand. "I don't know who you are," he said. "I don't know where you come from. But you haven't been in this city for a very long time, and everyone can tell that."

Riyad said nothing. It had been more than two decades since he'd moved to Los Angeles. He'd been so young then, just twenty-three. He'd returned to Raqqa twice to visit, but the fact remained: He'd spent half his life in another country. In all those years, though, he'd still often thought of himself as a visitor in the United States, no matter what his address or his citizenship papers said. He lived in the United States, sure, had raised a family there, built a business and a life. But he'd always imagined that if life got difficult, he could eject himself, that somewhere on the other side of the world, in a small city on the banks of the Euphrates and the edges of the desert, there was the place his ancestors had built, a place he could always return to. Now, though, sitting on this familiar road with this man who'd immediately identified him as an imposter, Riyad realized he'd become a stranger in the place he still called home.

The driver continued, "Wherever you go, whatever you do, just be careful. Please."

He pulled up to the precinct, just steps from the Alkasem house. Riyad became nervous as he approached the front door. Would his family still be here? Were they still alive? Flowers had wilted. The beauty of the courtyard had begun to erode. Perhaps it wasn't his home anymore, but still, he thought as he lifted his arm to the door, there was no mistaking this place. He knocked.

CHAPTER

2

The guards were gone. That's how Bashar Alkasem could tell that something was not okay. When he had left his home in the center of Raqqa just before seven o'clock that morning, at first glance all appeared in order. He wandered Raqqa's calm and quiet streets, past schoolchildren and farmers, vendors preparing their shops for the morning rush. The city pulsed with a familiar movement, and yet, Bashar could tell its texture had shifted, its rhythms scattered.

Every few blocks he would see someone walking with an urgency uncommon at this hour, gait quick and eyes darting. That seemed odd. But he was less concerned with what he saw than what he didn't. On a typical morning, he would pass by armed guards stationed outside the courthouse and the schools and all other government buildings, glaring at pedestrians, Kalashnikovs in hand. Their presence wasn't even unique to wartime. In Syria, for as long as Bashar had lived, the sight of a massive gun on a disgruntled guard was nearly as common as that of fresh shawarma roasting on a cone in a market stall. Often the guns weren't even loaded. The guards would serve as little more than decoration, paid by the regime only to stand and glare. Bashar actually didn't mind them, if he was being honest. They were little more than a nuisance, there only to remind the people of Assad's strength.

But that was the thing. Today there were no guards, no guns. All of a sudden, on a quiet Monday morning, the human symbols of regime power had disappeared.

Bashar kept walking. He had to. Today, strange or not, was a big day. He had a test this morning, for a class called Internet Knowledge. The law school hadn't offered it back when he'd been a student, long before the internet existed in its current form, so he had to take it now. If he passed this test, he would move one step closer to becoming a judge. That was his dream. Or at least his current dream. He understood that dreams should be malleable, fitting within the strictures allowed by reality. His older brother, Riyad, kept his eyes on the sky above him; Bashar, on the earth beneath his feet. Bashar didn't need to envision another life when he could live the one he already had. So even if he'd long ago imagined himself as a doctor, or perhaps teaching philosophy, or maybe even building a small business like his brother in the United States, he now dreamed of becoming a judge. It was a respectable profession, secure and stimulating. Now he was in the running for an alternate seat on Syria's Supreme Court.

The opportunity had been created by crisis. Syria was now two years into what already seemed an interminable civil war, and much like so many soldiers, some judges had defected from the regime to the rebels. Others had fled Syria altogether. Now the Ministry of Justice was scanning the country for replacements, talented lower-court judges and high-level attorneys. Bashar fit the latter description. He'd dedicated most of his adult life to legal practice, becoming one of his country's foremost experts on inheritance law. He was brilliant, fair, and, perhaps most important, unlikely to cause trouble. While his brother had always defied authority, Bashar had spent his life working to please it. He just had to pass this test and a couple more oral exams, and then he would be well on his way.

He saw the irony. When he was appointed to the bench, Bashar would be serving a government that had driven his brother out of the country years earlier; he would be working under a president whom many in Syria wanted to see removed from office—or, better yet, from this earth. Bashar, though, had long ago learned to view the Assad regime with more complexity. All institutions carried capacities for good as well as evil. He'd seen both in Syria, and he'd seen both in his years abroad. Assad was corrupt, yes, but Syrians knew how to navigate their country's corruption. Bashar preferred the regime's familiar cynicism to the rebels' chaotic idealism. Besides, Bashar believed he could serve the government and the common good at the same time. Show up every day, treat people with respect, and rule with a commitment to justice. He could do that, he believed, no matter which ruler's portrait hung on the courthouse walls.

He was happy. Was that strange? Even amid war, Bashar's tiny corner of the world was still filled with daily joys. His city had seen little violence. The government had remained in control here, and life continued as it always had. Bashar had a brilliant and beautiful wife, Aisha, who'd stepped away from her own legal career to raise their brilliant and beautiful girls. Jenan was three years old and already talking like an adult; Wajid was a year younger and finding the world a place ripe for mischief. Bashar and Aisha spoke often of trying for another child, hopefully a boy, someone to carry the Al-kasem tradition in this city. Riyad had long ago departed, and the last few years had sent his other brothers scattering around the globe as well: one in the Gulf, another in Sweden. The family needed a boy, someone to keep their name alive in the city their ancestors built.

Now he continued walking to Ittihad Private University, where he entered his assigned classroom. The test started at seven-thirty, and Bashar was never late. He took his seat amid other midcareer attorneys—some he knew, others not. The proctors had been sent by the government all the way from Damascus, and now they passed out the tests and instructions.

"Finish these quickly," a proctor said as he distributed the exams.

Bashar got to work. He went through question by question, answering with confidence. He loved the law, both its rigidity and its mystery. In preparing for this test, he'd seen how ancient principles mapped themselves onto modern technologies. His answers were concise, accurate, and clear. All around him, the scratching of pencils on paper filled the silence, while the proctors paced the room, row by row.

About ten minutes before they were supposed to finish, one proctor spoke up. "Hurry," he said, tapping a pen on a desk. "All of you need to finish right now."

Bashar looked up from his test. Maybe, he imagined, the government proctors were just tired and ready to return to their families, annoyed by this trip to the desert, eager to get away from the *sha'awi* and back to the cosmopolitan capital where they lived. Bashar wasn't sure. But as he handed in his test and walked out of the room, he heard the proctor's voice one more time, carrying an angry edge: "Now!"

Bashar walked out of the building and back into the city, still strangely empty of government guards and their guns.

HE FELT GOOD. He'd passed—he knew it. And yet the mood of the morning still unnerved him as he walked across the university's campus and back toward his office. Typically at this hour, the streets would be filled beyond capacity. Syria's internally displaced had swelled the city. They came here from Homs or Deir ez-Zor, seeking refuge from their own homes on the war's front lines, giving the city a nickname: "the hotel of the revolution." They came for one reason: Raqqa was safe. No one, the thinking went, would ever fight over this remote desert outpost.

But today the crowds were sparse. Bashar saw occasional cars and buses speeding out of town, packed with people who seemed to know something he didn't. He walked into his building, up the stairs, and into his office, with its balcony that overlooked one of the city's most prominent squares. He took a seat at his desk and answered his phone when it rang.

It was his friend Walid. "Where have you been?" he asked.

Walid was a fellow attorney, a few years older but at the same stage in his career. He was like Bashar: calm, deliberate, a pragmatist. He was not prone to panic or hyperbole. But now he said he'd been calling all morning. And in his voice Bashar heard some newly uncovered angst, an urgency approaching fear.

"Can you run home?"

Bashar hesitated. Yes, of course he could, but he'd just arrived for a full day's work. He had cases to prepare for, was expected in court later that morning. "Why?"

"The city," Walid said, "has fallen."

RAQQA DIDN'T SO MUCH collapse as begrudgingly lie down. For months, the regime had been decreasing its forces in the city, dispatching soldiers to other regions of the country, throwing them into higher-stakes corners of the fight. Now control of the city slipped into new hands after only a few clashes. Many of the remaining regime soldiers had fled all at once. This was Syria's first provincial capital to fall into rebel hands, and the rebels had gained control after a few days of fighting on the outskirts of the city and then waking up one day to find that the regime's workers had packed their bags and fled.

Bashar did not yet know these details, only that something drastic had changed. *Is my family okay?* He rushed downstairs, taking nothing from his office. Every file and photo and book felt too important on its own for him to choose any one thing to bring with him. He walked back outside, into a city transformed in the course of a morning; its streets were now fuller, its people racked with fear. Bodies moved in scattered directions, vacant casings rushing without patience or purpose. They knew only to move, not where to go.

He walked past the courthouse and saw a regime guard, the first he'd encountered all day. At first, the sight calmed him. Here, finally, was a guard with a gun.

"What are you doing?" Bashar heard a man ask the guard. "Don't you know you're about to be killed?"

Civilians encircled the guard and put their arms around his shoulders, rushing him away from the square and out of sight of rebel eyes, to somewhere he could change out of his government uniform. It was a little strange, yes, to see people rally around a symbol of their oppressive government. But even if regime soldiers often served only to menace, many people in Raqqa saw them as no more than working men with impossible jobs.

Bashar's eyes scanned the square, plotting his path home, and there, on the other side, for the first time he saw them. *The rebels*. He couldn't tell which faction they claimed. Syria had no comprehensively organized opposition. The regime fought the rebels; the rebels fought both the regime and one another. Maybe these men came from the Free Syrian Army, a group preaching democratic values. Or maybe they were Islamists affiliated with the Muslim Brotherhood's allies Ahrar al-Sham. Or perhaps they came from the more hard-line faction Jabhat al-Nusra. To Bashar, at this point, it mattered little. All rebels disrupted the city's order. They carried dangerous weapons and more dangerous ideas.

They also carried the arrogance of winners, even if there had been no prolonged battle for them to win. The ones Bashar now saw were riding around the square in a pickup truck, windows open, wheels spinning slowly. Two sat in the front, one at the wheel and the other leaning out the window with an AK-47. Another sat in the back, manning a *doshka*—a massive heavy machine gun that nearly filled the entire bed of the truck. They wore black boots and black berets, big beards and bigger smiles. They looked giddy. They looked proud. Today, for these men, was a very good day.

"Hello!" the one with the *doshka* shouted, and some in the streets nodded in their direction, a little nervous. "Don't worry!" he added as they continued rolling, all the way around the perimeter of the public square, their faces bright, weapons pointed to the sky. "We are here to liberate you!"

Bashar kept walking. He tried not to show it, but inside, he fumed. He didn't want to be "liberated." No one had ever been liberated without violence. Life under a dictator had been difficult at times but, for him and his family, altogether *fine*. Life under these insurgents was sure to bring chaos. He didn't want this. Not now.

Bashar held up his hand to hail a taxi and watched as the cars flew by, never looking in his direction. He rushed to the nearest market for meat and produce and found the store packed with people, pulling anything they could grab from the shelves. He mapped a path home that kept him in alleys and side streets, tucked away from the action. He did not know who these new people were or what they wanted, how long they'd be in power or what ideas they espoused. He knew only that they were happy, and that so much of his city was not, and he felt, as he approached his home and his waiting family, suddenly very afraid.

THE MOMENT HE STEPPED through the door, Bashar's wife rushed to him. Aisha wasn't sure what to think. She'd heard only that the city had fallen, and she'd been terrified until the moment her husband returned. The life they'd built felt suddenly fragile. Even amid war, up until today Aisha had felt secure. She'd spent so many of her days walking with her daughters to and from her own parents' house across town, where she watched them play with their cousins while she sipped tea with her siblings. It was a joy, building a home of her own while remaining intertwined with the family of her birth.

Now she didn't know when she'd return to her parents' house. Now she didn't know when she'd next walk outside. She didn't know who would rule them or what they'd demand, or to what lengths the regime would go to retake the city. But she knew that Bashar was finally here, and that at least for now they were safe, and she wrapped her arms around him the moment he walked inside.

The girls were in the den, playing. It was best to keep calm, best not to let them know anything had happened. And so they sat together for a while, waiting for Bashar's mother to cook dinner and watching their daughters watch cartoons, trying to laugh when they laughed, to smile when they smiled, to shield their ears from talk of war and mime the routine joys of an ordinary day.

———

THE NEXT MORNING, BASHAR awoke restless. What did life look like in a city without government? How could he work as an attorney with no one enforcing the rule of law? The regime's departure meant no police or Mukhabarat, yes, but also no judges, no bailiffs, no one staffing the courts at all. He would stay clear of his office, at least for now. Best not to announce himself as an attorney or, worse, as a soon-to-be judge. He tried to treat the day as he would a weekend, sipping coffee, talking with his family, watching his daughters play. They knew nothing of what had happened the day before, were barely even aware their country was at war.

Sometime around midmorning, though, he decided he'd had enough. "I'm going outside," he told his mother. "We need bread."

She and Bashar both knew they had plenty to get through the day, but Bashar needed to get out of the house. He needed to see what his city had become.

He stepped out into the cool air, the streets even quieter than they were yesterday, the few people he saw walking quickly, eyes cast down. Just around the corner, there was the bakery his family patronized nearly every day, with dough whipped together daily, oil and salt and yeast, then placed in massive tandoor ovens until it formed and rose. But the bakery was more than where people bought food; it was where they gathered, stitched together by a shared need, and spent minutes or hours in conversation with friends and strangers, trading news of deaths and of weddings. Here, Bashar knew, was the best place to hear news of what had become of their city. He took his place in line and listened.

"The regime will be back by the end of the day," said one man.

"No," said another, shaking his head. "They won't be back at all. They don't care about us. They'll just leave us to the rebels."

Both arguments had merit. Raqqa was, after all, the first provincial capital to fall. Its collapse signaled a weakness on the regime's part, an inability to maintain control of the biggest city in the desert region. And yet, capital or not, Raqqa still belonged to the "forgotten territories," a land divorced from politics due both to governmental neglect and to local culture. Would Assad care enough to reclaim it? Maybe not. His soldiers, after all, had just packed their bags and left.

Up near the front of the line, Bashar saw the rebels' boots and beards, their guns and their berets. He braced himself.

"Hello!" said one. He was tall and fit, with the posture of a conqueror and the satisfied face of a man who hadn't even had to fight for the city he'd conquered.

People in the crowd nodded back at him, some smiling with polite curiosity.

He repeated the party line: "We came here to liberate you!"

More nods. The people stayed quiet, as if hoping the soldier would leave but never daring to ask him to go away.

"This is your city," he said. "Raqqa belongs to the people. Never to the regime."

He and the other rebels said they were from the Free Syrian Army. This was the biggest rebel force in Syria's war, a coalition of democracy-supporting fighters—most Sunni Muslim, but some Christian or even Alawite, the same sect as Assad—led in large part by former Syrian military personnel, including some high-ranking officials who'd defected from the regime. The Free Syrian Army drew support from the West and was seen by many as Syria's greatest hope, leaders and soldiers who could overthrow an autocrat and remake the country into something more just.

At least in theory. In practice, the FSA was less an army than a cadre of interlocking and overlapping rebel groups with various allegiances and motivations. Some were secularist, others were Islamist; some drew support from Western backers, others from repressive Gulf states like Saudi Arabia and Qatar. Central leadership was barely existent, the chain of command a jumbled mess. Their distinguishing characteristics were minimal: They carried guns and wore boots, and from time to time, they overtook cities. And now they were standing at the front of Bashar's breadline, declaring that Raqqa had been freed.

And yet, Bashar imagined, this couldn't possibly be as simple as the soldiers suggested. Other rebel groups loomed in nearby cities.

Ahrar al-Sham, a group allied with the FSA but even more committed to the Muslim Brotherhood, had many soldiers scattered throughout the region. So did Jabhat al-Nusra, the Syrian rebel group connected to Al Qaeda. And then there was the regime. Assad's forces may not have put up a fight to keep Raqqa, but that didn't mean they wouldn't take the opportunity to exact revenge.

- - - - - - - -

A couple of days after the city had fallen, Bashar brought his family together for their midday "supper," determined to quell the world's chaos by keeping his house calm. They were a family that ate together, that maintained traditions. When Bashar was a boy, his father had called the family together for their meal and taken a daily silent roll call, making sure every member was present, that everyone spoke. Now this was Bashar's duty.

"*Bismillah,*" he said. "In the name of God, the most merciful, the most benevolent."

He scanned the table, looking at the faces of those he loved. Across from him sat Aisha. She was terrified. Terrified and, if she was being honest, a little thrilled. Violence could arrive at her doorstep any day, but somewhere in the recesses of her mind, she loved the fact that Raqqa had fallen. The regime had killed untold thousands, tortured many others. It had been kidnapping innocent civilians for as long as Aisha had been alive. When she was a girl, members of her family had been arrested on trumped-up charges. She wanted Assad out of power. She wanted to see what else her country could become.

Bashar looked down to the end of the table. There he saw his *mama,* digging into bowls, scooping out rice for others around her.

"Please," she said, gesturing to Bashar, "pass your plate."

She'd been steady since the moment the city fell. She had to be. Ever since her husband died, Bashar and Riyad had been the patriarchs of the family, but as her sons branched out to pursue their own dreams, she became its stronghold. Bashar was like her, secure in himself and deeply practical, but she wondered if, when the time came, he might be a bit indecisive. She would guide him. She would push him. Together they would make the right decisions to keep their family safe.

Bashar regarded his daughters at the table. Jenan sat up straight, patiently waiting. She was the elder. Three and a half years old, and already so much like Bashar. He couldn't think of a time when she'd ever disobeyed him. She picked up all her toys the moment she was asked, worked dutifully in the kitchen whenever her grandmother needed help, and seemed to live in terror of disappointing the adults around her, on a constant quest for order and approval.

Now he turned to the baby. Wajid was two and a half, only just beginning to understand the world around her. She spoke rarely, often relying on her big sister to communicate on her behalf, but she wandered wildly, toddling from room to room and out into the courtyard whenever she could. Bashar saw curiosity in her eyes, some inborn restlessness that seemed to be satiated only when she ventured beyond her parents' grasp.

They ate. Nothing special. Some bread and olives, some *labneh* cheese, a few tomatoes and cucumbers as well. Everyone reached for the serving plates in the center of the table, chattering, occasionally laughing, until, at almost exactly noon, they heard a blast so loud it annihilated all other sound.

YOUR FIRST BOMBING could be anything. That was how Bashar came to think of it in the years to come. When it hits, some part of the brain says it's no more than a car crash just outside the front door. Or maybe a building being demolished for new construction. The mind tries to tell itself quick, comforting lies.

This bomb arrived loud and angry, shaking wall and earth and bone. Bashar froze. Across the table, Jenan reached for her grandmother and yelped, while Wajid buried her head in the body of her mother and screamed. The ground shook for another split second, and now Aisha was screaming, too, and for a moment Bashar and his mother let the fear overtake them, and now the girls saw that the adults were afraid, all of them, in a way unlike anything they'd ever seen, and so their screaming and crying grew until it consumed the entire room.

After a few seconds, the room was filled with dust, something shaken upward by the impact of the explosion, rising from the earth to the air and through windows and doors into their home, their eyes and lungs. They coughed. They wiped their eyes and their noses and coughed some more. And then, for a few seconds, silence. Now the mind played catch-up, realizing that this was not some accident, not some fluke, but the noise of an instrument designed to kill, something dropped nearby that had perhaps killed some other family, gathered around some other table in some other home.

At least that was how it worked for Bashar. For his children, ignorance still served as an inhibitor of greater fear.

"What was that?" asked Jenan.

Bashar rushed to give an answer. One of the lies the mind tells now passed from his brain to his lips to his daughters' ears. "They're doing construction," he said, and this was correct; technically, there'd been construction all over the city for months. "A building fell down." The other adults nodded, and Jenan nodded too. It sounded comforting. It sounded true.

He dismissed them from the table, sent them with their mother into another room. "Watch TV," he told them. "Turn the volume all the way up."

When they were gone, Bashar's *mama* fixed her eyes on his. "So," she said, "what are we going to do?"

She knew already that they needed to strategize, that they lacked the luxury of spending another second overtaken by fear. But Bashar wasn't sure what to do. He was racing to process the reality of what he'd just felt. His city was under attack, bombed by its own government. Bashar knew it. This had to be Assad, bombing either to retake the city or just to get revenge. Bashar assumed, for the moment, that the bomb had dropped a few feet from his doorstep. Only later that day would he find out that it had hit a mosque, right next to an old prison that had been used as a meeting point for rebel soldiers, nearly a kilometer from their home. He assumed they would wait, see how things developed, then decide how best to proceed.

"Remove your emotions," his *mama* said. The look on her face showed that she'd already done just that. "You need to make every decision wisely."

Bashar nodded.

"They are trying to paralyze us with fear," she continued. "Don't let them."

Soon they lost power. The lights went out. Bashar spent the afternoon alone in his study, weighing terrible options while his daughters played, all of them gathered together in the dark.

So this was war. Finally, Raqqa began to experience what its citizens had heard so much about. Living under a dictatorship had been one thing. They'd long ago learned how and when to dispense the necessary bribes, how to keep their cool in a country where cronyism was rewarded and hard work often ignored. Bashar had made himself a master of never saying the wrong thing, never aggravating the wrong person, keeping his complaints to himself. This was how he'd thrived in the country his brother had left behind.

Surviving a war, though, presented an altogether different challenge. For so long, the war had seemed a distant thing, arriving only in the tales of the internally displaced, the men and women from Deir ez-Zor and Homs, who'd been expelled from their homes and filled Raqqa's vacant buildings, bringing with them stories of neighborhoods flattened, innocent women gunned down, children who'd witnessed horrors that would leave them forever changed. And now with the very first bombing, Raqqa would endure these horrors too.

The bondage of tyranny had felt, most of the time, quite peaceful. This so-called freedom invited death.

BASHAR CHECKED IN with friends and neighbors. Most were afraid, some less so, but all consoled themselves with the same hope. Soon, they imagined, the regime would return to Raqqa. Then things would be better. They just needed the forces who bombed them to become, once again, the forces who ruled them. A perverse logic, sure, but right now it felt like the quickest path to peace. Assad would have no reason to bomb a city he again controlled.

But that night more explosions arrived, this time in the form of Scud missiles, bombs shaped like massive sharpened pencils, launched from the ground and ripping holes through the sky. Days passed, and the shelling continued. Sometimes the family knew to be ready. Perhaps regime soldiers had been murdered in nearby cities, provoking anger. Or perhaps rebels had been inching their way toward a regime stronghold, drawing rebuke. Or maybe someone had driven through the desert and seen a Scud launcher pointed at their city. Phones rang. Men ran from home to home, shouting warnings: *Take cover. Now.*

They would rush across the street, where their cousin had a basement that could be used as a bomb shelter. They went time and again, whenever they heard the hum of an airplane overhead, until, after two days, they decided the shelter wasn't worth the hassle. Endure enough bombs, run panicked enough times, and eventually the panic itself becomes exhausting. Sure, they could run. Or they could stay. But death could find them anywhere. It was amazing how quickly terror turned into resignation. In their homes, in their shelters, or in between—it didn't matter where they were. As long as their city remained under attack, any day felt like the day they could die.

Bashar told himself the city would settle. Probably. Eventually. The regime would prevail, and he would pick up his old life again. He would finish the exams and take the oath, ascending finally to the bench of a judge. If the regime didn't succeed, though, then the new occupiers would likely form new courts. And the way things were going, it looked like those courts might be built entirely around sharia law. Attorneys trained in Syria's secular system would be viewed as threats. It didn't matter that Bashar was a devout Muslim, that he spent his Thursdays in prayerful meditation just to prepare for his Friday prayers, that he'd lived a life so pious that friends often teased him, nicknaming him "Sheikh." None of that would satisfy the fanatics, he knew. Nothing would. So for at least a time, he would have to give up his legal practice. Days ago he'd been preparing to become a judge. Now he wasn't even an attorney. He had other identities, though. He was still a father and a husband. He was still breathing. This was still a life.

AND YET HE HAD to consider that he might be wrong. This life might grow untenable. If it did, he'd have a few options. They could flee for a regime stronghold. Perhaps Latakia, the Alawite-dominated city on the Mediterranean coast. Or maybe even to Damascus, a city that had enchanted him ever since he'd lived there while serving in the army decades ago. As a last resort, perhaps they'd have to flee the country. He couldn't imagine this, felt ashamed to even consider the possibility. Leaving Syria's borders would mean giving up on a future for his homeland. But his brother Kasem had carved out a life for himself in the Gulf, and Keith had found safety and security in Sweden. And then there was Riyad, all the way in America. He knew his older brother wanted to bring the whole family across the Atlantic. He wanted Bashar to work in his restaurant, Jenan and Wajid to study in American schools.

Bashar could imagine this, sure. But for now they would stay. They would wait. They would hide during bombings, and he would hold his daughters when the missiles flew. This was their home. No government or rebel army could sever the Alkasem family's connection to this land.

It was getting late in the day. Dinnertime approached. Sometime after that, he imagined one or two more bombings would come. He had been sitting in his den—his vast collection of books had always been his refuge for critical thinking, being transported by stories, or simply sinking into the beauty of words. Now he stared at the words but did not read them. Instead, he took a moment to indulge his own panic while pretending to read. His daughters would never know the difference. But soon he smelled his mother's cooking and rose to find out what she'd made.

On his way to the kitchen, he heard a knock at the door. He made a move to answer but saw that his little sister had beaten him to it, scurrying out the main door and into the courtyard, all the way up to the gate. Soon he heard a squeal, and for the first time in days it was a sound not of terror but delight. Bashar poked his head out the door, and then he saw him. *Riyad.*

CHAPTER

3

Riyad began this day just as he began most others, waking to the sound of the neighborhood's rooster, then rolling out of bed and heading out the door with his father for the Eastern Market. The morning was hot. It was 1977 and Riyad Alkasem was ten years old. As they walked across Raqqa in the predawn darkness, they heard a voice, gorgeous and quivering, singing over a loudspeaker, calling Muslims to prayer. Riyad and his *yahba* did not pause to join the faithful; their morality was built less on religion than on tribal code, a sense of honor not beholden to any book or prophet. If pressed, Riyad's *yahba* would say that yes, sure, he believed in Allah, but he didn't pray, at least not five times daily as Islam required. He had far too much else to do.

They entered the market and found a feast for the senses. Farmers filtered in from the desert, leading horses and donkeys and sheep, riding motorbikes and *trezina*—exhaust-belching vehicles that lurched through the city on three wheels, laden with produce and weaving between pedestrians. A breeze floated off the Euphrates and through the three-mile stretch of vendors, carrying the smell of spices and sand.

At the end, beyond the Gate of Baghdad, the road wound across the river and eventually into Iraq, connecting Raqqa to the rest of the world. But Riyad's father, a stout and rough-handed man named Abdul-Rahman, had no need to venture outside the city. Out there, he was just another *sha'awi*, but inside this gate, he was a man of great importance. Farmers nodded with deference when they saw him. Shop owners went out of their way to show him respect. Riyad beamed as he walked alongside him, chest out and eyes glowing, looking up as merchants and shoppers greeted his father.

"Good morning, *mukhtar.*"

Mukhtar. Similar to "mayor," it was a title bestowed on Riyad's *yahba* even though he held no government title. He wielded his power within Raqqa's tribal structure, an informal government far more important than any erected by the state. As *mukhtar*, he ratified contracts and settled disputes. He held the tribal seal, necessary to lend legitimacy to property transfers and divorce settlements, or to record the founding of new businesses or the births and deaths of Raqqa's people. The city had an actual mayor, supported by the Syrian government and its ruling Ba'ath Party, but no one held any illusions about that official's power. Abdul-Rahman was the city's true *mukhtar.* Someday, Riyad imagined, he or his brother Bashar might take their father's place.

Riyad's *yahba* had the market memorized. Abdul-Rahman knew who had the fattest cucumbers and the freshest eggplant; he knew where to find the highest-quality garlic or turmeric or chilies. The Alkasem family owned one of the oldest and busiest shops in the city's center. They sold dairy from the desert, produce from the farmland that ran along the Euphrates, and canned foods brought in from a wholesaler in Aleppo. So Abdul-Rahman began every morning here in the market, buying in bulk to stock his shelves. If a farmer sold him something subpar, Abdul-Rahman would never return. He had too many other options. The Euphrates, after all, had been the river that led to Eden; its banks yielded wonders. He need not waste his time with overripe beets or flavorless *baharat*. Often, when he approached a stall and asked for produce, a shop owner would tell him, "Not today, *mukhtar*. It's a bad harvest. Come back next week." Honesty earned Abdul-Rahman's loyalty, and in Raqqa, his loyalty was one of the greatest resources anyone could have.

Soon the sun turned the sky orange, then blue, and the market emptied as farmers returned to their fields. Riyad and his *yahba* walked to the family shop. There they found Bashar, dusting and tidying, making sure to keep the shelves organized and the floors pristine. Bashar didn't care that he had to stay behind while his older brother got to explore the market's sprawl. He loved the solitude of the shop, the metronomic rhythm of his own mornings. He swelled with pride when customers walked in while his father and brother were still out, only to find that Bashar, just eight years old, could help them find any product they needed, walking them along the shelves he'd organized all on his own. Once Riyad and Abdul-Rahman returned, they served a steady stream of customers, and before long it was time to close for supper and siesta.

They returned home to find their *mama* preparing for supper. Soon they would sit down for their *yahba*'s roll call, registering the presence of each family member at the day's most important meal. Everyone had to be home. If you were playing with friends, you came home to eat and then returned. If you were sick, the entire family moved into the bedroom to eat by your side. The meal was their anchor, a moment in the middle of the day when they would come together and tackle plates stacked high with rice and yogurt, pitas packed with spiced lamb. Afterward they would nap, spending a few hours in the dark and out of the heat before returning to finish their work for the day.

And yet today, about an hour before supper, Riyad found himself restless. From his doorstep, he watched the Euphrates, fat and crawling, stretching away from Raqqa and into other lands. He knew he shouldn't go. His father had always said that dangers lurked on the other side of the river: young hooligans from the city, agitated members of adversarial tribes, the river's own aggressive current. Riyad, though, often thought caution inhibited joy. Home bored him. Per-

haps his family could relax in their rooms in the dark, but for Riyad
to relax, he had to wander. He had to leave.

He headed down the hill toward the river. At this hour the streets
were quiet, shop doors closed, the city settling into its afternoon
languor. When Riyad reached the base of the hill, he crossed the
city's Old Bridge, which had been built by the French during colo-
nial rule and led to the road that connected Raqqa to the rest of the
world. As he crossed, he passed a stream of American cars carrying
travelers into town, alongside merchants on foot with camels or
donkeys and cargo in tow. On the other side of the river stood remnants of an old French army outpost, a small shack with one window just big enough for a guard to stand watch, rifle raised. It hadn't
been used for those purposes in years. French troops had left Syria
back in 1946, and today Raqqa seemed like the last city any army
would ever target. It was too small, too inconsequential, not worth
the effort or time. Riyad still liked to hang out in the shack, though,
imagining the soldiers of years long passed, but he could never stay
for long; it reeked of urine.

If he kept going, deeper into the desert, soon he would arrive at
the ancient city of Resafa, long ago abandoned by civilization, built
above a network of caves. Just inside the caves, in the spots where
the sunlight could still reach, grew bright and gorgeous flowers, like
hibiscus. In the spring, Riyad would go there with his mother and
his grandmother to pick them and bag them and haul them back
home to keep for the winter, when they would be used in a healing
elixir known as sick tea.

But Resafa was too far for today. He couldn't miss roll call. So he
settled for the far banks of the river, still close enough for him to
rush back when needed. He scooted downward, over stone and
brush, careful not to scrape knees or elbows, until he reached his
favorite spot at the water's edge. Here there was a spring, tucked just
off the Euphrates itself, spitting water into a small lagoon. This, he
thought, was the best spot on the entire river. The water's temperature hovered just above freezing, so cold that he'd seen people dunk
watermelons under the surface to watch them crack wide open when
submerged. It was like a Jacuzzi, he would think many years later

when he first saw one in America—only instead of submerging him in heat, the water provided a jolt of cold.

He sank his feet in, and the chill shocked and then spread, running all the way from his toes to the crown of his head. He couldn't figure out why his father said this place was so dangerous. As the sun prickled his neck, he felt fully at peace. This was "heavy water," with more than the normal amount of the isotope deuterium, its texture thick, its taste sweet. When he got out, he knew he would dry but still feel the water's weight, the Euphrates following him back across the bridge and into his home, staying with him all day and night, until bedtime. This was just what he wanted. His shoulders slumped, and he turned his face to the sky.

He gazed across the river at his city. From here it looked smaller somehow. He walked the streets of Raqqa each day staring upward—at his father, who held his hand as they wandered the Eastern Market; at the farmers, calling out prices for their daily produce; at the donkeys that carried goods through the streets; at the posters and statues of President Hafez al-Assad, who lived in Damascus but ruled all of Syria, even Raqqa, even him. From this side of the river, though, Riyad saw Raqqa as a singular organism, its people less individuals than pieces of a collective whole.

He moved down the river and dove in, swimming out to the farthest spot where his toes could reach the bottom and then, for a few moments, just beyond. He floated on his back, ears underwater, eyes closed. After a while, he looked up to see the sun slanting downward, still high but creeping toward the horizon, and he began to wonder if he'd been gone from home for a little too long.

He swam to shore and climbed back up the banks, sensing that he needed to hurry. He rushed back across the bridge, up the street toward his home. The sun dried him as he walked, just as it did every other time he sneaked away to the river, and by the time he reached his doorstep, his hair and clothes looked no different than they had when he'd left. He walked in. The room was full and quiet. Not only his parents and siblings but his uncle, too, all of them staring. They'd been waiting. They looked angry.

Riyad was late.

He'd missed roll call. In the Alkasem household, you never, ever missed roll call.

His father marched over and grabbed Riyad by the forearm. He ran his fingernail down the arm, scratching skin. Typically, when scratched, the skin turns white for a brief moment before returning to its natural complexion. But Riyad's skin stayed white. It was an old trick in Raqqa, passed down since long before Riyad was born. The heavy water of the Euphrates kept the skin white longer when it was scratched, and now his father looked him in the eyes, and Riyad knew his *yahba* knew.

He pulled out his belt. Never in his life had Riyad received a spanking—not because he followed the rules, but because he was a master of never getting caught. But now his father smacked him across the backside, one lash after another, and the pain grew, and Riyad winced until his uncle and mother told his *yahba* that was enough, it was time to stop.

His father breathed heavily, then looked at Riyad, finger raised. "Never," he said, "cross that river by yourself."

He stopped and shook his head, near tears. They'd sent people looking all over the city, he explained. They'd worried that Riyad was dead. They'd even thought about sending someone to look in the river, but they hadn't dared. They imagined that if Riyad had been foolish enough to go there, they would arrive to find nothing or a corpse.

"If you ever go to that river," he said, "you can't go alone. And you can't go with just anyone. Only cross that river with blood."

Riyad nodded.

His *yahba* continued, "Family will save you. No one else will."

Riyad said he understood. His *yahba* volunteered to go to the river with him, and sometimes they went out there and swam to the deepest parts together, staring at the sky, finding a similar peace. Every now and then, though, Riyad still found himself feeling that familiar pull during nap time. Those days he rose and sneaked outside, aware of the risks but still compelled by some restless churning he couldn't quite understand, and he crossed the bridge, stuck his feet into the water, and looked back at Raqqa, all alone.

Most nights Riyad went with Bashar and his *yahba* to the tribe house, a gated home just blocks from their own. They passed through the gate and the garden, toward a grand room Riyad could smell before he saw. Fire crackled, big enough in the winter to keep visitors warm, small enough in the summer to boil coffee without overheating the home. Pillows scattered around a circle, where men sat cross-legged, rolling cigarettes by hand and passing a pot of coffee around. When they laughed, they looked like mountains in an earthquake, massive trembling lumps of scarred and calloused flesh. Riyad loved them.

He sat and listened as they told stories, weaving together threads of tribal lore. Through their tales, Riyad could trace his ancestry back nine generations, all the way to Ibrahim, the man who'd been granted this land from the Ottomans, and to Taha, Ibrahim's great-grandson who had boiled coffee to welcome others to the city he planned to build.

Their tribe was built on extremes: loyalty to members, hospitality to strangers, vengeance to enemies. The desert's tribes were often locked in low-simmering wars with one another. A single crime, such as a street fight turned fatal, could echo across generations.

Tribal code demanded an eye for an eye, as it had since the Code of Hammurabi, inscribed on stone some four millennia ago, right here by the Euphrates, in ancient Babylon. There was an ordered ruthlessness to the tribal code, trading murders between rival groups, killing women who'd lost their virginity before marriage, even those who'd been raped. They could be brutal. Even as a child, Riyad saw this.

And yet he saw so much goodness in his tribal culture too. He learned from his grandmothers a sense of care, which went into the ways they nourished relatives and welcomed strangers, into the extravagant hospitality passed down from Taha and still pervading all aspects of tribal life. When Riyad was a boy, a table fell on his toes and broke them, leaving him immobile for weeks. He passed the time in the kitchen with his father's mother, who would smoke roll-up cigarettes and teach him how to peel eggplant and chop squash, how to make ghee and cheese, separating milk from cream. Riyad assisted while she cooked, and they would work together until the afternoons, when they'd sit and watch their family feast. When he was a little older, he found himself drawn to the kitchen of his mother's mother, who continued his education. She taught him how best to mix spices, peppering him with short lessons—"Helba kills the cumin"; "Save the coriander for the end"—that Riyad would never forget. To Riyad, this was less about cooking than about history. These were dishes that dated back to the time of Taha; Riyad saw a story on every plate.

In the tribe house with the men, Riyad saw that same sense of hospitality take other forms. When someone from another village or city arrived, no matter who they were, they were greeted with tea, a hot meal, and an offer of a bed. If they were sick, they would be nursed to health; if they were afraid, they were offered comfort and protection. Many applied the same rules to their private homes.

And so one night when Riyad settled next to his father by the fire, he understood why the tribal council had turned angry, throwing beads and slamming fists. Someone had proposed a plan they could not begin to fathom, something so egregious it could barely be spoken aloud.

Riyad's cousin had come to tell them that he planned to open a hotel.

"Are you serious?" someone shouted.

"You are a disgrace!" yelled another, his fists balled.

The rest nodded in agreement. This was unconscionable. For centuries, they had housed and fed travelers in their homes as a matter of honor. The mere suggestion of accepting money in exchange for hospitality would make them no better than the snobs of Damascus or Aleppo—or worse, London or Paris. It could not be tolerated. It would invite a deep and enduring shame.

Riyad sat and watched, eyes darting around the room, until finally his father said, "Let the westerners open a hotel."

His words were measured compared to the others, but he said that word—*westerners*—with derision. It referred not to the globe's "west" but to Syria's, to the moneyed elites of cities on the other side of the country who traveled to their city for business but preferred to remain cloistered off in hotels of their own.

His cousin remained resolute. He hadn't come here for permission. He just wanted to let the tribal council know. For Riyad, though, the night felt instructive. It was a lesson that he belonged to his family first, his tribe second, his city third. He was an Alkasem, a Taha al Hamed tribesman, and a Raqqawi. Somewhere beyond that, though far less important, he was also a Syrian. But his lessons about his country came not from anyone connected to the intimate realities of his life. They came directly from the regime.

Riyad knew that there existed, somewhere outside Raqqa, a power higher than the tribal council, a man who carried more weight than even his father the *mukhtar.* Around age twelve he traveled, along with several hundred other boys, deep into the desert, well past the Old Bridge and the French military outpost, over the mountains that overlooked his city and into a desolate stretch of stone and sand and occasional trees. It was time for Talaal al-Ba'ath, a summer camp sponsored by the Ba'ath Party that was required for every boy in the country.

Morning broke daily with a bullhorn at five o'clock, when the boys would wake up, don their camp uniforms—khaki shirts with blue pants and blue scarves—and step outside for a routine of Swedish calisthenics. They would eat a quick breakfast of bread and cheese and olives in the makeshift mess hall, then go back outside to exercise even more. They jogged to and from the Euphrates and sprinted up and down hills. They raced across monkey bars and did squats and push-ups while the sun glared down on them, high and malevolent. Some boys collapsed. A few cried. Later they packed into trucks and rode still deeper into the desert, where they learned to take apart and reassemble automatic rifles, and then they lay on their bellies and felt their bodies jolt as they learned to shoot.

In the afternoon they gathered under oak trees, the shade protecting them from the sun. A counselor, tall and fit, called them to attention. "Today," he said, "we're going to talk about our country's leader."

The counselor had an angular jaw and an omnipresent smile; when he spoke, his voice soothed and energized, somehow all at once. Riyad listened, transfixed, swatting occasional flies and mosquitoes, moving out of the way of the odd scorpion.

"Our leader's name," the counselor said, "is Hafez al-Assad."

Riyad knew what to do next. They all knew what to do next. They'd been doing it in school as long as they could remember, had it drilled into their heads by Ba'ath Party officials who taught them their country's required rituals alongside reading and math.

They clapped, loud and enthusiastic. No one questioned whether this custom was odd. Anytime someone spoke the name of Syria's president, everyone within earshot had an obligation to offer applause.

"Good!" the counselor said. "That's what I like to hear."

He smiled, and Riyad smiled too.

"That was really good," he said, "but I think you guys can be even louder." His eyes scanned the group. There were about thirty of them, sitting packed together. "I think you can be louder than any group in this whole camp." The counselor paused, and his silence seemed to pull the boys upright, backs erect.

Riyad could clap louder than anyone under the tree—he knew it. He just needed the chance. He stiffened his shoulders and held out his palms, anticipating the magic words.

The counselor spoke again. "Today, I'm going to tell you all the reasons why Hafez al-Assad—"

Now Riyad rocketed his hands together, again and again, smiling and cheering along with every boy who sat around him, while the counselor stopped his sentence to soak in their waves of noise. He stood before them and beamed and shouted, "Yes! That's it!"

They were at their best, as Syria was at its best, when they were cheering as one, fully united, so he said the name just one more time, inviting everyone to join.

"Hafez al-Assad."

They all clapped together, whooping and whistling until Riyad's palms stung and his throat ached, and he was sure, now more than ever, that they could be heard all the way across the desert.

The boys were natives of an ancient land. Here in what was now called Syria, humans had been breeding cattle since the Neolithic era of the Stone Age, ten thousand years before Christ. Their land had belonged to the Sumerians and the Assyrians, to the Egyptians and the Babylonians, to the Persians and later the Romans, and still later to the Umayyad Caliphate and the Ottoman Empire, and eventually, in the first half of the twentieth century, to one final vicious and obstinate occupier: the French. In all this, tribal ties had endured wars and deaths and replacements of many rulers. That's why Riyad had been taught by his family that tribe mattered more than country or even religion.

But his counselors taught a different lesson. They taught that today, with Syria growing into a good and powerful force, nationalism was more important than anything else. The Ba'ath Party, they explained, had been their country's savior. Syrians had fought for independence from the French and were granted it in 1946, and the political chaos of colonialism soon gave way to the political chaos of a newly formed state. In its first decade of national autonomy, Syria cycled through four different constitutions. Three years after independence, in 1949, the country endured three separate coups d'état.

Five years passed until the next coup, in 1954, and with so much instability, Syria decided briefly that perhaps independence wasn't all they'd hoped it would be, and the country merged, in 1958, with Egypt to form a new combined nation called the United Arab Republic. The merger failed, and in 1961 Syria seceded to become independent once more, this time following yet another coup d'état.

In this chaos, a group of leaders and warriors emerged, ready to take over the country and instill a sense of stability, fostering growth and maintaining peace. They called themselves the Ba'ath Party and were connected to the party by the same name in neighboring Iraq. They laid out a vision of a Syria whose people were defined not by tribe or religion or ethnicity or sect but by a sense of pan-Arab identity. Syria, the counselors taught Riyad, then took a turn for the better, and in 1971 it settled finally on a leader who was fit to rule the country with justice and might, a man prepared to carry them into a phase of growth and prosperity that, as long as he and his party remained in power, would never end. This man, of course, was the one they all clapped for, their president, Hafez al-Assad.

Assad had been fair, the counselors taught. He'd been just. He had protected Syria from its enemies, both foreign and domestic. Israel threatened to wipe Syria off the face of the earth, but Assad had intimidated the Israeli government into submission. "Terrorists" in Aleppo had tried to take over the government and slaughter Syria's people, but Assad and his forces had defeated them all. He seemed like a man greater than anyone Riyad had ever known.

AFTER THE CAMP ENDED, Riyad returned home and told Bashar and the rest of his brothers all about how he'd shot guns and stayed up late each night in his tent, telling jokes with other boys from around the desert region. He started showing interest in life outside Raqqa, realizing that there were powers even greater than the tribal council and that he shared with the Iraqis and the Lebanese a sense of Ba'athist Arab identity.

He thought back to the lessons he'd been taught about the uprisings in Aleppo, the ways the regime's soldiers had defeated the terrorists and protected the people, and he imagined himself fighting alongside them, marching into battle in the name of President

Assad. The man seemed amazing: a pilot who'd been a great warrior for the country, who'd then seen Syria heading in the wrong direction and stepped in to right its course. Riyad wanted to know everything there was to know about him. But whenever he giddily rambled about Assad, his parents just nodded politely, saying little. When he asked them questions, they stiffened, offering only terse and vague answers. And when he pressed his father for details about Assad's rise to power, asking, "How did Hafez al-Assad become president?" his *yabba*'s eyes could have cut him.

"Shhh," his father said. Then he bent down to his son and whispered, *"Hidtaan elha athan."* The walls have ears.

Riyad grew into a teenager and continued his restless wandering, spending mornings in the shop, afternoons on the river, and evenings roaming the city with friends in search of mischief. Then one day he could wander no more.

He lay in bed for days with an aching throat, but then his throat healed, and he still could barely move; his ankles swelled, turning fat and then throbbing, and soon the pain crawled up to other joints, knees and elbows and wrists, turning even more painful with every movement he made. Doctors told his family they were not sure what was wrong, but to wait, that the pain would subside. Instead, it lasted for months. Riyad retreated into himself, barely able to get through the school day, otherwise never leaving home. He felt ashamed by his pain and weakness, never told his friends that anything was wrong. He simply told them that he no longer liked to play basketball, that he no longer had any interest in roaming the city or the desert. He found new friends who enjoyed sitting inside smoking cigarettes and playing cards. He gained weight. He became bored, depressed.

Doctors in Raqqa told him to travel to Damascus and consult

with physicians there. So one morning in February 1982, he and his mother took the first bus out of the city at six A.M. His mother was a warm but fierce woman, tough and hardworking, devoted fully to her family's well-being. She took joy in creating a sense of order and acted as the family's moral center, guided partly by tribal code and Islamic teachings but mostly by her own intuition. She taught Riyad and Bashar to cook and to clean up after themselves, to tell strangers their family name tracing back seven generations, to offer extravagant hospitality to guests and never expect anything in return. She made sure that they sat down and did their homework every night, and after they finished, she would pore over their assignments, pointing to answers and saying, "That's not right. Do it again." Only years later did they realize that she'd never read a single word—she was illiterate. She'd just been telling them to do better to make sure they were trying as hard as they could.

So it was nothing for her to travel for fourteen hours round-trip to get Riyad to a doctor.

They arrived at midday, and the doctor told Riyad he had rheumatic fever, a disease resulting from untreated strep throat. He prescribed penicillin and told him that if he could find ways to manage the pain, eventually he'd be fine. They walked outside, a little disappointed. Riyad had hoped for relief, not just vague assurances that eventually he would be okay. But the wonders of Damascus distracted him from any pain. The city had always thrilled him, with an energy and aura far grander than any he'd felt in Raqqa. Today it was cold but not too cold, and it was raining but not too hard, and the rain smelled sweet, and the people walked through puddles in Western jeans and boots, carrying a confidence unlike anything he'd seen back home. In the shops and the restaurants, Riyad sensed traces of a life he'd imagined as off-limits to tribal boys like himself. He stopped in a café with his mother for espresso and paninis and other things he'd never tried, and as they sat by the window, he watched the city fully alive.

Soon it came time to leave. They boarded a bus, and he sat with his *mama*, three or four rows behind the driver, Riyad by the window and his *mama* on the aisle, empty seats all around. If they had taken the early morning bus, they would have been surrounded by government workers. The midday bus attracted farmers; the late-night bus, soldiers. But this one, late in the afternoon, carried scattered travelers on the road for scattered reasons.

Memories of that bus ride would stay with Riyad for decades. Some details would harden; others would turn fuzzy and drift away. The trip started peacefully, the bus moving slowly with lights low and soft music playing, the driver knowing that soon they would slip out of the city and the bus would go dark and the passengers would nod off to sleep. Riyad would remember the curiosity he felt when he saw the first armored Humvee truck, driving along the outskirts of Damascus, windows tinted so heavily he could see nothing inside. Soon the bus stopped at a checkpoint, and two members of the Mukhabarat came on board. The Mukhabarat was Syria's not-so-secret secret police, officers in plainclothes who gathered intelligence on the country's people and reported it up the chain of command to the regime. They walked through the bus. One searched luggage, the other checked passengers' IDs. This was typical, nothing out of the ordinary. They even had a member of the Mukhabarat riding along with them on the bus.

"Have you picked up anyone on the street?" one of them asked the driver.

"No," he replied.

"Good. Don't."

Riyad would remember that his curiosity grew into confusion when they reached another checkpoint with two more guards. They came on board dressed in full fatigues and carrying Kalashnikovs, and they marched down the aisle checking IDs until they reached the passenger who was himself part of the Mukhabarat.

"You're coming with us," one guard said. He was short and young and muscled, his words matter-of-fact.

"Wait, what?" said the passenger. "I'm Mukhabarat! I'm one of you!"

The guard shrugged. "You're from Hama, yes?"

"Yes," he said, and Riyad saw a pistol in its holster on his hip. "I'm from Hama."

Riyad had never been to Hama, but he knew about it. It was Syria's fourth-largest city, with just under 200,000 people, situated 120 miles north of Damascus. The Orontes River snaked through its center, in contrast to the way the Euphrates wrapped around Raqqa's edge, and when the sun reflected off the water onto its buildings in the late afternoons, it could be one of the most beautiful cities in all of Syria. It held neither the tribalism of Raqqa nor the cosmopolitanism of Damascus, defined instead by a deeply conservative religious culture, its population predominantly Sunni Muslim. The Muslim Brotherhood, whose members had been the "terrorists" defeated by the regime several years earlier in Aleppo, maintained a strong following in the city, and many of its members called for overthrowing the government and replacing it with an Islamist theocracy.

The bus would pass through Hama soon, and the guards seemed insistent that this man—the Mukhabarat from the city—would not be going. "Come," one said.

"No," the man responded, and as Riyad watched, the guard slapped him across the face. The man doubled over, and the guards dragged him down the aisle, his gun hanging impotently in its holster, until they pulled him off the bus and shut the door.

Riyad would remember the silence that followed, the bus continuing to roll north as the sun set to their left, bathing the arid earth in its glow before disappearing. As the bus approached Hama in the dark, still hours from its destination, it stopped again, and another guard told the driver and passengers that they couldn't continue. The road was closed.

"No one," he said, "is allowed inside Hama."

And Riyad would remember the route they followed, not along a paved road but out deep into the desert, along a path used typically by donkeys and camels, rattling up and over rocky hills at perhaps ten miles an hour. His body jangled with nerves and with the contours of the desert road. He wondered what had happened. Had there been a natural disaster? An earthquake or a violent dust storm?

Maybe Israel had attacked. Maybe his country was now at war. His mother said nothing, and Riyad didn't ask. The moment he announced his fears would be the moment they became real. But soon he realized that the driver was wondering, too, because now he flipped through radio stations in search of information, finding nothing. Some stations played music. A French-owned news station carried reports from seemingly every other corner of the world. Something was happening out there in the dark all around him, but he didn't know what. He couldn't see.

"Pray," the driver said. "Please pray for safety."

Riyad looked up at his mother, but she did not look down at him. She, Riyad knew, was the strongest person in his family. His *yahba* was the skeleton; his *mama* the muscle and the nerves. Her family carried the blood of the Prophet Muhammad, and she knew the Quran better than Riyad's father, but at heart she was a pragmatist, more focused on the world in front of her than on a spiritual plane she couldn't see. She'd had no patience for the guards and their checkpoints, shown no sense of intimidation when they'd walked aboard carrying their guns. She had taken her boy to Damascus to see a doctor. And now, regardless of what else might be going on outside those windows, she would take him back to Raqqa where he belonged. So when the driver asked them to pray, she locked eyes with him in the mirror, held his gaze for a moment, then told him flatly, "Just get us home."

Riyad would remember wondering at age fourteen if he was old enough to lead his mother off the bus and into the desert and trust that together they could find their way. He wondered where they would go and what they'd find, whether there was a nearby city where they could stay the night or a distant relative who might take them in; and as he wondered these things, he realized that no, they were foolish; they were on a bus headed in the direction of Raqqa, and there was no place safer than here, in this seat, riding along. He repeated these words in his mind until suddenly the bus stopped near a ditch and his body jolted forward. That was when he saw them, the women, and they were screaming and running and then banging on the bus's door.

He would not remember how many. Three? Four? But he would remember the colors: bright reds and yellows in their robes, traditional dress for the Hama region; deep brown in their eyes, set inside pale white; and red on their tongues, which Riyad could see as they screamed.

Some held children. Others waved arms. All begged the driver to open the door, until he did, and then they pleaded with him in full hysterics. Riyad would not remember the particulars of what they said, only that they were in danger. The driver told them that they could not board, that they were *all* in danger, that he needed to leave them there; and Riyad would remember that they seemed fine with remaining there in the darkness, but that they would not, could not, let the driver continue without him taking their babies with him wherever he was going.

He would remember his confusion. Take their children? Where? They said to take them to any mosque in any city, anywhere in the country, and that someday a relative would find them, and as he sat next to his own *mama*, Riyad wondered, what could be so terrifying that it would make a mother give away her child?

"If I take even one child with me," the driver said, "then every single person on this bus is going to die."

And Riyad would remember that the driver closed the door and pressed on. Riyad did not turn around to see the women wailing but looked straight ahead as the bus approached another group of women and swerved right past them.

"We would die," the driver said to the passengers, and no one responded. "We would die, we would die, we would die."

Riyad would remember more checkpoints with still more aggressive and antagonistic guards, but he couldn't get his mind past those women in that ditch. When they switched buses in Aleppo, people said there had been some sort of uprising in Hama, but something had gone terribly wrong. When they finally arrived back in Raqqa, a little after midnight, he stepped off the bus and into his home and his bed, and he felt as if he could drown in his own shame.

For weeks afterward, he couldn't sleep. He replayed the images and sounds. The robes' colors, the women's fear, the children's confusion. He told himself the driver was a coward. The passengers were cowards. *He* was a coward. Why hadn't he stopped it? If only he had said something, their lives might have been saved.

News trickled out slowly. On the Syrian Arab News Agency television network and in the *Tishreen* and *Al-Ba'ath* newspapers, all owned and operated by the government, the media painted a picture of what had happened. The Muslim Brotherhood— "terrorists," the regime called them—had taken over portions of Hama, but the people had no reason to worry. The regime had defeated the enemy. The nation was safe. Assad and his army had everything under control.

And yet to Riyad, it didn't add up. He'd seen the regime's soldiers and Mukhabarat patrolling the road to Hama with menace. He'd seen their guns and their force, their armored Humvees. And besides, he knew a little about terrorism. There had been sporadic attacks throughout the region several times during his life. Terrorists tended to strike quickly, creating chaos and carnage in an instant, without warning. But these women knew some great danger was coming. Their fear spoke of something deadlier than a run-of-the-mill car bomb.

But he did not know exactly what had happened in Hama. He heard whispers, sometimes from friends, sometimes from men who came in and out of his father's shop. The whispers supported what he'd suspected ever since that night: The people of Hama were not afraid of terrorists; they were afraid of their government, of the Syrian Arab Army. Those women and children had become enemies of their own state.

If Riyad had had access to the news that would later be reported by Amnesty International and by journalists in contact with American diplomats in the region, he would have learned that he had witnessed one of the world's great humanitarian catastrophes of the late twentieth century.

The Assad regime had long seen many in Hama as a threat, with good reason. Parts of the city served as hotbeds of the Muslim Brotherhood, a group with roots in Egypt that aspired to turn Arab states into theocracies. In 1979 the Brotherhood massacred a military school in Aleppo, killing eighty-three people. These were the "terrorists" Riyad had learned about in his summer camp. That part of the lesson had been true; the Brotherhood and affiliated groups had been responsible for regular acts of terror throughout Aleppo and Damascus. In March 1980 the Brotherhood took over the main commercial district in Aleppo, and the regime responded by swooping in and killing up to two thousand people—many of them Brotherhood members, but some not. Later that year Brotherhood members attempted to assassinate Assad with grenades and gunfire. The regime responded by pulling as many as one thousand suspected Brotherhood sympathizers from their prison cells and executing them in the middle of the night. The violence continued. Throughout the fall of 1981, the Brotherhood car-bombed government and military targets—and even, reportedly, a shopping center—in Damascus, killing hundreds.

And so in early 1982, right around the time Riyad and his mother rode south to Damascus, Assad assigned his brother Rifaat to take care of the Brotherhood for good. He sent five hundred soldiers into neighborhoods where the group had influence, carrying names and addresses of members' homes and hideouts. The Brotherhood met the soldiers with resistance, and by dawn the soldiers had retreated. Voices over mosques' loudspeakers declared that Hama had been liberated and was no longer under government control, that the people, all the people, now needed to rise up with arms against the regime in jihad.

The violence grew. In showing themselves to be formidable, the Brotherhood awakened a terrible anger in the regime. The group had risen with guns and was now met with tanks. Rebel grenades and Molotov cocktails were countered by regime artillery fire and bomb-dropping helicopters. Soon enough Hama was in flames. Regime forces no longer cared about targeting individual members of the Brotherhood; instead they leveled homes throughout Brotherhood-dominated neighborhoods, indiscriminately. They blasted minarets off mosques and shot down civilians suspected of even being related to Brotherhood members.

At the time, Riyad heard nothing of this. No news of the battle, nor of the horrors that came next, events that would cement Hama's legacy as the site of one of the planet's worst massacres of the modern age. Regime soldiers flooded Brotherhood districts, pulling families from homes and gunning them down in the streets, before dumping their bodies in mass graves. They connected cyanide gas containers to entrances of buildings and then turned them on, killing everyone inside.

No one would ever come up with a definitive total for the number of dead. Access for journalists and human rights groups remained limited. Bodies could not be counted in mass graves. Amnesty International would estimate the deaths at between 10,000 and 25,000. The Syrian Human Rights Committee would claim the number was even higher. When Western journalists arrived in Hama two to three months later, they found entire neighborhoods leveled, blood still streaking the sidewalks and streets.

RIYAD KNEW NONE of that. He knew only what he saw. He knew that those women couldn't possibly be terrorists, that their fear and desperation spoke of some violence he could barely fathom. He started talking. He had to. He told his uncles, his brothers, his friends. He described the ditch, the faces, the sound of the women's screams. The children, confused. The driver, apologetic. Himself, worried and ashamed. Over and over people told him the same thing: *You must have been confused. Surely it wasn't that bad.* And Riyad wondered, *Are they right?* It was easier to mistrust himself than to mistrust his family or his government. There was safety in self-delusion. If Riyad was wrong, he just needed to change his perceptions. If his family and his president and everyone he trusted to protect him were all wrong, then what might he risk in being right?

He told himself that President Assad would make everything okay. He was a good man. A hero. Riyad imagined he would issue an apology, express regret at the innocent lives lost. Instead, though, the president traveled to Hama to celebrate a great victory. Women danced for him in the streets as he paraded through the city, a conqueror in his own land. He never indicated that innocents had been lost in the fight, never suggested his regime had done anything but win a just battle over a wicked rebel enemy.

Riyad felt the confusion and rage of being told his reality was false, and a desperation for someone—anyone—to tell him that what he'd seen had been real. That the women's fear had been grave and warranted. That their neighborhood had likely been destroyed, themselves or others close to them killed. He wanted to hear that his president was a murderer. "Listen," he sometimes imagined a grown-up saying, "what you saw was correct. This man is not a good man."

His father came the closest. He told Riyad that his intuition had probably been right, but that it wasn't their concern. "Politics," he said, "is not our problem." This was the tribal way. "We are all the way here in the desert," his father said. "This is not our fight." Bashar believed the stories Riyad told him, but he offered little comfort. Riyad was too young to fully wrestle with the reality of his government's terror, and Bashar was two years younger than *him*. He didn't want to think about politics, barely wanted to think about life outside their family's home. Bashar stayed in his room with his books. He preferred to lose himself in the latest Agatha Christie novel, not to consider the gravity of what Assad's regime had done.

On the bus that night, his mother had said little. Once they arrived at home, he'd asked her why the driver had said the entire bus would be killed if they took any children. What had made everyone on and off the bus seem so afraid?

She didn't say. She told him there was nothing to gain from wondering what had happened and said only that she'd felt sad for those mothers, that they faced an awful situation she couldn't fully understand.

But when Riyad begged to know when someone would be held to account, she stopped him. She looked him in the eyes, her gaze firm. "Life," she said, "is hard."

They never spoke of Hama again.

TIME HARDENED RIYAD. Anger took the place of confusion. Defiance masked soon-buried fears. All the traditions he had followed so enthusiastically before—clapping whenever anyone said Assad's name, showing respect for the president's image in his school and in the streets—he now made a show of ignoring. Riyad became one of the most dangerous kinds of people in all of Syria: a loud-mouthed kid with a hatred of the regime.

As he grew older, he heard more whispers, more news of the regime's abuses of power. Assad's spies monitored his own people more closely than they did foreign enemies. Thousands of Mukhabarat scattered throughout the country. They listened to phone calls and read letters, eavesdropped on public conversations, and reported any expressions of dissent. Syria's people could be arrested for "threatening public order" or "disturbing public confidence"—in essence, speaking out publicly against the regime. Protests had been banned since 1963. The lucky violators were arrested and imprisoned, the unlucky ones "disappeared."

Now when others applauded Assad, Riyad scoffed, laughed, then ranted. The man was a buffoon, he said. The further he got from Hama, the less he could talk about that night, so now he pointed not to Assad's evils but rather to his incompetence. The Syrian economy was still struggling. Its army could be annihilated by any enemy who thought the country worthy of attack. Syria, he declared, was doomed with Assad in power, and anyone who accepted his reign was complicit in their own oppression.

He made a decision and announced it to anyone who would listen: He was moving to Europe. First he would have to finish high school, and then he probably would need to go to college, but after that, he would be gone. He just needed money and a passport. Maybe he would go to Germany, or Sweden. When expats from Raqqa came back home to visit, he showed up at their doors and peppered them with questions about European life. He wanted to know about visas and jobs, about universities and new languages, about Berlin's metro and Stockholm's winters. He let himself sink deep into their stories, imagined himself in their lives, in anyone's life but his own. Yes, he thought, that was what he needed. Someday he would leave this country behind.

CHAPTER

4

In college, Riyad became a problem.

In 1985, he moved two hours away from home to study law at the University of Aleppo. He planned to earn his law degree in a four-year undergraduate program, then spend two postgrad years training to become an attorney. He liked the law and loved his new city, massive and layered, deliciously chaotic at nearly every hour of every day. Aleppo was home to much of Syria's wealth and nearly all its finest restaurants, some with miles-long wine lists and fancy tablecloths, others no more than shacks serving falafel or kebab. Riyad felt the city tingle with possibility. Here was a city divorced from Raqqa's tribal culture. Here no one cared who his great-grandfather was or whether he'd come from Taha's lineage. He felt he could be anything, anyone. And who he became, quickly, was a rambunctious kid from the desert who wouldn't shut up about the regime.

He was sometimes annoying. He knew it. Even worse, he could endanger himself and anyone who dared agree with even a sliver of what he said. But he couldn't help himself. He hated Assad, hated his eggplant-shaped head and his dictatorial mustache, hated his portraits hanging over buildings and streets, the sneering taunts of a pathetic man. He hated the Ba'ath Party and anyone who defended it, and he felt ashamed of how much he'd enjoyed its summer military camp when he was a little boy.

By now, most of his peers had begun to realize that the regime was far from perfect. They were older now, and they'd heard enough whispers. They knew the government functioned as a kleptocracy, doing little to help its own people. They'd heard the stories of dissidents tortured or disappeared. They'd asked questions as children, and they'd been given the same answers as Riyad: "Hush. The walls have ears."

So now they hedged. "Assad is good," they would say. "He's just surrounded by corrupt people."

"So," Riyad would respond, "do you think he's stupid?"

Either he didn't know about the corruption, Riyad argued, because he was too stupid to see it, or he knew and approved, making him every bit as bad as the most crooked bureaucrat or most menacing Mukhabarat. Riyad criticized the regime in classrooms and in restaurants, in private homes and in public streets, with friends and uncles, with strangers, with the elderly and with kids. Once in a class on Syrian socialism, he was asked on a test to write quotes from Assad's most famous speeches. He refused, instead filling in quotes from other historical figures—Churchill and Chairman Mao, JFK and Gandhi—and attributing them to Assad. The professor approached him, confused. "Why would you write this?" he asked. "You know Assad never said any of this."

Riyad grinned. "Are you saying you don't think our leader is capable of such wise and inspirational words?"

"No," the professor said, "of course not."

"You don't think President Assad is smart enough to say these things?"

The professor's face reddened. "Of course he is!"

"I don't know what you want me to say then."

Riyad passed the test.

Some friends rolled their eyes at him. Others left the room during his rants. When Bashar was around, he would sometimes place a hand on Riyad's shoulder, as if to quiet him, not because Bashar supported the regime but because he preferred that his brother remain alive.

His father was less gentle. "Who do you think you are?" he asked Riyad in their family's den one afternoon, while Riyad was home from college on break. "You think you're Che Guevara or something?"

Riyad rolled his eyes. He didn't imagine himself a revolutionary— at least not yet. He was just someone who'd found lies beneath the reality his country had constructed. He wanted those around him to experience the rage and terror that would come when they discovered those lies too.

"No," he told his *yahba*. He wasn't Che Guevara. "All this stuff is just bullshit. Assad, the whole Ba'ath Party. It's bullshit, and everyone acts like it's okay."

His *yahba* let his shoulders slump. Never, not since Riyad was a kid coming home from that night in Hama, had his father tried to defend the actions of the regime. Barely anyone in Raqqa cared much for Assad at all. Theirs was a city concerned only with governing itself, and they knew the best way to maintain autonomy was to keep quiet. Dissidence invited violence.

"You're putting yourself in danger," his *yahba* told him, and Riyad shrugged.

In truth, it was his father's name that kept Riyad out of trouble. He'd avoided the wrath of the regime only because he'd been born to the *mukhtar*.

"I'll be fine," Riyad said.

For his final semester of college in Aleppo, Riyad found himself curious about one particular class—International Law: American Government. He had never met anyone who'd been to the United

States. As a boy, he'd learned in school that it was an evil nation full of imperialist politicians spreading toxic power. As he got older, he'd learned from popular culture that it was an extravagant nation full of gorgeous people, spreading the music of Madonna. When he watched American movies, he found himself transfixed, not by the beauty of the celebrities or the wildness of their culture but by what he saw in the background: the streets. They were gorgeous. Whether it was Sylvester Stallone running through Philadelphia in *Rocky* or Burt Reynolds speeding away from cops in *Smokey and the Bandit,* all of America seemed paved with obsidian, deep black and pristine, nothing like the graveled and sand-strewn roads that stretched from Raqqa to the rest of the world. So America had (1) evil imperialists, (2) talented singers, and (3) gorgeous highways. He signed up for the class, eager to know more.

Riyad knew the professor from a civil law class he'd taken before. He was brilliant and tough but fair, a man in his fifties who wore a blazer and button-down but no tie, who commuted from Damascus to Aleppo each week, taught his classes, then returned home. "By choosing to take this class," he said, standing before a sparsely populated room on the first day, "you are choosing knowledge that can be beneficial for your country."

Riyad perked up. He liked this thought. He wanted to make Syria better. "By learning how other systems of government work," the professor continued, "we can learn how to make our own government even better than it already is." Riyad rolled his eyes at the last part—perhaps he and his professor had different ideas about the present quality of their government—but still, this was something. An acknowledgment that Assad's regime might fall short of perfection was an idea both dangerous and intoxicating.

When Riyad started reading the textbook, he soon came to understand why so many of his fellow students had avoided this class. American democracy seemed inaccessibly complex, a tangle of statutes and systems he couldn't fully understand. He read about the multiple branches of Congress and the differing laws from state to state. He tried to understand the Electoral College, the United

States' system of electing a president by assigning electors to each state based on its population, then determining a winner based on who won the most electoral votes. *What a ridiculous system*, Riyad thought. Why didn't America go by the popular vote just like everyone else?

The textbook encouraged this line of thinking, that American law was backward. It was Syrian-written and regime-approved, emphasizing the slog by which bills became laws and the overlapping and sometimes contradictory layers and branches of government. It detailed America's history of slavery and its pitiful record on civil rights. It explained how many potential laws failed to pass through Congress or were vetoed by a sitting president. It made the whole country seem like a needlessly complicated mess.

Yet the more Riyad read, the more he was drawn to this description. He found a certain beauty in America's complexity. He came to realize that America had been built in direct opposition to the system he'd inherited, that it had been founded on the idea that concentrated power represents a threat to a nation's people, and that for a nation to flourish, it must make its powers diffuse.

And then, midway through the book, Riyad encountered a paragraph that left him stunned. The United States, the book explained, allowed for a process called "impeachment."

What?

He took a second look.

Impeachment.

The book explained that if a president violated the law, Congress could vote to remove him from office. This wasn't theoretical; Americans had actually done it. In the nineteenth century, the House of Representatives impeached Andrew Johnson for unlawfully firing his secretary of war. The Senate had kept him in office, but still, that was something. And in 1974, President Richard Nixon had resigned, knowing that if he didn't, he'd soon be impeached for his complicity in unlawful spying on political opponents.

Riyad couldn't believe it. *Is this real?* All his life, he'd seen Syria's president treated like a deity. In America, though, a corrupt president could lose his office; some constitutional scholars believed the nation's leader could even be thrown in prison.

Riyad marched to his professor's office. "Is this true?" he asked.

"Yes," the professor said, a little startled. "It's true."

"How is that possible? I mean, the president gave these people their positions, right? How can they have the power to question him?"

Now the professor shut his door. He seemed both excited and unnerved by this conversation. He reminded Riyad that legislators were elected in their own individual races, then mentioned the concept of congressional investigation, and finally told him that even presidential appointees could find avenues to power that would hold the president who appointed them to account.

"Okay," Riyad said. "So is the president like the queen of England? With no real power?"

The professor laughed. "No, he's a very powerful man." And then his voice dropped, just barely. "But he's not more powerful than the system."

Riyad walked out of the office dizzy, almost shaking. Here was the procedure Syria needed to right its government's wrongs, sitting on a page in a textbook in a library for anyone in the entire country to read. He would someday think back on that afternoon as one where he fell under a spell, feeling no cold and no warmth, no hunger and no fatigue, where he felt nothing at all but the consuming force of a single question: *How can we get this here?*

And he realized that he would have to do it. He would travel to America and become an expert on its constitution, and then he would bring that knowledge back home.

Riyad thought he knew a secret. All around the world, people imagined America to be a powerful nation because of the size of its skyscrapers, the wealth of its cities, and those gorgeous, immaculate highways. Others looked to the strength of its military or its ability to export culture. All of them, Riyad thought, were missing the point. Those cities and those riches, that might and cultural bravado—all of it existed only as a result of the U.S. Constitution.

Without the checks on power, America would be no different than anywhere else. Riyad knew he had to go.

IT WASN'T EASY. He would have to get a visa, and to get one, he would have to be accepted by an American college, and it all required sending letters to far-off places in a language he didn't speak. So he found help. An acquaintance who lived in Chicago sent him an American college catalog. He took the catalog to two other friends— one with a typewriter and the other with an English degree—and they began crafting letters, explaining Riyad's dream.

Riyad knew it might not work. If it didn't, he would remain in Syria and become an attorney. Here at home, there was another possibility: The Ministry of Justice was offering an exam that would determine fitness for becoming a judge. The only requirement to take the exam was that you had to have a law degree. It didn't matter how long you had practiced as an attorney or even if you'd practiced at all.

So even before he graduated in the fall of 1989, Riyad had decided he would take the test. It seemed wise to pursue this backup plan while he waited to hear from American colleges. But he also drew motivation from some strange combination of curiosity and ego. He'd grown into one of the law school's star students, and now he wondered: Could he compete with people who'd been practicing law for decades? Could he jump ahead of all of them, landing a judicial appointment just months after he finished school?

That summer, he studied in the private legal library of a friend of a friend. Every day for a month he sat in that room, sun blasting through the windows, a single pitiful fan spinning hot air while sweat dripped down his back, and read the works of legal minds across the Middle East, diving deeper and deeper into the history and philosophy of the law.

When the day arrived, a few months after his graduation, he took a bus to Damascus to take the test. He walked into the Ministry of Justice, its ceilings high and columns imposing, alongside men and women with gray hair and tailored suits, walking with the purpose and confidence that could come only from a life spent walking into official buildings and knowing that you belonged. In his wrinkled shirt and ill-fitting khakis, his hair short and curly and his frame thin and wiry, twenty-two-year-old Riyad joined them, there in the same room, taking the same test.

WEEKS LATER, back home in Raqqa, he was sitting in a coffee shop with friends when a neighbor walked in carrying a newspaper from Damascus. He slammed it on the table, right in front of Riyad.

He sat up straight, startled.

"Look!" the man said, thrusting his finger onto the middle of an open page.

Riyad looked. There was his name, "Riyad Alkasem," in a block of text, surrounded by other names he didn't recognize.

"What?" he asked.

"That's you. Congratulations."

It was a list of the top forty scores on the judge's exam, the ones who'd be granted an interview with Syria's minister of justice and, with it, the chance to become a judge. Riyad felt hot, flush with pride. He'd done it. He'd beaten out attorneys decades his senior, proven himself to be among the brightest legal minds in his country. He could barely grow a decent beard, and here he was, set to be offered a position so many spent their entire lives working toward.

Moments later the phone at the register of the coffee shop rang.

"Riyad Alkasem?" asked the attendant, and Riyad nodded.

"Your father is on the phone. He says to come home."

He walked into the house, and there was his father, along with his mother and his brothers and sisters, even some uncles, scattered around the room and waiting, much as they had been on that afternoon he'd disappeared to the river so many years before. Only now he saw no anger, felt no lashings. His *yahba* wrapped his arms around him and told Riyad that he was just so very proud.

Soon neighbors showed up, and still more uncles and aunts and cousins, all eager to offer hugs and congratulations. Riyad soaked in the attention. He'd spent so much of his life angry for reasons he couldn't fully explain, rebelling against a system that everyone around him seemed to accept. It felt justified and necessary but, at the same time, exhausting. He'd angered his father with his incessant railing against the government, had alienated cousins and uncles who couldn't stand to hear him complain, had pushed away friends who worried they might be in danger just for listening to his rants.

Now he thought, *Maybe this is okay.* Maybe he could stay here, among his loved ones, and help Syria's system from within. As a judge, he would have influence. And as perhaps the youngest judge in the entire country, he would have years to rise through the ranks. Maybe he could ascend to one of Syria's highest benches, perhaps even to its Supreme Court. Maybe he could help to bring an end to the Ba'ath Party's chokehold on power, could introduce a multiparty system. Maybe, he imagined, he could even work toward instituting checks and balances. Perhaps as Riyad's power grew, Hafez al-Assad's would wane. Riyad floated around the room returning smiles while his mother prepared a meal, everyone passing around tea and congratulations, thinking that maybe he could remain in his country after all.

DAYS LATER RIYAD RECEIVED a piece of mail from California State University, Los Angeles. He had been accepted into an English as a Second Language program. If he could get himself to the United States, they had a place for him. He could study English for a year, then whatever else he might want in an American university. The welcome packet included I-20 immigration forms, a course catalog, and photos of the campus. He looked at pictures of the Hollywood Hills and felt unable to imagine life there. His acceptance letter was real, but America still seemed to exist only in a dream.

Besides, after a successful meeting in Damascus with the minister of justice, Riyad's path to a judge's bench appeared clear. Syria's constitution said he was too young to take the bench right away, but he could apprentice under Raqqa's prosecuting attorney, and over time, he'd make his way to a judgeship.

He reported to the courthouse on a Monday, walking through the lobby on the way to the prosecutor's office. The courthouse was modest, nothing like the opulent lobby at the Ministry of Justice, but still, it had the air of a place filled by important people making important decisions. Now, in his ill-fitting professional clothes that hung on him like a clown costume, Riyad was one of the building's important men.

But on his way in, he heard a voice call out, "Stop!"

Riyad followed the voice to a middle-aged man with blank eyes, sitting at a desk in the middle of the lobby. He beckoned, and Riyad approached, the man's eyes tracking him the entire way. "ID," he said.

Riyad showed his ID, and the man made no effort to check it against any list, just writing Riyad's name in a notebook, which Riyad assumed had a record of everyone who came in or out.

"Okay," he said, returning Riyad's national identification card. "You can go."

Riyad picked up his accent: Alawite. The Alawites were a minority sect in Syria, but they had a few powerful members, most notably the president, Hafez al-Assad. *Ah,* Riyad thought. Now he got it. This man was no legal assistant or low-level bureaucrat. He was Mukhabarat.

He took his ID back and continued into the prosecutor's office, uneasy. Why, he thought, did the courthouse need a spy?

He went inside to meet the prosecutor, a kind man with a soft voice who wore a jacket and tie and had flecks of gray in his hair.

"Welcome, son," he said. "Congratulations." He was honored, he said, by the chance to help Riyad adjust to life in the courtroom. They had a few cases already under way, and he handed Riyad some documents to study, then pointed him to the desk that was to become his.

Before settling in, Riyad told the prosecutor he had a question. He nodded in the direction of the Mukhabarat. "Is he always here?"

The prosecutor looked at the Mukhabarat, then back at Riyad, and nodded.

"Why?"

The prosecutor walked over to Riyad and lowered his voice. "Well," he said, "here's the thing. In the courtroom, we make our case. The defense makes their case. Sometimes the judge rules whatever he thinks is fair. But sometimes the Mukhabarat just hands the judge a piece of paper that tells him the ruling. And he rules like that."

Riyad's face went hot. *Is this possible?* he thought. *Yes, of course it is.* He felt ashamed for even imagining things might be different.

"Really?" he said, hearing the defeat in his own voice. "So judges don't even get to do what they believe is right?"

The prosecutor shrugged. "Sometimes yes, sometimes no."

Riyad went quiet. He felt angry tears rushing to his eyes. When he got home that evening, he sent a letter to Cal State Los Angeles and told them he was on his way.

RIYAD HAD ONE MORE meeting scheduled in Damascus with the minister of justice. They'd planned to discuss the details of his appointment and the possibility of accelerating his rise to the bench. He rode south on a bus with his father, who'd decided to join him for the trip to the capital.

As they approached the sprawl of the city, Riyad turned to his father, heart sprinting, a jangle of nerves. "*Yahba,*" he said.

"Yes?"

"I'm not going to the meeting."

Abdul-Rahman looked confused. "What do you mean?"

"I'm going to the American embassy instead. I'm going to get a visa so that I can move there and go to school."

His *yahba* looked at Riyad, then away. He knew his son had talked about leaving Syria for years, but he had now come to imagine him right there in Raqqa, a pillar of the community and the tribe, just as he himself had always been.

"Why?"

"You know why."

His *yahba* said nothing. Yes, of course he knew, had seen the unquenchable fire burning in his child ever since that bus ride through Hama. Lately, though, he had thought perhaps Riyad was getting past it and was ready to accept his country's faults, to stay.

Riyad took his father's silence as an invitation.

"Here's the problem," he said. "If I stay here, I won't keep my mouth shut. I can't. And I can't work for the government. I can't work for that son of a bitch."

His father knew who Riyad meant. For years, Riyad had never referred to Assad by his official title or actual name.

"If I'm a judge, everything I do is for him, and I can't do it. That's not a life."

His father nodded, and Riyad could tell that he understood.

"Your brothers—" his *yahba* said.

Riyad interjected. "I know."

They were nearing Damascus, the countryside outside their window a whir of green and brown. Riyad's father knew his son was right. If Riyad kept blasting Assad, eventually he would anger the wrong person. And the regime wouldn't just come after him. It would come after the whole family. He regarded his son at that moment. He was no longer the child who'd gone off to the regime's camp in the desert, nor the confused teen who'd stumbled off the bus from Hama, glassy-eyed. He was a man with a law degree who'd earned the right to become a judge. Who'd earned the right to start his life wherever he wanted, even if that meant leaving his *yahba* behind.

"Okay," he said. "You go."

HIS *YAHBA* GOT OVER his sadness quickly. His son was no longer going to be a judge, but he was going to America! He told friends. He told strangers. By the time Riyad got back to Raqqa, it seemed like the whole town already knew.

"Take me with you!" said one of his friends.

"You're not cool enough for America," joked another.

They imagined what his life might be like, spending all day by a pool in California or at the top of a skyscraper in New York. One mimed a scene of Riyad dancing in a club, mimicking the way he'd seen Americans dance in movies, all hip thrusts and shoulder twitches and flailing limbs.

They laughed enormously, and Riyad did his best to laugh too. He didn't know what life in America would be like, but he imagined he'd see little of nightclubs. And now, with his flight just days away, a sadness crept in alongside the excitement. He was really leaving. He knew he would miss this place. So he sat and ate and laughed but didn't quite know what was so funny, didn't know exactly what to feel.

His *mama* told him she disapproved, that America was an imperialist country full of crime.

"I'm sick of this communism bullshit," Riyad told her. "Maybe imperialism is better."

Besides, his country's president was a criminal. How much worse could America's crime be?

BASHAR TRIED TO BE supportive. Really, he did. "I wish you didn't have to leave," he told his brother, "but I know you do." His body, though, told a more complicated truth. When Bashar saw Riyad's visa, his lungs deflated and his shoulders collapsed. He smiled without joy, offered congratulations with no conviction. His brother was leaving. He knew what this meant.

"You have to care for the family," Riyad told him. Their father was getting older, had already suffered a stroke. While the boys were in college, the family shop's revenue had dwindled. Both had already begun thinking about how they could keep their siblings and parents afloat. Riyad imagined that in America he'd send money back to Raqqa. Bashar had once dreamed of becoming a doctor, but now he'd decided to study law instead, not because he wanted to follow in Riyad's footsteps but simply because becoming a lawyer required fewer years of schooling. Bashar could get through his degree and his mandatory military service, and then he'd make enough money to help the family get by.

Riyad had begun to feel guilty for leaving his brother behind. He knew that Bashar would have to become the oldest brother, a big responsibility in their culture, where the oldest son was seen as responsible for maintaining a family's good name. In truth, though, Bashar had always functioned as the oldest. He'd been the one who listened to their parents when they were boys, stayed inside during siesta, and worked dutifully in the shop; the one who'd earned the highest grades and buried himself in books, who could someday inherit their *yahba*'s position as *mukhtar*. Bashar belonged in Syria; Riyad belonged anywhere else.

In some ways, Bashar had been preparing himself for this day ever since the night his brother returned from the road through Hama. He hadn't known where Riyad would go, but he had always known his brother wanted to leave. While Riyad was in Aleppo for college, Bashar continued to live at home, commuting to the same university from Raqqa. Now, though, the reality of Riyad's looming departure knocked him sideways. Bashar could try his best to care for their family in Syria, but who was going to care for Riyad in America?

"How will you get by when you don't speak the language?"

"I'll learn it."

"Who will you call if you get in trouble?"

"We have cousins in New York. I'll find them."

"When will you come back?"

"I don't know."

Bashar couldn't care for his big brother in America, but he could make sure he had all he needed before boarding that plane. And so he took Riyad on a final tour of Raqqa, making sure he said goodbye to friends and relatives, teachers and neighbors, anyone in their hometown he imagined Riyad might not see again.

One day he took Riyad to see their grandfather, the grand mufti of Raqqa, one of the most respected religious leaders in the region. He led a large community of Sufis, a sect of Islam that embraces the mystery of God, finding communion with the Holy in personal experience alongside the words of the Quran and the Hadith. The Alkasem brothers had grown more religious as they got older, finding a goodness in Islam that contrasted with some of their city's more ruthless tribal traditions. Bashar had found himself drawn to Sufism and to his grandfather's teachings. He saw God as a mystery, himself an explorer in search of divine truths. He memorized the works of the great Sufis, and he spent hours at their grandfather's side, listening to him speak, communing with his followers. Riyad, though, preferred his Islam straightforward. Pray five times daily, fast during Ramadan, avoid alcohol and pork, and give to the poor. He saw no need for much else.

Still, the grand mufti was their blood relative. Riyad had to say goodbye. The brothers arrived one afternoon to find him dressed in a white turban with a red crescent in the middle, face locked in a gleaming smile. Some muftis wore signs of wealth, but Riyad's grandfather, tall and thin, preferred to dress as if he lived among "the meeks." He spoke, though, in a way that betrayed his influence, as if every conversation were a speech before hundreds in a great hall.

"Welcome, son," he said.

Riyad sat with him for several minutes of polite conversation before standing to hug and kiss him in his final goodbye.

"You know," his grandfather said as Riyad let go of his embrace, "I hear they like our food in the West."

Riyad nodded politely, but inside he was ready to turn and leave, to say his remaining goodbyes. "Okay."

"Yes," his grandfather said, as if emphasizing the profundity of his last statement.

"Okay." Riyad smiled and pulled away.

"Cook them food," his grandfather continued, his words spilling out like divine commands. "Cook them food, and teach them about Islam."

Riyad stopped, feeling his face flush. He wanted to be polite, to nod and to quietly leave, but he had to say something. He liked to cook, sure, and he'd grown in his faith as he aged, but now he needed everyone—even his harmless grandfather—to know exactly why he was leaving home.

"You know," Riyad told him, "I'm going to be an attorney. That's the whole reason I'm going. To be an attorney and learn their government so I can bring it back here."

His grandfather nodded. "Good, good. But also, cook them food and tell them about Islam."

Riyad started to shake his head, but he felt Bashar's hand on his shoulder. "Okay," he said, "I will."

A DAY LATER, as Riyad sat with friends outside Sinbad Falafel, the chef, Abu Mohamed, came out to greet him. Abu Mohamed wore black pants and a white button-up jacket with pockets on its side and chest. His food was the best in all of Raqqa. He'd been recruited from Aleppo by Riyad's uncle, who wanted to open a restaurant here in town. But Riyad's uncle's partners had tried to scam Abu Mohamed out of his share of the business. Helpless, Abu Mohamed had taken the matter up with the *mukhtar*. Riyad's *yahba* ruled in his favor, choosing fairness over family.

Abu Mohamed had never forgotten. "I have something to show you," he told Riyad. "Come with me."

Riyad followed him into a back room. He walked into unrelenting heat, barely any light, a smell so pungent it turned him dizzy.

"You smell that?" Abu Mohamed asked.

Riyad didn't have to answer. Of course he smelled it.

"That's the smell of wealth."

Abu Mohamed pointed at a tub of boiling yellow liquid. "You see that?"

Riyad saw.

"That's money."

He called Riyad closer. "I'm going to show you how I make my hummus and my falafel."

Riyad said nothing. The room was hot, the smell unbearable, and the lesson likely worth little.

But Abu Mohamed's eyes flashed urgency. "No one knows this," he said. In the past, a few of his employees had come close, but Abu

Mohamed made sure he kept some steps to himself. "Someday," he told Riyad, "I will show this to my children. But that's it."

Riyad was hot and restless but now just the tiniest bit curious. "Why?"

"Your father is a good man. I want to give him something. This is the only thing of value I have to give."

Riyad nodded.

"Besides," Abu Mohamed said, "you're leaving the country, so I don't have to worry about you opening a restaurant down the street."

Abu Mohamed could see that he was skeptical. Riyad had only so many hours left in Syria and wasn't sure he wanted to spend any of them learning how to prepare food.

"My son," said Abu Mohamed, hand on Riyad's shoulder, "never say no to knowledge."

He walked back over to the vat of hummus and gestured toward Riyad. "Come," he said, and so Riyad went. He watched as Abu Mohamed cooked the chickpeas and moved them from one vat to another, as he mixed in the tahini, added the citrus and the spices, and whipped the ingredients together until they combined to make something new. Abu Mohamed held a seriousness on his face the moment he began working, his eyes searching the bowl before him for imperfections no one else on earth could ever see, and Riyad knew that he was witnessing something special, that the lines of customers out the door existed only because of the obsessive work done in the dark of this room. In Abu Mohamed, Riyad saw the same care and sense of duty that he'd seen in his grandmothers in their own kitchens. As Riyad watched and listened, his curiosity turned to awe, and Abu Mohamed's instructions lodged themselves somewhere deep in his mind, where they would stay dormant for many years.

RIYAD ROSE EARLY the day he was to leave Raqqa, body electric, heartbeat quick. He ate a breakfast prepared by his mother, bread and olives, coffee and cheese. By now she'd resigned herself to the

reality of his departure and had begun to see it as a blessing, knowing his antiregime rants could bring unwanted attention to her family. He hugged her, long and tight, and when he leaned over to kiss
her head and her hand, she cried.

Riyad picked up his suitcase, which held his travel documents,
one shirt, one pair of pants, a change of underwear, and a prayer rug.
He'd buy a toothbrush when they stopped in Aleppo, but not much
else. He'd inherited the mentality of Ibrahim and Taha, nomads
who roamed the world, never packing so much that they couldn't
vanish from any place at any time. He walked out of his house and
down to the bus station, alongside Bashar and a group of his friends.
He was set to travel by bus from Raqqa to Damascus with Bashar,
his cousin Thayer, and his friend Ahmed, where they would take
him to the airport and deliver him to the plane.

He expected to meet his father at the bus station. Instead, when
he arrived, he found his father and dozens of other men, uncles and
tribal elders, all gathered in the parking lot and in the coffee shop
next door, smoking and sipping coffee and talking while the sun
rose. When he arrived, they surrounded him, offering hugs and
kisses, pats on the back and on the shoulders, and declarations of
abundant pride.

"America," said one, shaking his head as if he couldn't believe it.

"The American land," said another, nodding as if he could.

One of their own, a boy from the Taha al Hamed tribe, would
soon be living in the most powerful nation on earth. Riyad would
achieve something monumental simply by setting foot on that plane.

"Talk about us," one told him. "Tell them about our tribe, who
we are."

Said another: "Show them our generosity."

And another: "Represent us well."

Riyad nodded and said he would. Even if he hated so much
about Syria, he loved Raqqa, and he loved even more the men and
women of his tribe.

Riyad stepped onto the bus, just behind Bashar, Thayer, and
Ahmed. As he boarded, a fellow passenger, a businessman from

Aleppo, laughed and asked him, "Are you the first person from your city to ever leave or something?"

Riyad grinned, a little embarrassed. Even to other Syrians, the desert culture seemed quaint. He couldn't imagine how foreign it would feel to people in the United States.

"Not exactly," he said. Others from Raqqa had moved abroad, yes, but it was still a city where moving to Aleppo for college was seen as cause for celebration. Even if others had done it, few here could fathom getting on a plane that would fly halfway around the world. And besides, Riyad wasn't just anyone. He was an Alkasem, son of the *mukhtar*.

He found his seat. Abdul-Rahman followed him, and they sat together for a moment, quiet and still. Then his *yahba* leaned over to hug and kiss him, and Riyad felt something drop inside his body, a weight tumbling through his insides and spilling out. For the first time since he'd made the decision to leave, he wept.

"Wipe your tears," his *yahba* said. "It's time."

His father said again that he loved him, that he was just so very proud. And right before he stood to leave, he leaned back toward Riyad and held him close. He spoke into his son's ear: "Just remember, you have to be careful. Every day where you are going, you have to be careful."

He was going far across the river. He was going without blood.

"For every one friend you make," he said, "you will have a thousand enemies."

Riyad nodded, kissed his father goodbye, and wept some more.

RIYAD RODE BESIDE BASHAR for hours, stopping in Aleppo to change buses and to pick up nail clippers and a new toothbrush and a few knickknacks he imagined he might need along the way. Bashar rode mostly in silence, leaning over once or twice to remind Riyad to be careful, to call the family if he needed anything, not to assume that every stranger he met would offer him the kindness he'd come to expect at home.

He told Bashar and the others he was less worried about his safety than his ability to function in a foreign country. "I don't drive, and I don't speak English." He laughed. "Other than that, I'll be okay."

His cousin Thayer shook his head and patted Riyad's arm. He mentioned a distant cousin, a few years older, who'd moved to America years ago. "He's an idiot," Thayer said, "and he's okay." He squeezed Riyad's shoulder. "Do you really think you're dumber than him?"

Riyad chuckled. He supposed not.

"Believe me," Thayer said, "you'll be just fine."

They arrived at the Damascus airport, and Riyad said goodbye to Thayer and Ahmed. Then he turned to Bashar.

They hugged wordlessly, Riyad holding his little brother while Bashar gently cried. They let go, and Riyad stepped onto an escalator. He turned with his bag and looked down behind him at his brother and his cousin and his friend, unsure when, if ever, he would see them again. He smiled and waved and felt himself about to cry, as the escalator lifted him up, higher and higher, until they vanished from his view, and Riyad turned, now knowing no one, unsure of where to go next.

CHAPTER

5

Riyad stepped off the plane at Los Angeles International Airport, in October 1990, and walked into a scene of confusion. He did not understand the words spoken all around him, nor much of what he saw printed on the airport's signs. He still spoke English at only a third-grade level, so all he knew was to follow the mass of people until they stopped, standing together in a long and winding line. Customs and immigration. He'd prepared for this. He pulled out his passport. One last step, and he would officially enter the United States.

Riyad was tired. He'd been called a "terrorist" by another passenger while changing planes in Rome—the insult confused him, as he'd most often heard it deployed against the Muslim Brotherhood by Assad. But that didn't bother him nearly as much as his experience at an airport coffee shop, where he'd approached the counter famished but unsure how to say what he wanted. Before him in line, he heard another customer ask for a "cappuccino" and receive both a drink and a pastry, and so Riyad stepped to the counter and said "cappuccino" too. Seconds later he walked away, defeated and embarrassed, when he was given no pastry but only a cup of creamy coffee unlike any he'd tasted at home.

He'd nearly been stranded in Rome, bumped from his flight for reasons he didn't understand by a gate agent who said he could fly to Los Angeles next week instead, and who shrugged when Riyad asked her where he should sleep until then. A young African American man had overheard and intervened on Riyad's behalf, causing a scene and refusing to shut up until the agent guaranteed Riyad a spot on the plane. He didn't know why the man had helped him, didn't know why he'd been bumped in the first place, but when he took his seat on the plane, he didn't move, not even to go to the restroom, scared that the moment he stood up, someone else would take his place.

And yet, still, here he was in Los Angeles. He waited his turn, fidgeting, nervous. A friend who'd traveled abroad told Riyad that when they gave him a customs form, he should answer no to everything, and so Riyad had done just that, clutching the paper in his hand. Soon enough the agent called him forward. She was young, African American, heavy. She sat in a chair and peered up at Riyad, studying his face, then his passport and visa, and then his face again.

"You're here to study?" she asked.

"Yes," he said.

She nodded and flipped through his passport in silence. "Legal residence?" she asked, eyes unmoving.

Riyad shook his head. He did not understand.

"Legal residence?" she asked, now glancing upward, just for a second meeting his eyes.

Riyad took this in for a moment. He understood one word: *legal*. He'd learned it in college, where, after all, he had studied law. She must be asking if he had studied to become a lawyer, he thought. Of course. That was it.

"Yes," he said, "legal residence."

Now she looked down at him, amused and impatient all at once. "What is it?"

"Yes," he said, "legal residence."

She shook her head again. "Do you speak Syrian?"

"No," he said. There was no such language as Syrian. "Arabic."

"Okay." She called someone on her phone, and Riyad assumed

she was asking for a translator, but soon she sounded agitated, then hung up and shook her head once more. For one reason or another, Riyad assumed, no translator was coming.

"Let's try this again," she said. "Legal residence?"

Riyad held up his finger. One moment. He would find what she needed. He just had to look through his bags. He pulled out his I-20 form, the one issued by Cal State Los Angeles that had helped him secure a visa. He handed it to her and waited.

She read. Then spoke. "No."

Now she sighed, and Riyad could see her amusement evaporate and her impatience grow.

"What. Is. Your. Legal. Residence."

He reached into his bag for another document, then handed it to her. His law degree. He smiled, pleased to show her that she was welcoming to America a man of letters.

"Legal residence," he said.

She looked down at the document. It was written entirely in Arabic. She shook her head, and he could tell by the way she shook it that she was not impressed, was actually still quite annoyed and, more important, convinced that he was the dumbest person she had ever met.

Riyad realized, of course, that she held his entire future in her inkpad, that if she chose not to stamp his passport, he might never enter America at all. And after more than twenty-four hours in transit, many of them spent missing his family and his city, Riyad now realized that he'd made a mistake. A massive, life-ruining, suddenly obvious mistake. Why on earth would he ever have believed that he could just *move to America*? Surely he couldn't navigate this strange country with its strange language. Surely any ambition of finding his place here had always been a fool's dream.

He felt panic rise, then consume him. His hands vibrated; his mind jangled. He did not know where to go or what to do, only that he definitely couldn't stay. *I'll go back,* he thought to himself. He had $900 in his wallet. His flight here had cost $1,400. How close to Syria could he get with $900? he wondered. Italy, maybe? Egypt? If he could just make it to a country where enough people spoke Arabic, he'd be fine. He'd get a job, find a place to stay, save a little more money, pay for a flight all the way to Damascus, then take a bus back to Raqqa. Maybe he could even still become a judge.

"Okay," he said to the woman. "No problem." He reached for his passport, hoping she would give it back to him and let him return to the terminal. Only she didn't. She just looked at him again, and he looked back, and neither said anything, and Riyad had no idea what to do.

Finally, he heard a voice from behind him: *"Enwan!"*

Riyad's breath left him. He couldn't believe it. Someone was speaking Arabic. He turned around to find a man with brown skin, perhaps Syrian, looking at them both in exasperation.

"Your address!" he said in Arabic. "She wants you to give her your address."

Oh! Address. Riyad knew *this* word, even in English. He'd learned it in school, years ago. He had on a piece of paper the address of a family friend, Nidal, who'd agreed to pick Riyad up from the airport and let him stay in his house while he got settled. Riyad handed her the paper. It had a number, and then a street, and then a city: Glendale.

She looked, read, then grinned. "Yes," she said. "Legal residence."

She stamped his passport and waved him through, and Riyad entered, a resident of the United States.

ENTERING THE TERMINAL, Riyad was struck by the space—vast and cavernous and filled with bodies of all colors and shapes, all of them united by the fact that they seemed to know where they were going. Riyad, carrying his suitcase, did not. He was supposed to meet Nidal. He knew this. Nidal was the brother of one of Riyad's best friends back home in Raqqa. He'd seen a photograph of Nidal, and Riyad assumed they'd find each other with no problems, but now he just wandered around, directionless, scanning the room, until he ran, abruptly, smack into a portly and gray-haired white man.

"Hey!" the man said, and Riyad apologized, and all around him people snickered, a few making comments to the man as if they knew him. Riyad gathered himself and continued.

"Riyad!"

He heard the voice calling from near one of the walls in the terminal. He walked over to two men, both middle-aged. One was tall and light-skinned, the other short and brown and wearing glasses. Neither looked like the man he'd seen in the photograph who was supposed to pick him up.

"Nidal?" he asked.

They both laughed. "No," they said, but they waved him over all the same.

"Two things," said the tall and light-skinned man. "First, do you know who you just bumped into?"

Riyad shrugged.

"That was Tommy Lasorda."

Riyad shrugged again. Lasorda was the manager of the Los Angeles Dodgers and a legend in American sports. Riyad had never heard of him, had barely heard of baseball, which he'd seen only in American movies. "Okay," he said.

"Number two," said the light-skinned man, "you need to understand that Nidal is a liar. The quicker you get that, the better off you'll be."

Riyad nodded, not quite sure what to make of this, as the men introduced themselves. The tall one was Warkase, the short one Abdul Hai. Both had spent many years living in Raqqa. They'd heard from family members that the Alkasem boy was moving to Los Angeles, so they'd gotten his flight information, and now here they were.

"Come," Warkase said. "You're staying with me."

Riyad shook his head. He was supposed to meet Nidal. The woman at customs had let him into the country only after he'd shown her Nidal's address—he didn't know what laws he might be breaking if he spent his first night in America at someone else's home. Maybe he'd be arrested, even deported.

"No," Riyad said. He showed the men Nidal's address, an apartment in the suburb of Glendale. "I'll just walk to his house."

They laughed, first gently, then uproariously. Then they turned gentle again, and Warkase put his arm around Riyad. "Do you know where you are?"

Of course, Riyad thought. "Los Angeles."

"Yeah. But do you really know where you are?"

Riyad said nothing.

"Because you must think you're still in Raqqa if you expect to walk to that apartment." Warkase gestured all around them. "This *airport* is the size of your entire city." He grabbed Riyad's suitcase. "Come on."

As they walked to Warkase's car, Abdul Hai explained further. He'd gotten a call from his father, telling him that Nidal, whom Abdul Hai's family knew from Raqqa, was scheduled to pick Riyad up. But this was unacceptable. Nidal came from a good family but had developed a bad reputation. He couldn't be trusted to care for anyone from Raqqa, much less the son of the *mukhtar.*

"He can't sleep anyplace except yours," Abdul Hai's father had told him. "If you let anyone else take care of him, you will bring shame to our entire family." Even on the other side of the world, tribal code remained law.

The moment they stepped outside and into the car, the pain of Riyad's travels melted away. He felt the southern California air, warm and dry and perfect. He scanned the surrounding hills, jutting dramatically from the earth, green and gorgeous. And then there were the streets, pure black, smooth, and organized, just as he'd seen in the movies. They drove north on the 405 and west on the 10, and Riyad felt dizzy at the sight of so many cars all moving in the same direction, weaving in and out of lanes as if in some improvised dance.

They took him to Hollywood and rode down Sunset Boulevard, and he stared at the iconic sign perched in the hills. The dream he'd seen in brochures now blurred with reality. Riyad felt ravenous and dizzy, as if his mind couldn't keep up with all his body saw and smelled.

———

HE STAYED IN GLENDALE with Warkase for one night and then in Long Beach with Abdul Hai for many more. He planned to spend a couple of weeks there, getting on his feet. After he got established, he would start taking the bus to East L.A., where he'd register at Cal State Los Angeles and begin English classes in the next term.

Abdul Hai had two roommates, brothers, both Syrian. One was a civil engineer by trade but was currently unemployed; the other, a college student studying computer science. Both had ample free time, which they spent, every single day, sitting together and sipping coffee while they read the *Los Angeles Times*, front to back. Riyad didn't get it. They knew the language, sure, reading the newspaper had helped with that, but what did it matter that they could speak English when they spent all day staring at the same four walls? Riyad couldn't bear it. He had to explore.

One morning he just put on his shoes and walked out the door, into the world. Warkase had told him he'd be immobilized as long as he didn't have a car, and the moment Riyad tried to navigate Long Beach on foot, he realized those words had been true. The city was a whir of moving metal—sidewalks minimal, streets acres wide. There was one place he could go, though. Just across the street from his apartment complex was a massive expanse of parked cars in front of a series of interconnected brown buildings, each with a different-colored sign, with names like Dollar Tree and Circuit City, Burlington Coat Factory and Hallmark. And sitting there in the center stood one building that loomed taller than the rest. It had a red and white sign, three circles, one inside the other. Riyad felt drawn to it immediately. *Target.*

He walked through the doors and into another world. Row after endless row of mixing bowls and lawn chairs, baseball gloves and underwear, boxes of cereal and batteries, all of it bathed in the glow of the store's fluorescent lights. He'd never seen anything like it, had never known such a thing existed. The movies about America showed sheriff's departments and skyscrapers, baseball fields and high school hallways. Why, he wondered, didn't they show *this*? It was gorgeous.

He walked slowly, first around the perimeter of the store and later up and down its many aisles, touching the merchandise briefly, just getting a feel for the wonders it held. He saw six-packs of soda and bags full of rice, bread sliced and wrapped in plastic, nothing like what was in the bakery back home. Every now and then he would pass one of the store's employees, and his eyes would turn downward, so as not to draw suspicion. He didn't know what he was doing wrong, but something about the whole experience felt decadent.

A thought struck him: *Can I work here? I should work here!* He'd need a job to support himself while he went to school. But that dream left him almost the moment it arrived. He saw one of the workers, dressed tidily in his red vest, navigating the shelves with an expertise that Riyad couldn't fathom. The workers here probably all had degrees from American universities, he reasoned. Riyad was still years away from being qualified to stock these shelves.

So he'd look elsewhere in this strip mall. Somewhere there had to be a job suitable for his skills. He walked out of Target and all across the shopping center, avoiding the businesses that seemed to demand qualifications beyond his own (Circuit City, Burger King) and into smaller shops selling hardware or cheeseburgers or anything in between. In each storefront, he arrived armed with a single sentence, in his best English: "Do you have a job?"

Most did not. They shook their heads, some more politely than others, and sent him on his way. After more than an hour of walking in and out of restaurants and stores, growing accustomed to rejection, he opened the door to an Italian deli, walked inside, and marched straight up to the most important-looking man he could find.

"Do you have a job?"

The man stared at him, face blank.

Riyad wondered if he'd misspoken. "Do you have a job?"

The man's eyes grew. He was short, perhaps forty, with a bald head and olive skin, body hair so thick, Riyad could see it through his shirt, which was clean and well-pressed, a shirt that spoke of wealth.

"Are you kidding me?" he asked Riyad.

Riyad tried to shrug and to shake his head but instead just awkwardly flinched.

The man continued. "You just came in here an hour ago!"

Riyad racked his brain. Here every building, every storefront, looked the same. If he was honest, most of the managers of most of the stores all looked the same too. Back at home, shops and restaurants all looked different, each of them set in buildings that dated back centuries, most manned by owners he'd known since he was a little boy. In Raqqa, he could tell businesses apart, no problem. But not in Long Beach. Not today.

"My answer," the man told him, "is the same right now that it was the first time. No."

Riyad returned home that night still unemployed, and he rose the next morning to hit the shopping center again. He popped in and out of any storefronts he'd missed the day before, until he entered a small restaurant with brown walls and a few scattered tables, a counter at the front for taking orders. Only then did it hit him: This was the same Italian deli as the day before. Without thinking, he'd walked in again. Only now, instead of the original important-looking man, Riyad saw a different important-looking man. Perhaps this man had more interest in bringing on a new hire.

Riyad took a chance. "Do you have a job?"

He got the same answer, no. Riyad nodded and thanked him for his time, then turned to leave. Before he reached the front door, it opened, and in walked a short man, bald head, glowing skin.

"You!" the man said. "What are you doing here? I told you yesterday—*twice!*—we're not hiring."

Riyad apologized and continued to the door, ready to slip back outside and into the strip mall.

"Wait," the man said.

Riyad waited.

"You know what? I actually kind of like you."

Riyad stood in the doorway, quiet. He felt a sense of pride. An American—*an American who wore expensive shirts*—liked him. This was something.

"Do you want to wash dishes?" asked the man, who soon intro-duced himself as Raffy.

Riyad said yes.

"Okay, then. Tomorrow you come back in here, and you wash dishes."

RIYAD SHOWED UP the next day wearing his other change of clothes: a white button-down, black slacks, and black Italian loafers.

"What are you doing?" Raffy asked.

"I'm here to work."

He laughed. "Are you serious?" He looked at Riyad's shoes. "In those?"

Riyad shrugged. He had sneakers back home in Raqqa, but it had never occurred to him to bring them to America. He was here to learn about democracy. He needed to look his best.

"They're the only shoes I have."

Raffy shrugged and began training his new employee. He showed him their system for washing and drying dishes, which Riyad picked up in a matter of minutes, no problem. Raffy explained that he would also need Riyad to work as a prep cook, helping him before they opened to ready the kitchen for each day.

Riyad knew how to prep. He'd done it as a little boy, dicing to-matoes and peeling onions while his mother and grandmothers floated around the kitchen. But he'd never cooked like *this*. He'd never even seen some of these ingredients. Raffy took him on a tour of the kitchen, introducing him to meats and cheeses and fruits and vegetables he'd never heard of, explaining how each one fit into the meals they prepared. Riyad learned that avocados were green and mushy, that Swiss cheese had holes, and provolone came in circles.

Raffy showed him sliced meat. "This is turkey."

"Turkey?"

"Turkey."

Riyad was confused. He'd never heard this word applied to a food. Perhaps he was saying the meat came from Turkish cuisine, but Turkish and Syrian dishes overlapped in many ways, and Riyad had never seen meat sliced like this.

"Like the country?"

"No. Like the bird."

Riyad shrugged. Whatever. In Syria they called the same bird *deek musri*—Egyptian chicken. He got to work, prepping food before the restaurant opened, washing dishes throughout the day, closing down the kitchen at night. By the end of his first day, his shoes were ruined, his shirt filthy, and his body exhausted, but still he felt eager to return the next day.

A couple of days later, on a Sunday, the phone rang at his apartment. One of the brothers answered, then rustled Riyad from the couch. He held his hand over the phone, eyes serious, and whispered, "It's your boss."

"Hello," Riyad answered.

"Get dressed," Raffy said. "I'll be there in twenty minutes. We're going shopping."

Twenty minutes later Raffy pulled up in his truck. Riyad hopped in, and off they went to a place called the "flea market." Raffy walked with him through a cavernous warehouse, scooping up a couple of old T-shirts and even older pairs of pants, and then the item Riyad needed most of all: a pair of white LA Gear high-tops.

"Wear this tomorrow," he said, and Riyad nodded. "Now you're ready to wash dishes."

He had a job. Soon he would have money—about $250 a week. Back home in Raqqa, that would have placed him squarely in the professional class. Here in Los Angeles, it positioned him just barely above the poverty line. But that, for Riyad, felt like plenty.

NOW HE NEEDED a bank account. One afternoon Riyad walked into the Wells Fargo across the street from the deli. Inside he saw a young woman sitting at an open desk in the middle of the room. She had redder hair than any he'd seen in his life, and she wore a sleeveless shirt, revealing arms covered in freckles. He'd never seen anyone like her—not back home in Raqqa or in his weeks here in America, not even on TV. He approached and she smiled.

"Hello," he said. "I need a check."

"Okay," she said. She studied him, seeming to surmise that this man was new to America and that this transaction would not be completed with ease. He saw a flash of confusion cross her face, quickly replaced by a warm smile.

"Cash a check?" she asked.

"Yes," he said, "cash a check."

She reached out her hand for Riyad to hand her the check. He did not. He had no check. The confusion returned, and then, again, the smile.

"Money order?"

"Yes. Money order."

She waited for Riyad to tell her more about the money order, but he did not.

He stared at her.

She stared at him.

He fidgeted.

She smiled.

"I don't understand," she said.

"I don't understand," he said.

They sat, quiet for a few moments, each one thinking. Riyad didn't know what to say, had no clue how to explain to her the thing he needed. He wanted a bank account, a place to put the money he would soon be earning, a place where he could watch that money grow over weeks and months and even years while he lived in this country, paying for his college tuition and his future car, perhaps someday for a house. Something to make him feel like finally, for the first time since he set foot on American soil, he was rooting himself in this strange land.

Instead all he had was this, a few moments at a desk sitting in awkward silence, trying his best not to stare at the hair and the freckles on the very nice woman who looked very, very confused. He slumped a little, sighing. He could have been a judge back in Syria. *A judge*. He would have been assigned his own personal assistant, someone responsible not only for taking calls and greeting visitors to his office but for anything Riyad wanted—buying him clothes or groceries, chauffeuring him around town, running any errand, personal or professional, that Riyad could ever have imagined. Instead he was here, washing dishes, with no place to put his money.

But that was the thing, he told himself. He had a job. In America. He'd made it through the confusion at customs on his way into the country, had figured out how to get hired after stumbling into the same restaurant three times. He'd decided that if he just waited, just kept trying to say what he needed and refused to be embarrassed by his lack of language, he would be okay.

He sat upright. "Check," he said.

"Check," she said.

They both went silent again.

She smiled, and in her smile he saw a warmth unlike any he'd felt since arriving in this country. They were doing this together, Riyad and the red-haired bank worker. He could tell that she wanted to understand him every bit as badly as he wanted to understand her. She sat there across the desk from him, her eyes tilted upward as if to reach back into her brain.

While she continued thinking, he tried to construct a sentence. "I give you money," he said, holding out a few bills of cash. "You give me check." He tried to think of what use he might have for a check. "I write check for phone company."

She nodded. "So you want a money order? For the phone company?"

By now Riyad realized that the phrase *money order* was not useful. This was progress. "No money order," he said.

"Okay."

While he sat thinking of what to say next, she bolted into an upright posture, a curious smile grabbing hold of her face.

"You give me money," she said. "I give you account."

Riyad nodded. Her smile grew.

"I take money slowly," he said.

"Yes!" she said.

"Yes," he said.

Now she beamed with a mix of sympathy and relief. "This," she said, "is called a checking account."

They were off. She took Riyad's ID and spent several minutes writing in a notebook. Soon he was all set up, with a place to deposit his cash and with checks he could use anywhere he needed. She finished up, gave him some paperwork, and looked him in the eyes.

"Riyad," she said, and it felt so nice to hear someone call him by name, "you should be very proud of yourself."

Riyad nodded and cast his eyes down at the floor. He felt tears creeping toward the edges of his eye sockets, but he pushed them away and smiled.

"Thank you," he said. He walked out of the bank and into the southern California sun, feeling, at least for the moment, that his life in America might still come to resemble his dream.

HE GOT HOME and told Abdul Hai. "I opened a checking account!" he said, speaking Arabic.

Abdul Hai nodded. "Okay, that's good."

Riyad smiled goofily, unsure how to deal with the fact that his friend's excitement did not match his own.

"So," Abdul Hai said, "now you have a job and a bank account. Are you ready to find your own place to live?"

Riyad nodded. "Yes."

Abdul Hai had been patient, the two brothers less so. Either way, Riyad knew that no one loved a stranger sleeping on their couch. It was time to move on. He and Abdul Hai scanned the newspaper for housing ads, and they found one offering a single room in a four-bedroom house, about three miles from his job.

They pulled up into the driveway, knocked on the front door, and were greeted by an older white woman who looked to Riyad like every older white woman he would ever meet in California. She was thin, wirily muscled, with curly hair and a massive smile and skin that both sagged and shone.

"Hi," she said. "I'm Helen."

Riyad introduced himself and stepped inside. There was a den area just before them, then two wings of the house—one a master suite where Helen lived, the other a line of three bedrooms and one bathroom, which she rented to tenants. She showed him to the available room. It was small, lightly furnished, with a twin bed, a small dresser, a nightstand, and nothing else. Rent would be $350 a month.

"This is good," Riyad said. "I like to live here."

Helen smiled, and when she did, Riyad felt like he was being wrapped in a mother's hug. "Wonderful," she said. "Just let me know what time you want to move in with all of your stuff."

Riyad didn't understand. "My stuff?"

Abdul Hai translated. She meant the rest of his possessions.

Riyad shook his head and held up his suitcase. "This is my stuff."

Helen looked at his suitcase, then at Riyad, and then at his suitcase again. "Really?"

"Yes."

Riyad stood there waiting, suddenly embarrassed. Helen looked like she might cry. He did not want her to cry. "It's okay," he said. "I'm okay."

He slept that night on a bare mattress, with wadded-up clothes as his pillow. The next morning he rose and walked forty-five minutes to work, where he prepped and washed and dried, and then he walked all the way home. When he walked into his room, he found the space transformed.

A pair of sheets and a comforter were fixed neatly on the bed. At the foot, there was an electric blanket, unplugged and nicely folded. At the head was a pillow, covered in a case, and sitting on the nightstand he saw an alarm clock, set to the correct time. While he'd been working, Helen had gone shopping.

He told Abdul Hai the next day.

"What?" Abdul Hai responded.

"Yeah," Riyad said. He'd been in America for just a few weeks. His boss had bought him clothes, and his landlord had given him a bedroom full of necessities he lacked. "Is this just how people are in America?" Riyad asked. He assumed the country must have a culture of generosity, not dissimilar from the tribal customs back home.

Abdul Hai shook his head. "No, this is not normal. Not at all."

Riyad had been lucky, Abdul Hai told him. This country could be wondrous but also cruel, and Riyad shouldn't expect his luck to last.

RIYAD SETTLED INTO LIFE at the restaurant, walking three miles every morning, along sidewalks and under overpasses, feeling the warmth of the southern California sun and the wind whipping off of cars as they sped by. On his walk each day, he encountered flocks of crows perched on the phone lines, staring down at the world below. In Syria, crows had always been considered a bad omen, and he wondered if their presence meant he'd made a grave mistake, that he didn't belong here. America seemed like a place of adventure, but so far life looked far different than he'd expected. He tried to register for classes at Cal State, but when he met with officials, he realized he'd lost his I-20 form, an essential document for enrollment. Suddenly, the whole process of starting school seemed byzantine and overwhelming, as if simply getting himself into a classroom were his first test, and he could not pass it. So he decided to focus on his job, to spend some time saving money, and eventually he'd figure out the paperwork he needed to begin school. But as he walked, seeing the crows overhead and wondering when he'd ever undertake an American legal education, his eyes would move to the palm trees and the cloudless sky, and he knew he was right where he should be.

Once at the restaurant, he would get to work prepping ingredients before it opened, then stay late washing dishes until it closed. He would walk home, and into his small room, and fall into a deep sleep, prepared to do the whole thing again the next day.

One day he was back at the sink, washing plate after plate in the midst of the lunchtime rush, when he heard shouting coming from the other side of the kitchen. Raffy's wife, a tall and severe woman named Rachel, was at odds with the sous-chef. They were shouting in Italian, with occasional expletives in English.

"Fuck you!" shouted one.

"Fuck you!" shouted the other.

Soon enough the sous-chef was taking off his apron and throwing it on the floor, walking toward the back door of the kitchen.

On his way out, he stopped and looked Riyad in the eye. "If you're smart," he said, "you won't stay here." He pointed at the boss's wife. "That woman will make your life miserable." And then he left.

Raffy himself had gone out that morning for a trip across town to his favorite grocer. His wife managed the front of the house but had no clue how to cook. Apart from one server, Riyad was the only other person on shift.

Riyad looked at Rachel, and she began to cry, and he felt embarrassed watching her, unsure how to make her stop. Finally he offered, "I can cook."

She looked up at him, skeptical. "You've never cooked here."

He shrugged. "No, but I watch."

In his mornings while prepping the kitchen, Riyad had learned the ingredients. From his post at the dishwashing station, he'd seen enough dishes plated to know which words correlated with which actions. He couldn't read the order sheets—kitchen shorthand eluded him—but if someone called out the name of each dish, he felt confident he could make it.

"I know what to do," he said.

"Okay," she said. She had no choice. "Let's try."

The first order came in from the front of the house, and she called it out: "Turkey and avocado sandwich."

Riyad got to work. He grabbed an Italian roll from underneath the counter, then sliced it open and slathered it with house-made mayonnaise. He topped that with lettuce he'd shredded just that morning, then a few sliced tomatoes and a drizzle of Italian dressing. He reached into a bin for the turkey, the sliced meat he thought of as "Egyptian chicken," then spread out a few slices of provolone, which he knew only as "circle cheese." He scooped out an avocado, then took a spear of pickle to top it off. He sliced the sandwich down the middle, diagonally, and handed it to Rachel, who was now on the phone with her husband.

"He really knows how to do this," she said.

And so it went. He made turkey and sausage sandwiches, prepared spaghetti and lasagna. He even remembered to sprinkle some pepper flakes on top of the pasta, which Raffy liked because one in every few bites shocked the palate, drawing diners back away from their thoughts or conversations and deeper into the dish. He got tripped up when asked, on a roast beef sandwich, to "hold the au jus," but that was his only mistake. When given an order for an Italian sausage sandwich, he prepared it as he'd studied, steamed it until the cheese began to melt, then sent it out into the dining room.

Minutes later the server came back to the kitchen. She held a dollar in her hand.

"This is for you," she said, handing it to Riyad. The customer who'd ordered the Italian sausage sandwich wanted to tip the "chef" and called it one of the best sandwiches he'd ever had. Riyad took the dollar and smiled, then returned to work.

Soon enough Raffy returned to the kitchen, his face glowing. He took Riyad by the hand. "How did you know all this?"

Riyad shrugged. "I watch."

Raffy beamed. "You're never washing dishes again."

And Riyad didn't—at least not at the deli. The next day Raffy began training him as his apprentice, teaching him how to make everything, from the pasta to the sauces, completely from scratch. He even taught him how to talk to customers. "You have to use your accent," he said. "White people love that. It makes the food seem more authentic." Never mind that the restaurant was Italian and Riyad was Arab. In Raffy's vision of his white customers, all darker-skinned foreigners were the same.

A few days into Riyad's new gig, Raffy said to him, "I'm teaching you everything I know. But you have to promise me that when you get ready to open your own restaurant, you won't do it right across the street from mine."

Riyad rolled his eyes. "I'm never going to open a restaurant. I'm here to study."

BUT THAT WAS the thing: Riyad still hadn't enrolled in a single class. He'd lost his I-20 form almost immediately upon arrival, and he hadn't made the twenty-mile trek from Long Beach to Cal State to figure out his options. Even when he figured out the paperwork, he wasn't sure how he'd make it to classes. He needed to work every shift he could get, and he had no clue how to commute to and from campus. He didn't even know how to drive.

He still felt he was here on a mission, but with every day he spent slicing prosciutto and folding tortellini, his goal of studying foreign politics to revolutionize his own country felt more and more distant. The restaurant ate up the hours of most days; Sunday was his only day off, and he often spent it hanging out with Abdul Hai and other Syrian friends.

Among his fellow countrymen in America, Riyad felt like an outsider. The Syrians who moved to the United States came mostly from the upper crust, the sons of diplomats or international businessmen, people who'd grown up shuttling back and forth across continents. They were all enrolled in American colleges or had graduated into white-collar jobs. They took vacations. They drove new cars. Riyad's world barely expanded beyond a restaurant kitchen and rented bedroom walls. Even here, on the other side of the world, he was still a desert boy, a *sha'awi*.

Still, it felt nice to speak Arabic for a few hours every week, and besides, he didn't have any other friends. On his weekly visits to Abdul Hai's apartment, he got to sip coffee and play cards and speak Arabic, and it almost felt like home.

Occasionally they talked politics. Once someone said, "Our country is in great shape." He was an Alawite from Latakia, the son of a prominent regime leader.

"Whose country," Riyad asked, "your Syria or my Syria? Your Syria is wonderful, yeah. Mine is shitty."

And then—nothing. No gasps, no anger, no ominous silence for fear of a visit from the Mukhabarat. The other man just said, "Hey, we're all Syrian in this room. Let's respect each other." And he left it at that. They returned to their coffee and their card game and set talk of politics aside.

Once Abdul Hai came into Riyad's restaurant with a couple of friends, rich kids who were the sons of a Syrian consulate official and dressed like American preppies.

"Look at this guy," Abdul Hai said when Riyad emerged from the kitchen. "He would have been a judge in Syria, and instead he's here washing dishes."

The friends chuckled, and Riyad couldn't quite tell what their chuckles meant. Were they mocking him? Or just showing some perverse admiration?

Soon they turned serious. "You know," one said, "you can still go back." Riyad's rejection of the judgeship had come with a grace period. If he wanted, he could return home and resume his previous plan.

"Yes," Riyad said. "I know." Bashar had been telling him the same thing. Riyad didn't care. "I'm fine here."

They shrugged, chuckled, and left, and after they walked out the door, Raffy saw a pained look on Riyad's face and asked him what they'd said.

After Riyad told him, Raffy stood quiet for a few seconds. "If it's okay with you," he finally said, "I'd like to ban these boys from my restaurant."

The next time Abdul Hai showed up with his Syrian buddies, Raffy told him he wasn't welcome.

"No one should ever talk to you like that," he told Riyad.

RIYAD DIDN'T KNOW when he'd enroll in an American college, nor how he'd work toward mastering his new country's constitution, but he began to feel like he might be able to make a life here. The country revealed itself to him in new ways daily, and with each shift and rent payment he made, each day he spent walking to work in the southern California sun, Riyad felt more and more as if he could make this place his home.

CHAPTER

6

Riyad drove to the airport one evening in January 1993, the faintest buzzing in his belly, not quite nervous but not quite calm. He was here to meet a woman. Her name was Linda, and she was a good friend of his roommate Mike, whom he'd moved in with sometime in the two years after he left Long Beach to live closer to the heart of L.A. For weeks, Mike had been telling Riyad about Linda, that he might like her, that she was different from the flighty Americans and the sheltered Arab immigrants Riyad had encountered in his floundering attempts to date in L.A. They'd talked on the phone a couple of times, and he found her warm and kind.

Now he pulled up to the curb, waiting, Mike beside him in the passenger's seat. Linda was flying back with her young son from her grandfather's funeral in Tennessee, and Mike had convinced Riyad to drive them both to pick her up.

Mike pointed out the window. "There she is."

Riyad looked up to see a mass of red hair, big and alive, luminescent, resting atop a slender woman who walked and smiled with equal ease. He watched her, transfixed. When he first arrived a little more than two years ago, the chaos of this very airport had overwhelmed him, but now the world around him blurred as he watched Linda walk toward them. She held the hand of her eight-year-old son, Jorel, and Riyad introduced himself to them both, grabbing bags and loading the trunk and allowing a faint grin to linger on his face.

They climbed into the car, an old Mazda that Riyad had bought for nine hundred dollars. It had been so cheap because someone had been shot and killed in the backseat and blood still stained the upholstery. Mike had promised to sit in the bloodstained seat, with Jorel next to him in the back and Linda up front by Riyad. They rode north toward Van Nuys, chatting about the flight and the funeral, and Riyad noticed how Linda floated from the trivial to the grave as if weightless, and he thought he could listen to her talk for hours.

They stopped for dinner at Chuck E. Cheese. Mike took a cab home, leaving Riyad with Linda and Jorel, and they sat and continued their conversation over pizza while Jorel played. Linda told him about her home, Tennessee, a humble place with simple people, its culture built on hospitality. She talked about her childhood spent running wild through woods and rivers, and Riyad thought that her home sounded much like Raqqa. She told him how she'd left Tennessee to become a flight attendant soon after high school, living in New York and traveling all over the world. She'd spent a month shuttling back and forth between Libya and Saudi Arabia, taking Muslim pilgrims to Mecca for the *hajj*. In New York, she'd met a man and had Jorel. The relationship didn't last, but Jorel had come to feel like her entire world.

Riyad watched them, mother and son. Linda delighted in her child, who ran giggling from his pizza to the ball pit to the Skee-Ball and back again. She explained that she'd moved to L.A. because Jorel had become a child actor and model, appearing in TV commercials and print ads. When she talked to Jorel, she spoke fast, in a thick accent that Riyad couldn't comprehend, but when she talked to Riyad, she spoke slowly, and she watched him as he listened, and sometimes he nodded, but she could tell he misunderstood her, and so she slowed down further and explained herself again.

They were both foreigners, her world nearly as different from Los Angeles as his own. And they were both wanderers, people who loved their homes but found themselves called to explore. She was eight years older than he, and in her he saw evidence of a life fully lived. She told stories from worlds he never knew existed. She teased him gently, and she listened intently, and she held in her a curiosity unlike any he'd ever known. In a matter of hours, he felt like she understood him more than anyone—man or woman, Syrian or American—he'd ever met.

He wanted to tell her his story. He wanted to tell her everything.

SO HE DID. He told her about his home in the desert, about the ambitions that had brought him to America, and about the joys and struggles he'd found upon arrival in this strange land. Life had been hard, these last two-plus years in Los Angeles, harder even than in the first days after he arrived. He'd given up his life in Long Beach, drawn to the potential for greater opportunity in downtown L.A. That had been a mistake. He bounced from home to home, sleeping on couches and milk crates and, for one stretch of several weeks, in the front seat of a friend's car. Fellow Syrian immigrants had lied to him, promising jobs that never materialized. Impatient Americans had dismissed and confused him, refusing to help him navigate their world.

The America he'd discovered on arrival—a world of generous bosses and kind-eyed bankers and landladies who cared for him with a mother's love—that was not the America he knew now. By the time he figured out how to get the documentation he needed for college, his life had become more about survival than revolution. In the last two years, he'd worked the graveyard shift in gas stations. He'd served doughnuts and pizza. He'd gone months allowing himself only six dollars a day for food, which he spent at a burger joint called Troy's, drowning his bread and beef in condiments just to pack as many calories into his body as he could.

He hung out with other Arab immigrants, young men who'd

come here from cultures much like his own. So many, he thought, seemed drawn to the America they'd seen in the movies. They went to clubs and bars, chasing women and fleeting highs. Riyad served as their designated driver. He loaded them into his blood-streaked car and listened from the periphery of their conversations. The nights drained him, but they were better than sitting at home.

Alone in his room, he would stare at walls and read letters from his family. He'd called a few times after he arrived in America, but the calling cards were too expensive. Besides, his *yahba* had scolded him once on the phone. Don't call, he said. *Write.* "I want to smell you on the page."

So they sent letters to each other, written in quiet moments, then delivered across the world. As tough as life had been for Riyad in America, it had been just as bad back home. His father's shop had fallen on hard times, and even as Riyad struggled to survive in Los Angeles, he still scraped together money to send home. Bashar had finished college, earning a law degree, and had moved to Damascus to serve in the Syrian Arab Army, as most Syrian men are required to do. Bashar loved the city but hated the military. He ached to return to a life of the mind, refused even to carry a gun.

Riyad thought, occasionally, of returning to Syria, even if he'd missed the chance to reclaim his judgeship. But going home would feel to him like failure, and besides, he had found some strange beauty in his poverty. The world still thrummed with possibility as long as he ached for what he did not have. So instead he just lay in bed and read his family's letters over and again, sometimes five or six times in the same night, inhaling the love in the words and the scent of the paper, until finally he would drift to sleep.

Then things took a turn for the better. Riyad had met a Syrian Christian named Sam, who owned a number of liquor stores around town. Sam asked Riyad if he drank, and he said no, and then asked if he smoked, and he said no, and Sam said, "Good. That means you won't steal from me." Then he offered Riyad a job. The liquor business offered stability, even if Riyad's faith kept him from drinking the product he sold. He quit the gas station jobs and ditched the graveyard shifts, even enrolling in English classes at a local community college. He clung to the dream of learning how to lead a Syrian revolution, even as he found himself growing into a simpler and more stable American life.

Riyad and Linda fell in love. Their conversation at Chuck E. Cheese led to more dates, and then, on Valentine's Day, just a few weeks after they met, Riyad took her to a nice restaurant, got down on one knee, and offered her a gold ring. In Linda's culture, this was fast. Her friends told her not to go through with it. They'd seen the Sally Field movie *Not Without My Daughter*, in which an Iranian man takes his American wife and their little girl back to his home country and refuses to let them leave. Riyad, they said, would surely do the same thing.

But Linda was ready. She wanted this, wanted him. She was drawn to his ambition, soothed by his gentle spirit. Even though he was a nomad, he seemed unmovable.

She said yes. Eleven days later, on February 25, 1993, Riyad and Linda married at a local mosque. Traditionally, Syrian women do not take their husbands' last names, but this was not Syria. And so then and for many years later, she would joke that she must be the only Linda Alkasem in the whole entire world.

MARRIED LIFE BROUGHT delirious joys and inexplicable confusion, sometimes in equal measure. Riyad felt rooted to something in a way he hadn't been since the day he left Raqqa. Linda felt protected and supported, as if for the first time in her life she'd found someone she could trust. Both of them, though, brought their own cultures and priorities and their own expectations. Though Linda had converted to Islam, she didn't much like going to the mosque. Men prayed on one side and women on another, and she found herself surrounded by strangers, many of them speaking Arabic or Urdu or some other foreign tongue, all participating in a ritual prayer she could barely understand.

In their marriage's early days, she missed drinking beer, and one day Riyad caught her sneaking one in the garage, where she'd hidden a few bottles. He asked her, please, to stop drinking, and she agreed after a few months that yes, sure, she would. He talked to her about the hijab, the head covering worn by many Muslim women. He told her that he found it beautiful, and that if she wanted to wear one, he'd be delighted, but she said she didn't want to, and he never pressed the issue. That was that.

One day while Riyad was at work, Linda cooked dinner, turned out the lights, and lit candles all over their home. She set the table, and she waited.

Riyad walked in the door, saw the candles, and gasped, "What happened?"

"What do you mean?"

He gestured around to the candles. "Did we lose electricity?"

Before she could answer, he turned on a light switch, saw that it worked, and then rushed around the house, blowing out every candle, one by one.

Linda couldn't believe it. "Why would you do that?"

She had wanted a romantic dinner. She wanted her husband to be impressed.

Riyad, though, had never learned to associate dim lighting with romance. For him, candles were used only for families without electricity. Lighting a candle meant admitting poverty. In the months since he'd begun working for Sam in his liquor stores, he had tried hard to build stability. He was no longer skating on the edges of society.

"We're not poor!" he said. "We don't need these!"

Frustration, though, always gave way to delight. They laughed together at their own shared confusion. Even as she settled into marriage, Linda imagined, she could still enter undiscovered worlds, right there in her very home. She felt electrified by the sense that with Riyad, her life's possibilities seemed to have no limit. Once he told her, "There are some things about me that you won't know until we've been together for twenty years." This didn't scare her. It thrilled her. And she knew that he, too, would discover new truths about her long after their children had grown and their hair turned gray.

Their life together took on its own rhythm, with Riyad working in the shop and Linda taking care of Jorel. They learned each other's beliefs and quirks and bodies, coming to understand how to weld their lives to each other's. They each learned something about the other at 4:31 A.M. on January 17, 1994, when they awoke in the dark and felt the earth shaking. Riyad looked across the bed and saw Linda bolt upright screaming, and soon they were running, both of them, out of their bedroom and down the halls of the apartment, to grab Jorel and get outside. There had been an earthquake. It measured 6.7 on the Richter scale, among the largest in modern American history. It killed fifty-seven, injured more than eight thousand, and caused at least $13 billion in damage. Their apartment was deemed uninhabitable as long as the threat of aftershocks remained, so they lived for weeks in tents in the parking lot, and Linda was in constant fear.

"We have to leave," she said.

THEY MOVED TO TENNESSEE, back to Linda's hometown of Hendersonville, just outside Nashville. Riyad met his new in-laws and saw that Linda came from a tough but caring family. He won over her father after fifteen minutes of stories from the desert and jokes about California. He won over her mother and grandmother—who told him "Welcome to America!" even though he'd been in the country several years by then—the moment they watched how he cared for Linda and Jorel. At family barbecues, her relatives soon stopped serving pork, out of respect for Islam. Around town, they returned strangers' glares with their own dirty looks.

Tennessee was as different from Los Angeles as Los Angeles had been from Syria. California had been all palm trees and pavement, warm air and warmer exhaust, a place of beauty pocked with blight.

Tennessee was soft hills and quiet roads, houses that seemed miles apart. In Los Angeles, Riyad could go an entire day without speaking English if he wanted, floating from the mosque to Arab-owned businesses to the homes of Syrian friends. Here he lived in a county that was 85 percent white. Riyad suspected he was the only Middle Eastern man in the entire town.

Some landlords refused to rent to him and Linda; they only got a lease when she signed by herself, with Riyad hiding in the car. Employers ignored his job applications, and he filed three separate complaints at the Equal Employment Opportunity Commission. While filing the third one, a woman who worked there asked, "What county are you applying for jobs in?" And when he told her that it was Sumner County, the one just northeast of Nashville, she said, "Oh, honey, you're gonna have to move." One of his lowest moments had come when he overheard a UPS manager telling one of his colleagues, "I'm not hiring that sand nigger." Riyad was confused; he'd never heard the term before. When he got home and asked Linda about it, he watched her eyes go wide with anger as she said, "Riyad! He was talking about *you!*"

Finally, he found a job as an assistant manager at McDonald's. The pay was decent, the work never boring. Soon Linda became pregnant, and she gave birth to a son they named Kasem, after Riyad's brother. But just as they began to find a sense of belonging back in Linda's hometown, Riyad got a call from his old boss, Sam. After Riyad's year away, Sam wanted him back. But not as an employee. As a partner. He wanted him to take over a shop in Santa Barbara. Riyad missed California. Linda decided Santa Barbara was far enough away from the major fault lines. They both wanted a chance for him to earn more money for their family. And so in 1995 they returned.

Riyad took over one of Sam's underperforming shops and turned it around. Their bank account swelled. Linda got pregnant again. Another boy. And it was then that Linda's mother raised a concern. If something happened to Riyad, Linda might struggle to get benefits for herself and the children. She had an idea, though. Perhaps Riyad should become a U.S. citizen.

Riyad was ready. This country had confounded him, but it had also delivered delirious joys. It had given him Linda, in whom he found wells of support and endless laughter, someone who believed in a version of Riyad he often didn't know if he believed in himself. It had given him Kasem, the young boy he watched toddle through the world with wonder, and soon it would give him another son. He believed America still held within it possibilities no other place could match. Even as he'd struggled here, he was awed by this country's diversity and its spirit. He didn't know if he could still transform the world, as he'd once imagined. But he thought that here, in America, he'd found the one place that might give him that chance.

So he began the citizenship application process. He went through the interviews and took the test down at a local high school, answering questions about the Constitution and the original colonies and the flag. He'd spent hours studying but knew so many of the answers from years ago, from that classroom in Aleppo. And when the time came, he drove to the Los Angeles Convention Center to be sworn in as a citizen one morning in 1996, on the emotional border between laughter and tears. He smiled at the men and women who walked in alongside him, some of whom he recognized from the test, all of whom now formed a multiethnic caravan, heading toward the auditorium.

They were asked to take seats. They were asked, at various points, to rise and to sit once more. They listened to speakers who talked about honoring their home countries while embracing their new one. And then finally they were asked to take the naturalization oath.

So Riyad stood and recited the words. He swore allegiance to the U.S. Constitution and pledged to support and defend it from foreign and domestic enemies, even if required to take up arms. "I take this obligation freely," he said, "without any mental reservation or purpose of evasion; so help me God."

A representative from the Daughters of the American Revolution handed him a small flag, and he took it with him back to the parking lot and into his car and onto the 101 toward home. They had planned no party; he and Linda had few friends, and besides, he had to work. But as he drove, he let the weight of the moment overwhelm him. Even after six years in the country, so many filled with struggle, even though he still hadn't earned a law degree that he could take back home to fix Syria, he found that he loved America even more than he had sitting in that Aleppo classroom all those years ago. And so as he rode north up the coast, the Pacific Ocean to his left and the Los Padres National Forest to his right, he kept the window down and stuck his arm out the whole way, that tiny flag flapping in the wind as he drove.

CHAPTER

7

The happiest days of Riyad's life began around four, maybe four-thirty, when he awoke in the master suite of his home, lying in bed next to Linda, whose red hair seemed to shimmer even in the dark. He tried not to disturb the house as he crept out of bed and into the hall, tiptoeing to the kitchen for some water, maybe a piece of fruit. In one bedroom was Jorel, now in high school and years removed from his days as a child actor. Soon he would rise for a day of classes and show choir and wrestling practice, and maybe a shift at the local Subway if he was scheduled that night. In another bedroom slept Riyad's sons. Kasem was now six, almost seven, a bright and energetic boy who bounded around the house practicing moves he'd picked up in karate class. Sammy was four and a half, born just months after Riyad became a citizen, and like Riyad he found the world ripe for exploration, toddling all over the house and the yard with their dog, a husky named Krypto, who Riyad knew was still sleeping in his favorite spot, right under Kasem's bed.

This was his life—or a slice of it anyway. Waking next to his American wife, stopping on his way out the door to gently kiss his sons, all in his three-bedroom house on a gorgeous lot in a quiet suburb, Thousand Oaks, California. He was a world away from Raqqa, yes, but also a world away from the minimum-wage night shifts and near-homelessness of his early days in America. He hopped into the driver's seat of his black BMW 740 Li and pulled out into the driveway, past the peach and plum trees that rose above manicured bushes in his yard. He followed the Pacific Coast Highway north—the ocean to his left, the sun creeping up from the horizon on his right, the pavement before him a smooth black, the most gorgeous he'd ever seen.

Around five-thirty he pulled into Carpinteria, just outside Santa Barbara, where his day began at the local gym with a spin class, in a room on a bike next to a couple dozen of southern California's tanned and toned and blond, lighting his legs on fire and soaking his back in sweat. He showered and dressed, and at around seven, he pulled into the parking lot of the strip mall where he worked. A breeze wafted up from the beach, which sat less than a mile away, and overhead, the leaves on palm trees rustled. He unlocked the front door of M&R Liquors and stepped inside.

This was it—the place that had provided him a life he'd never dreamed of. A small wood-paneled shop on the outskirts of Santa Barbara, where he sold alcohol. This was the offer Sam had given Riyad to lure him back to California: become a full partner with no initial buy-in, with only the promise that he would put everything he had into the shop. And so that's what he'd done. Even though he didn't drink, he set about making himself something of a wine expert, touring as many of the region's vineyards as he could, chatting up salespeople and winemakers at every stop. It was no different, really, than what he'd learned from his father during those mornings in Raqqa's Eastern Market, sipping coffee with farmers while learning which of their crops had come in the best in a given season.

Riyad had taken over in 1995, and by the turn of the millennium, M&R Liquors was one of the highest-performing shops in the county. He occasionally struggled with the fact that he sold something he didn't drink, and this job certainly wasn't the calling that had pulled him to America, but it gave him time for English and political science classes at Santa Barbara City College. And besides, the liquor business had delivered him a life rich with unimagined joys.

So now he turned on the lights and began preparing for the day ahead. It was a Tuesday, typically a slow day in the shop. He got the shelves and the register in order, then walked to the back of the store, where he had a small office. He turned on the TV for a little white noise and lay down on a small couch for a quick nap.

Sometime in the next hour, just before the shop was set to open, he heard footsteps moving through the store. The door to his office opened, and a voice greeted him: *"Salaam alaikum."*

Riyad opened his eyes and looked up at the doorway, and there he saw Bashar.

BASHAR HAD NEVER PLANNED to follow his brother to America. In truth, he'd never planned to leave Syria at all. He'd always found comfort in the very environment Riyad had found oppressive. He could deal with the regime, as long as he could stay close to his family and his city and his books. He'd graduated with a law degree just a couple of years after Riyad, and then he'd gone off to Damascus for his mandatory military service, biding his time before he could start practicing as an attorney.

He loved Damascus but hated the army. The work drained him, body and soul. He rarely spoke of his service, then or in the years after. He tried to draw scant attention, to do the work he must, to fulfill the two-year commitment and move on.

After his discharge, Bashar moved back to Raqqa and began a life in the law. He started his own practice, focused on inheritance law, and traveled the country and the region, burying himself in far-flung libraries, working to become the country's foremost expert in his field. He made a comfortable living. He met a woman, asked her to marry him, and she said yes.

When his father's shop started struggling, Bashar kept the entire family afloat. And so when his parents started talking about taking a long journey to America, about spending a few months with their eldest son and new daughter-in-law and grandchildren, Bashar never considered joining them. Not yet.

THEIR *MAMA* AND *YAHBA* arrived at LAX one afternoon in early 2000. When they reunited with Riyad—the first time they had seen one another since Riyad had visited in 1996—they hugged and kissed and cried.

They reached next for their grandchildren. It didn't matter that they didn't share a language, nor that the boys were growing up on karate lessons and cartoons instead of strolls through the Eastern Market and swims in the Euphrates. They were Alkasems. They each had their own small plot on Raqqa's community land, just as Riyad and his father and the many men who came before them did. And when Riyad saw the way his sons melted into his father's arms, he knew that no distance of geography or culture could erase the connection they shared.

For a few days, all was joyous. And then within a week of arrival, Abdul-Rahman had a stroke. His fourth. And so they took him to a hospital, and soon he was transferred to another hospital, and over a period of months he made it to a rehab center, and then he had another stroke and nearly died, went on life support, back in the hospital again. Riyad and his *mama* did not know what to do, whether to let him die peacefully or to keep him alive knowing that he'd never get better, and so they reached out to Riyad's grandfather, the Sufi mufti, and he issued a fatwa, an edict based on Islamic law:

"Do not take death out of God's hands."

Translation: Do not remove him from life support. If he is alive, let him live. And so after trying for years to get a visa and then flying all the way across the world, Abdul-Rahman would now live, indefinitely, in an American hospital bed, as would Riyad's mother, who would not leave America without her husband. Riyad tried to care for his father and mother and his own family and own business, but it was too much. He needed help. He needed Bashar.

SO HERE HE WAS. Bashar left behind his legal practice and his fiancée. But he arrived in southern California with an open mind, curious to know if he, too, could make a home here. In truth, Bashar liked America. He liked the country's plurality, the way Los Angeles alone seemed to contain within it many worlds, pockets of disparate cultures hiding just off highways in the many strip malls that lined the city. You could be in Vietnam one moment and in El Salvador an hour later, could travel to the San Gabriel Valley and find storefronts all in Chinese and then to Glendale to find Armenians and Arabs, with a few Syrian-owned tea shops and hookah joints that felt like they'd been surgically removed from Damascus and dropped seven thousand miles away.

Bashar first worked at a gas station owned by Riyad's company—he was more devout than his brother and couldn't bear the thought of selling liquor—and he enrolled in adult education classes to improve his English. There he'd made a friend, a Chilean man named Carlos who shared Bashar's love for philosophy, and so after their classes, the Chilean and the Syrian would sit for hours and discuss the Germans, often Goethe and Nietzsche, debating each other in halting English. Bashar imagined that perhaps these were the kinds of moments that America promised, and he found himself hungry for more.

ON THIS TUESDAY MORNING, Bashar walked into the back office to find his big brother lying on the couch, paying no attention to the muted television. He greeted him and handed him a breakfast sandwich, prepared by their mother, with whom he shared an apartment just down the road. They sat together and ate, and then Bashar returned to the front of the store, where he would tend to a few minor tasks before leaving to man the gas station.

Riyad sat up on the couch, allowing himself a few more moments of quiet before he prepared to open. In the corner of the room, the television was on as usual. Riyad liked to watch morning reruns of *The Daily Show with Jon Stewart*. Sometimes he'd flip to the news, and out on the main floor, he often turned his other television to something apolitical, like VH1 or the Food Network, both of which educated him on corners of American culture he'd never known existed. Now he looked over and saw an image that surprised him—two skyscrapers, one engulfed in smoke. The television was on mute, and he assumed it was an action movie.

The phone rang, and he answered.

"Are you watching TV?" It was Linda. She sounded panicked.

"It's on," he said, "but I'm just trying to get the shop ready."

"Have you seen this plane?"

"What do you mean? On the movie?"

"No."

Riyad paused, silent, confused.

"No," Linda said again. "This is not a movie. This is real."

"What?"

"Change the channel. It's on everywhere."

Riyad flipped to the next channel to see the same buildings, the same smoke and fire, and he unmuted the television to hear every newscaster's voice describing the same horror. A plane had crashed into the World Trade Center.

"Bashar!" he yelled, and his brother rushed back to the office.

They watched. Riyad stood in disbelief, his mind struggling to catch up with his eyes. He looked on as a second plane flew into the second tower, and then as both buildings collapsed. Riyad was stunned. Bashar was thinking. He started to count: two planes, two massive buildings, right in the heart of the biggest and most densely populated city in the country.

"How many people are going to die because of this?"

Riyad only shook his head.

At first Bashar thought it must have been an accident, but he held a vague fear that it could be an act of terror, much like the sporadic bombings that dotted the recent history of the Middle East, carried out by men who called themselves Muslim but perverted Bashar's faith.

"What is going to happen next?" he asked his brother.

Riyad had no answer. All he knew was to open his shop and get through the day. But by the time their doors opened, some of Bashar's fears had been confirmed. The two planes had been hijacked, along with two others, one that hit the Pentagon in Washington, another that crashed in a field in Pennsylvania. The suspected hijackers were linked to Al Qaeda, the terrorist group helmed by Osama bin Laden, a Saudi national who'd spent decades fighting foreign powers on behalf of an extreme Islamist agenda.

Bashar decided to stay at the wine shop today, rather than leave for the gas station, so he could be near Riyad. Minutes after they opened, a regular customer named Greg walked in. Riyad liked Greg. Originally from Texas, he'd lost a hand in Vietnam but carried himself with the swagger of a man who'd never lost anything, not even a game of cards. He was tan and fit with an omnipresent smile, and now he approached Riyad and said hello, subdued but pleasant. Riyad rang him up and said nothing. Today, it seemed, there was nothing much to say. Greg took his purchases and walked to the exit, stopping to stare at the television before walking through the door.

"This," he said, and now he turned around to shoot his eyes at Riyad, "cannot stand."

He turned back to the television and shook his head.

On his way out the door, he shouted, "Kill them all!"

There were others. One man glared at Riyad the entire time he stood at the register, eyes inflamed and head shaking. A delivery man from Frito-Lay talked to Riyad amiably, trading information and expressions of anger, then nodded at the television and said, as if he thought Riyad would agree, "We should just drop a fucking nuke on Mecca, you know?"

And then there was the man who seemed to walk with a certain violence, staring at Riyad the moment he entered the front door. He was white and heavy-set, wearing a goatee and a tank top. He stomped from the door to the register, making a stop at the cooler to rip a Dr Pepper from the shelves. He approached Riyad.

Riyad felt himself stiffen. "Anything else?" he asked, and smiled.

"No," the man said.

"Cash or credit?"

The man smacked a couple of dollars onto the counter, eyes locked on Riyad's. Riyad nodded and reached down, grabbing the cash and opening the register to retrieve the man's change.

"You know what?" the man said. "Why don't you just go home?"

Riyad opened his palms, trying to ask for peace. "Hey man," he said, "I'm really upset about what happened today too." Riyad placed his change on the counter.

The man shook his head and grabbed it. "I'm coming back," he said, just before turning around to walk out the door. "I'm gonna blow this motherfucker to the ground."

RIYAD TRIED TO FORGET IT. The man was angry. Everyone was angry—including him. But another customer had heard the threat and called the police, and soon cops and news reporters came to his shop. Riyad said little about the man who'd made the threat, emphasizing only the fact that he, a Muslim and an American, was every bit as upset by the day's events as anyone else. He didn't think of himself as a man who shared a faith with the attackers. He thought of himself as a citizen of the nation under attack. Maybe he didn't want to nuke his religion's holiest city, or to "kill them all"—whoever *they* were—but he did want justice. He wanted the plotters found and arrested, properly tried.

Bashar, though, watched the day unfold with the rising sense that lines would soon be drawn, and that he and his brother and so many others like them would find themselves on the wrong side.

"It's going to get bad for us," he said.

Riyad shrugged him off. "People are angry. They just need to vent."

Bashar was less sure. He didn't view America as his brother did.

Bashar loved the freedoms and opportunities and diversity, yes, but as he scanned the world around him, he found societal cleavages by color of skin. People who looked and worshipped like him, even those who'd been born and raised in America, were still viewed by many as visitors, given permission to live here as long as they respected the order of things. And when one member of a minority group committed a mistake or a crime—or, God forbid, a massive act of violence—then all others were left to answer on his behalf.

This wasn't unique to America. Humans were tribal. It was every bit as true in the Syrian desert as it was by the California coast. No one was immune from the thirst for vengeance when wronged. Americans would need an enemy, and the men who'd organized the attack were too few and too far away to suffice. Soon, Bashar believed, the country would turn on everyone who looked and prayed like the Alkasems.

ON THE MORNING of September 12, Riyad insisted on keeping to his routine. He woke and prayed and left home, driving back up the coast to Carpinteria, where he went to the same spin class as the day before. In Santa Barbara, he parked his car in the same spot as he did every day, well within his line of sight when he stood behind the register. Most days the lot was empty. But today, sitting there in the middle, he saw an old Ford truck.

He recognized it by the color and by the dents scattered across its body. The truck belonged to Dave, a Korean War veteran, now perhaps in his sixties. Dave worked in agriculture and came in often to buy a snack or a soda, rarely liquor. He was exactly the kind of customer Riyad had hoped to attract when he revamped the store, someone who saw the shop not simply as a place for alcohol but as a pit stop for the needs of their everyday lives.

Now Riyad walked toward the truck, curious. He saw Dave in the driver's seat, leaned all the way back, asleep. Next to him was Dave's adult son, whose name Riyad couldn't quite recall. Riyad had never seen Dave or his son this early. He'd never seen *any* customer lying in a vehicle in his parking lot, asleep. Then he saw, sitting on the console between them, long and black and polished, a twelve-gauge shotgun. He felt his body go hot, just for a moment. And then without thinking, he knocked on the window and woke Dave up.

Dave's eyes opened, and he looked a little rattled as his brain worked to make sense of the world around him. He sat erect and brought his seat upright, and he rolled down the window, slowly, with his left arm.

"Hey," Dave said.

"Hey," Riyad said.

"How you doing?"

"I'm okay."

Riyad eyed Dave's son, still asleep, and then his gun, and then returned his gaze to Dave. "You okay?" he asked. "Can I help you with something?"

"Oh!" Dave said, seeming a little surprised by the question. "Well," he said, and he looked down at his hands for just a moment. "We heard about what happened on the news. About you getting threats and all." He looked at his gun, then back at Riyad.

"Okay," Riyad said slowly.

"And, well," he said, "*you know.*"

Riyad shook his head. "Know what?"

"Oh," Dave said, as if it were finally registering. "Well, we just decided that we'd come down here to protect you."

Now Dave opened his door and exited his truck. He stood and hugged Riyad, and as they stood there in the strip mall parking lot, both men held on to each other and cried.

RIYAD HAD NEVER THOUGHT of himself as a "Muslim American." Muslim, yes. American, yes. But the two words had never needed to be deployed in combination to describe a group to which he now belonged. In truth, since his earliest days in the country, Riyad hadn't spent much time with other Muslims. He would show up to the mosque for Friday prayers, popping in and out and then heading home, rarely trading more than polite small talk with those who shared his faith.

Really, the only Muslims in his life were his family. Aside from his time spent with them, Riyad's life revolved around the wine shop. His partner, Sam, was a Syrian Christian. He assumed his customers were mostly Christian or Jewish or belonging to no faith at all; matters of the soul were not often discussed when ringing people up for a bottle of scotch or sauvignon blanc. Riyad felt no need to connect to a larger community of American Muslims. In general, he had no more or less in common with a college student from Somalia or a mother from Indonesia than he did with anyone else. Praying to the same God was not, on its own, grounds enough to build a friendship, in Riyad's eyes.

But now Riyad realized that Bashar had been right: The day the towers fell, the world had changed. None of the attackers were Syrian, but that didn't matter. They shared Riyad and Bashar's skin tone. They claimed to be fighting out of devotion to their faith. To many, walking through the world with brown skin, much less a belief in Allah, was now grounds for suspicion. To a few, it was even enough to invite violence. In Arizona, there was Balbir Singh Sodhi, the gas station owner killed by a man who told people he was going out to "shoot some towel-heads." In Texas, when Waqar Hasan came around to the front of the bulletproof cashier's area to help a customer, he was shot and killed, the customer later telling police it was an act of revenge for the attack on the towers. And just down the road in San Gabriel, California, Adel Karas was manning the floor at his International Market when two men walked in and shot and killed him there in his store.

As they watched the news, Riyad and Bashar saw a pattern. So many of these victims worked in shops like theirs: gas stations, convenience stores, liquor stores. Small neighborhood retailers had long served as a ticket to the middle class for newly arrived immigrants. This was how Riyad's partner, Sam, had amassed his wealth, and how Riyad had rooted his family in the middle class. In their shops, these men served as public faces of their home countries, but for so many Americans, they were interchangeable. Most of the 9/11 hijackers had been Saudi, but Sodhi was Indian; Hasan, Pakistani; and Karas, Egyptian. Sodhi was a Sikh, Hasan a Muslim, Karas a Christian. But all had brown skin, and all were now dead.

AFTER THE ATTACKS, the American government took action. First it launched a war in Afghanistan, then another in Iraq. Domestically, the Bush administration announced the National Security Entry-Exit Registration System (NSEERS), in which noncitizen immigrants from twenty-five countries—twenty-four of them majority-Muslim, plus North Korea—had to report to Immigration and Customs Enforcement, to be fingerprinted and interviewed by authorities, all for no reason other than the country from which they came.

As a citizen, Riyad was exempt, but Bashar was not. And so early one morning in December 2002, they showed up together at the immigration building in downtown Los Angeles. The morning was cold. The line was long. They'd debated coming in to register—some at the mosque had advised against it—but they'd both figured that it was best to follow the law. And besides, it wasn't every day you got to meet with immigration officials. Maybe they'd extend Bashar's visa. Maybe he would even get a green card.

The line snaked its way inside, and they finally made it into the lobby and then to a counter, where Bashar handed a man his passport and his visa. Together he and Riyad watched the man look over the documents, then look up at Bashar, then look back to the documents, and then, finally, point to the corner of the room at an armed guard.

"Go with him."

Bashar looked at the guard, then at Riyad. He felt the faintest twisting in his belly as he followed the guard upstairs and into a small office where they both sat, waiting, until another agent walked in. He looked at them both.

"Which one of you is Bashar Alkasem?"

Bashar raised his hand.

"Okay," the man said. "Bashar, we have a problem."

For a period of two weeks, earlier in the year, Bashar's visa had lapsed. His work permit had been renewed, but because of a misunderstanding in the immigration process, it was two weeks after his original visa expired before his next official document had gone into effect. It didn't matter that Bashar's documents were currently up to date, that he was in the country legally. For two weeks, earlier this year, he had lacked the proper documentation.

"Empty your pockets," the man said.

Bashar pulled out a Syrian passport, some prayer beads, a *miswak* toothbrush, used for cleaning the teeth before prayer, and about sixty dollars. He gave everything to Riyad.

Now the agent looked at Riyad, who felt a heaviness in the man's gaze.

"Where's your visa?" the guard asked him.

"I don't have a visa."

"Why not?"

"I'm a citizen."

"Okay. Then you need to leave."

Bashar looked to Riyad, hopeful. All their lives, his big brother always seemed to know how to slip out of trouble. He had managed to miss curfews and family suppers, to disrupt classrooms and mock professors, always unscathed. But now Riyad looked back at his younger brother with eyes that told him that he knew no tricks to break them out of this office. That he'd encountered an authority he could not challenge. He said in Arabic, "There's nothing I can do."

Riyad saw his brother's lips turn white. He did as the officers instructed, leaving the office and Bashar, all alone.

WHAT HAPPENED NEXT Bashar would have trouble discussing, even years later. He would say little to Riyad, less to his mother, and nothing at all to most everyone else. The memory would remain, though, at least in fragments. He would remember a guard asking him to see his hands. He would remember sticking them out and then being cuffed with plastic straps binding his wrists. He would remember feeling confused, frustrated by his weak English, and very faintly afraid.

"Come," he would remember them saying, and he would remember understanding that word clearly and doing just as he was told.

He would remember the guards escorting him down to the building's basement, and that there he found other men—some Syrian, others Egyptian, still others Saudi or Pakistani or Lebanese. All of them had believed this would be no more than a routine morning of bureaucratic drudgery, like a trip to the DMV, only to find themselves in handcuffs. They waited for hours, late into the night, until the guards returned and told the men to follow them out into a garage where several buses were waiting. They rode out of the city and through the Angeles National Forest's mountains, into a valley in the desert. They pulled into the Mira Loma Detention Center, where Bashar realized, finally, that he was in jail. He didn't know what he'd done wrong; didn't know how long he'd be kept. But he imagined he might be let go at any moment, that he'd return to Santa Barbara and assure his mother that this had all been a misunderstanding. Or maybe, he imagined, they would put him on a plane back to Damascus. That would be fine too. His fiancée had ended their engagement a few months after he left her for America, but he missed Raqqa, missed his home, missed the law.

For now, though, he waited. He was placed in a jail cell with a few others who'd been detained at the registration and with still others who seemed to be here for altogether different reasons, some with swastikas on their skin, many with muscles that suggested they were best left unbothered if Bashar wished to remain unharmed. He would remember just how many people were packed together in a small cell, with barely enough room to stand, flesh against flesh, no one able to lie or sit, and he would remember that his feet ached and his legs wilted as the hours wore on.

The officials seemed to delight in his pain and confusion. He would remember being called a "terrorist" and a "raghead," asking for food and being given a sandwich, and then the guards laughing when he realized that it was bologna, which was pork, which was for Muslims forbidden, *haram*.

And then he would remember things that he would tell no one, that he knew would rattle around in his mind for as long as he lived.

HE WAS RELEASED three days later, when Riyad came to pick him up and drive him home. He reflected on his own time serving in Assad's army and said to Riyad, "The United States should not be allowed to say anything about third-world regimes. Some of the things they did to us, they don't even do back in Syria."

Riyad couldn't bring himself to ask his brother to explain. He understood Bashar's anger, but he couldn't quite take it on for himself. This country that had given him so much still felt to him like the most wonderful nation on earth. And so they rode home together, quiet.

They told their mother what the officials had told Bashar: His time in America was coming to an end. He was one of about fourteen thousand people to enter deportation proceedings due to the NSEERS program. Not a single one of the fourteen thousand was found to have ties to a terrorist organization.

And so Bashar was going back to Syria. He was going back to his legal practice, with his father still connected to a tube in an American hospital, his brother still thriving in a country that had rejected him. And as he prepared to return, Bashar thought not that America had turned its back on him, not that he'd been an unlucky man in an unlucky time, not that this would all work out for the best and that it was good for him to return to his native country, but rather that, quite certainly, in some way he had failed.

CHAPTER

8

Bashar remained for a while, awaiting deportation. Over time the rest of the family scattered. Their *mama* was the first to leave. After three years in America, staying every day by her husband's hospital bed, and now having news of her younger son's pending deportation, she couldn't do it any longer. Her family back home was raising her daughters. She had to return to them; it was time. So one day she held her husband's hand to her face, then kissed his cheeks and his lips and told him goodbye.

Linda and the boys were next to leave. Both Kasem and Sammy had developed chronic immune issues, and with Riyad spending so much time in the shop or caring for his father, she decided she needed her family's support. So she packed up their home and moved back to Tennessee, until Riyad could join them. The distance between them was hard—Riyad on one side of the country caring for his father; Linda in her hometown, acting as a single mother. Riyad flew back every two weeks to see his family, his suitcase loaded with videogames and other gifts, but it never felt like enough.

Riyad sold the house in Thousand Oaks and moved into Bashar's apartment in Santa Barbara. They slept on twin beds in their own corners of the bedroom, much as they had as children. They spent their mornings managing their respective shops, their afternoons trading shifts by their father's side, and their evenings sipping tea in front of the television, watching the news coverage of America's war with Iraq, Syria's neighbor. The war was a disaster, built on the false pretense that Iraqi president Saddam Hussein held weapons of mass destruction. Now Hussein had been toppled and the country was ripped apart, and yet the war received still more funding, still plenty of support. Riyad found himself wondering if Bashar had been right, that America's Constitution had never held any magic powers, that a crisis could cripple institutions here just as it had all over the world.

AND THEN BASHAR LEFT TOO. He didn't even wait for deportation. One morning he just told Riyad, "There's nothing left for me here," and he booked a flight home. Riyad said he understood, but the night after his brother left, he curled up on his mattress all alone in the apartment and cried.

But Riyad still had his *yahba*. He visited Abdul-Rahman every day, sitting by his hospital bed for hours, telling him stories. He told his father about life in America, about the mundane rhythms of his days; he recounted stories of their life back in Raqqa, about their mornings in the market and their days behind the counter at the shop. He repeated the stories that his *yahba* had once told *him*, about Taha, son of Hamed and great-grandson of Ibrahim, the man who settled in a spot along the river and ground coffee in the desert, inviting wanderers to help him build the settlement that would centuries later become their home.

And he told his father about his dream. He'd imagined it since the moment his parents first applied for visas, years before they ever set foot on American soil. He wanted to take his father on a classic American road trip. Something like in the movies, the two of them in a rented red 1965 Mustang convertible, driving out of the city and through California's desert, going deeper and deeper into the country Riyad loved. They would marvel at the engineering of the Hoover Dam and the lights of Las Vegas. They would drive into Arizona and along Route 66, up to see the arches of Zion National Park in Utah and the Rocky Mountains of Colorado, land Riyad had only ever seen from the window of a plane. They would eat breakfast in diners and stay in highway motels. They would stop at a gas station to buy a giant road atlas, and they'd pore over it on the side of the road, debating whether to stop in Ticaboo, Utah, or Slick Rock, Colorado.

"You would love it," Riyad told his *yahba,* and even though his father couldn't respond, even though a nurse once asked who Riyad was talking to, Riyad believed that his father agreed. In the years after Riyad left Raqqa, his father had become a full-throated evangelist for American exceptionalism. He gobbled up every piece of American trivia he could gather. He spread his own version of pro-American propaganda—some of it true, some exaggerations or outright falsehoods—all across Raqqa.

"Did you know," he would ask friends, "that no American government leader has ever taken a bribe?"

"Did you know," he continued, "that the Americans built the Hoover Dam during the Great Depression?"

"Have you ever heard," he would ask them, "the greatest speech ever given by John F. Kennedy?" He would stiffen his back, then recite it. "'Ask not what your country can do for you, but what you can do for your country.'"

As he spoke, he would let a smile wrap around his face, beaming as if bragging about his own accomplishments, not merely the myths of the country where his son now lived. And now that they were here, Riyad wanted his *yahba* to see his new country for himself, riding in the passenger's seat of that Mustang, eyes feasting on the beauty of the land around him.

But he wouldn't. Sitting on a cheap chair by a sturdy bed in an Encino hospital, Riyad knew his *yahba* would never set foot outside this room.

ONE AFTERNOON IN EARLY 2006, a little more than a year after
Bashar returned to Raqqa, Riyad got a phone call while he was at
work. It was a nurse, a kind woman he'd gotten to know over his
years of visits to the hospital. She told him, in a gentle and sweet
voice, "You need to come to the hospital." His father was dead.

Riyad stepped into the room where he'd spent so many hours of
so many days, and he saw his *yahba* at rest. He did not cry. He shook.
His mind worked to process the image of the man who'd marched
him through the Eastern Market as a boy, who'd kissed him goodbye
on the bus before he left home all those years ago. Here was the man
he'd seen as his guide through this life and his protector from its
dangers, now lying before him, dead. The shaking started in his fin-
gertips, running along his father's still-warm skin, and soon it moved
up through his arms and all the way into his shoulders, until his
whole body was trembling, just slightly, as he leaned in to kiss his
yahba's head.

In his pocket, Riyad carried a scarf that had belonged to his
grandmother, his *yahba*'s mother. Riyad had been there when she
died, and he'd watched his uncle tie it around the bottom of her chin
and up to the top of her head, securing it so that her mouth would
remain closed. He didn't really know why. He knew no religious or
cultural significance. But this was the ritual of death that he'd
learned, and so now he grabbed the black and white scarf, which
he'd been saving for just this moment, and wrapped it around his
father's head, tying it at the top, gently, until his *yahba*'s mouth
closed.

He realized he needed to call the local mosque and to tend to
final matters with the hospital. He thought back to a moment when
his father had still been alive, when he'd been sick but functional,
not yet on life support, still able to speak. Riyad had leaned over to
kiss him, and his *yahba* had reached out and grabbed his son's head.
He pulled Riyad's ear to his lips, and he whispered, "My son."

"Yes?"

"Take me home."

They would bury his father in the dirt of Raqqa. This, Riyad knew, was the only place his *yahba*'s body could fully rest. Riyad didn't know what to expect as he prepared for a return to Syria. He had come to wonder, though, about his former vision of America. It was the country that had given him his wife and his children, and his freedom of expression, but it was also the country that had expelled his brother from its borders and had grown suspicious of anyone who shared Riyad's faith and complexion. He thought of Raffy at the deli, of Helen his first landlord, of the red-headed woman from the bank. Would they still be so kind to him today, now that the towers had fallen? Had 9/11 injected some disease into the hearts of otherwise kind Americans? Or had he just become more cynical the longer he'd lived in the United States? The uncertainty sent him to look for bigotry where once he would have seen none, questioning the motives of so many people he encountered. *Who is a bigot? Who is just a jerk? Does the difference matter?* The questions exhausted him.

He flew with his father's body from Los Angeles to Amsterdam, where he would connect on to Damascus. But in Amsterdam's Schiphol Airport, he experienced one of those encounters that left him in that in-between place, unsure of the line between standard rudeness and newly emboldened prejudice. He had exited the plane and wandered the airport until he reached his connecting gate. There, body sore and eyes bleary from ten hours in flight, he explained to the gate agent that he was traveling with his father's body. Could she make sure his *yahba* was on the plane?

She barely looked up at him. "We don't have time for that."

"Can you just check?"

This time she didn't look up at all. "No. Go sit down, please."

Riyad was stunned. He knew hundreds or even thousands would be waiting for his *yahba* back in Raqqa. He couldn't imagine showing up empty-handed.

"I need to know," he said, skin hot.

She kept looking at her computer, never up at his face. "Go sit down."

Riyad raised his voice, and soon another worker came over and said that yes, of course they could check on his father's body, and moments later they assured him that his *yahba* was on board. But the encounter lodged itself somewhere deep in Riyad's mind, and he played it over and over again on the flight, wondering, as he now so often did, if this was simply an unkind person, or a perfectly nice woman turning angry at the sight of a brown-skinned man.

HOURS LATER THEY LANDED in Damascus, the sky dark and the air cool. He'd flown all night, arriving just after four A.M. Once inside the airport, Riyad made his way through customs.

"Passport," the guard said, and Riyad handed him his American passport.

He flipped through its pages, peppering Riyad with questions. Why did he live in America? How long was he staying in Syria? Now that he'd returned, did he think he was going to live here again? Riyad answered as best he could, and the guard barely looked up as he listened, until finally he flipped one more page, stamped the booklet with a thump, and handed it back to Riyad.

"Thank you," Riyad said, and the agent said nothing.

As Riyad prepared to step away from his desk, though, he realized he didn't know where to go next. "One more thing," he said, and the agent's eyes lifted, lazily, back to meet Riyad's.

"My father is dead, and he was on that plane with me. Where should I go to get him?"

Now he watched as the agent's entire body slackened, shedding the suspicion that had gripped him from the moment he grabbed the American passport.

"Oh, sir," he said. "I am so sorry."

He stood up and walked outside his station, around to meet Riyad. He wrapped his arms around him in a hug.

"Come with me."

HE TOOK RIYAD BACK outside, and together they rode in a golf cart across an expanse of empty pavement, until they rounded a corner and approached the hangar. There Riyad saw a group of men, perhaps three or four, all wearing the khaki uniforms of the airport's workers. They were gathered around a water faucet that jutted out from the building's wall, washing themselves. Right hand, up to the wrist, three times, then the same on the left. They rinsed their mouths, then sniffed water to rinse out their nasal passages, then splashed water on their faces, then on their right and left arms. They washed each body part with precision and care, and Riyad realized that they weren't just rinsing off the filth of their jobs; they were performing the *wudhu*—the Muslim act of purification before prayer. Immediately, Riyad realized why. These were the men who were going to transport his father. They saw that task as something beyond the simple requirements of their jobs. They saw it, quite clearly, as something holy, an act of service unto God.

One by one they approached Riyad and hugged him. They all offered their deepest sympathies, and one of them looked to Riyad and asked, a little shyly, "Is it okay if we say a prayer?"

"Yes," Riyad said. It was. His father was on a gurney, inside a thin biodegradable casket. The workers turned him so that his right shoulder was facing south toward Mecca. One of the workers stood before the others and began to lead the prayer.

"Oh God," he said, "forgive our living and our dead, those who are present among us and those who are absent, our young and our old, our males and our females. Oh God, whoever You keep alive, keep him alive in Islam, and whoever You cause to die, cause him to die with faith."

They continued, onward, prone in the direction of Mecca as they repeated the prayer, until they finished, "Oh God, give him a better home than his home, and a better family than his family. Oh God, admit him to paradise and protect him from the torment of the grave and the torment of hellfire."

Riyad stood with these strangers, praying along with them. He was exhausted, trapped in a vise of jet lag and grief, but he continued with the men alongside him until they concluded their prayer: "Make his grave spacious, and fill it with light."

RIYAD FELT A CERTAIN IRONY in his return to Syria. The West was supposed to be open, the Middle East regressive and backward. Even Riyad often believed this. But while he prayed with these strangers back in the land of his birth, he felt a humanity unlike any he'd experienced for some time back in America, a sense of welcome that hinted maybe this was where he most belonged.

After they had finished praying, an ambulance pulled up, and there in the driver's seat, Riyad saw his brother Kasem. Kasem was the fourth-born, a doctor, and while Riyad and Bashar had been in America, Kasem had taken on the role of patriarch. Now he was here to help Riyad return their father to his city.

They loaded the casket and began to drive away, and then Riyad saw them—hundreds of people, all gathered here to meet them; uncles and tribal leaders, customers from the market, farmers who'd sold Abdul-Rahman produce. All had traveled hours from Raqqa to welcome back the body of the *mukhtar*. It was tradition in Raqqa for mourners to ride in a caravan from the home of the deceased to the graveyard, but Riyad had never seen something like *this*, a caravan at an airport more than two hundred miles away. Riyad's father hadn't set foot on Syrian soil in six years, but still he remained a giant among his people. Riyad rode for hours at the head of the caravan, his father's body behind him, a trail of cars farther behind him still, and as the sun rose and bathed the land around him orange, Riyad felt, somewhere inside, as if he were seeing Syria for the very first time.

———

THEY LAID OUT his *yahba* in the guest room of their home, surrounded only by Riyad and Bashar, their younger brothers and sisters, and their *mama,* who said her husband's face looked beautiful, as if he were still awake. She and her daughters stood over him and recited poems of mourning, and soon the tribesmen came to the house to pay their respects the best way they knew how, by shooting rifles into the sky.

"Stop that," Riyad told them, and he cringed a little when they laughed.

"Nephew," they said, "you have become too American." In Raqqa, men mourned with gunfire. And so they turned their rifles upward and fired once more.

Next they drove from their home to the graveyard, past streets lined with mourners who raised their hands at the passing caravan to say a prayer. And when they arrived at the burial site, Riyad jumped down into the grave, where he helped lower his father's body into the ground. He would rest in the same grave where his own father's body had gone, the same grave of his father's father, buried not in a casket but wrapped in cloth, so that he could dissolve into the dirt.

The imam said a short prayer, asking God to give him the strength to answer correctly the questions Islam taught that the angels would ask:

> What is your name?
> *Abdul-Rahman, son of Aisha.*
> What is your religion?
> *Islam.*
> What book do you follow?
> *The Quran.*
> What prophet do you follow?
> *Muhammad.*

And then they all prayed, asking God to help his *yahba* answer the questions correctly so that heaven's gates would open before him. They finished the prayer by returning dirt to the earth above his *yahba*'s body. This, Riyad thought, was exactly the burial his father deserved, on this hillside just beyond the city's gate, surrounded by thousands of people who had gathered to say goodbye to their *mukhtar*.

After the body was covered with soil, Riyad walked through the crowd and found himself covered by the hugs and kisses of the city's older men. He returned their smiles and grabbed their necks as they grabbed his, but he soon tired, wanting to be not with the people who populated his original city, but with the one man with whom he shared a home both here in Raqqa and so many miles away in California, the only person who'd been tethered to Riyad for almost his entire life.

"Bashar," he said, whispering in between the greetings of elders, "let's get out of here."

THE BROTHERS WENT to the tribe house and made a pot of tea, stirred in a couple spoonfuls of sugar, no milk, and sat on pillows and talked in person for the first time since Bashar had left California, a little more than a year before.

"Syria is changing, you know," said Bashar.

Riyad nodded. He wanted so badly to believe it. In his single day back on Syrian soil, he'd felt a peace he hadn't felt in many years. In the embrace of tribal elders and the prayers of airport workers, he felt a warmth and a belonging like he had in those earlier days in California, walking down the beach in Santa Barbara with Linda and his sons. He wanted to believe that this feeling could be sustained, that this country could deliver it. He wanted to believe that Syria had shed the elements that once drove him away.

"You really think so?" he asked.

Riyad held Bashar's eyes with his own. His little brother had always looked older than him. His frame was bigger, his face more serious. He was now thirty-seven years old. But Riyad saw in him a youthful earnestness, and he could tell how badly Bashar wanted to believe the words he spoke were true.

"Yes," Bashar said. "Things are getting better here."

Riyad had an opportunity, and Bashar thought he should consider it. Earlier in the day, a Ba'ath Party official had approached
him, telling him that the government was in a period of transition,
that they were looking for good and bright men to help shape the
new Syria. With Riyad's pedigree here in Raqqa, combined with his
fluency in English and his experience abroad, he would be a prime
candidate for a high-ranking government job. Riyad had been taking political science classes at Santa Barbara City College, but his
life revolved around providing for a family, not chasing his long-ago
dream. Still, he thought, that didn't mean he had lost his chance to
shape Syria's future.

He could move Linda and the boys back here to his homeland.
Let his sons grow up by the river that ran through their blood. Get
a sprawling house, a butler, and a chauffeur. Linda would miss her
family, of course, but perhaps this would satisfy the adventurous
streak that had sent her from Tennessee to New York and L.A. and
all the way to Saudi Arabia, all those years ago.

The country had a new president, Bashar al-Assad. Hafez al-
Assad had died in June 2000, and his son had taken his place. Yes,
the country was still ruled by the regime of a man named Assad, and
many of Hafez's cronies had remained in power under his son. But
still, things felt different.

"This new young man," Bashar said, referring to the president
who shared his first name, "we are giving him a chance. We think he
really wants to change things here."

The new young man hadn't been groomed for politics. The presidency was supposed to go to Bashar al-Assad's older brother, Bassel,
a vicious warrior who many in Syria had long feared. Bassel, though,
had died in a car crash back in 1994, leaving Bashar al-Assad to take
his place. The younger Assad seemed like a gentle soul. He'd been an
ophthalmologist, had married a gorgeous and sophisticated London-
born woman, Asma, with whom much of Syria—and the West, for
that matter—had fallen in love. He had gotten his start in government by running an anticorruption campaign in the 1990s, and now,
six years into his presidency, he continued to preach the need for
reform.

"The country you left," Bashar said, "is no longer the country where we sit."

Riyad told Bashar that he could never move back, that as long as the Assads and the Ba'ath Party ruled, this was still the hopelessly lost country that he'd known he had to leave. But still, in his mind, he considered it. The day had been sublime, from the moment he stepped off the plane in Damascus up until now, sitting in the tribe house with his brother. All day he'd been thinking, *This is what my father deserves.* And maybe, he imagined, this was what he deserved too.

HE RODE BACK to Damascus a few days later, and as he stared out the window, he began to think that somehow the country looked more beautiful than it had when he was a child. The desert's red shimmered. As they wound their way through Hama, Riyad found that he did not hold his breath, as he had on so many earlier drives through that city, but instead rolled down the window and studied the green hills, inhaling a sweetness in the earth he'd never smelled until now. The city looked serene. *What massacre?* Riyad kept the window down, feeling the air rush past him.

He'd always thought that in Syria, patriotism belonged to fools and to children. He'd tried to forget his own memories of clapping as a boy every time he heard Assad's name. Now, though, he wondered if this was what it felt like to have pride in his home country. He tried to ignore the massive portraits of Bashar al-Assad that hung over the streets in every city, just as portraits of Assad's father, Hafez, once had. He tried to imagine that his brother was right, that the new president was trying, that he could help Syria to shed the evils of its government's past. Maybe, he thought, his homeland held a potential for greatness he'd never imagined. The country outside his window appeared every bit as wonderful as the America for which he'd long ago departed.

He reached the airport and hugged Bashar and his cousins goodbye.

"What do you think of our country now?" his cousin Thayer asked him before they parted.

"It's so much more beautiful than I ever remembered," Riyad said.

"Good," Thayer said. "I hoped you would feel that."

Riyad nodded, and Thayer continued.

"You should come home."

RIYAD ENTERED THE AIRPORT and checked in for his flight. He went through customs and security, then stepped onto the moving sidewalk, letting it carry him to his gate. As he stood, he looked over his shoulder to see a man in his late twenties, wearing jeans and a sweater and a mustache, walking toward him. He held a familiar look in his eyes, the look of a man who believes he is owed whatever he wants. Immediately, Riyad knew. Mukhabarat.

"Come with me," the man said.

Riyad stepped off the moving sidewalk and over to a corner of the corridor, where the man began to pat him down. Riyad knew where he was headed. He was wearing cargo shorts, and in one of his side pockets, there was a noticeable bulge. The man's hands moved down Riyad's torso, to his hips and then his thighs, and then, as if he were completely surprised to find something worthy of his attention, he reached into the cargo pocket and pulled out a wad of American cash.

The Mukhabarat looked at the cash, now resting in his own hand, then back at Riyad. "How much is this?"

"Five thousand dollars."

I'm an idiot, Riyad thought. *What was I thinking, keeping all that cash in my pocket?* He'd borrowed the money from a friend, because so much of his own cash was tied up in his company's business accounts. He thought he'd need it, because you *always* needed cash in Syria, could barely navigate the country with only a credit card. But he should have thought to split the money up into different pockets of his luggage and his person.

The man considered the money in his hand, then nodded. "Okay," he said. "Just forget about it." He moved as if to put the cash in his own pocket, and he waved Riyad ahead. "You can go."

"What?" said Riyad.

"You can go," said the man. "Have a good flight."

And just like that, with one short encounter with one member of the Mukhabarat, Riyad was back. Back to the teenager who railed against the regime. Back to the college student, obsessed with plotting his own escape. Back to the man who hated this country, this irredeemably corrupt country, this place that he never should have let himself begin to imagine he might return.

He was not moving. The Mukhabarat could arrest him if he had to.

"You can't keep that money," he said. He felt his face go hot. "I just buried my father. I borrowed that money. I have to take it with me."

The Mukhabarat only smiled and said, "My friend, you need to move along." The Mukhabarat always considered the people they shook down for money to be great friends.

Riyad stood his ground. He'd never stood up to a Mukhabarat in his previous life, but now the highs of the week and the presence of his American passport gave him a new confidence. "I'm not moving."

The Mukhabarat appeared startled. "My friend, please. Move along."

"I'm not moving."

The guard slumped his shoulders, then rolled his eyes. He had no legal authority to take Riyad's money. This was simply the way that things had always been done.

"Okay," he said. He handed the money back to Riyad. "But you know, I would really appreciate some sort of gesture, for allowing you to keep this money."

Riyad felt shocked, then stupid for feeling shocked. *Fine.* He peeled off five one-hundred-dollar bills, then stuffed them into the man's hand.

Finally, in his last hours on Syrian soil, *here* was the country he remembered. He marched to his gate, looking at no one, ready to return to his boys and his Linda, his home.

CHAPTER

9

With his father now dead, Riyad had nothing keeping him in California. He needed his wife and boys; Linda needed her family. So he would move to be with them in Tennessee. One morning he packed up his apartment, taking only what could fit in his blue Chevy Silverado truck—the one he had nicknamed "Billy Bob"—and he set out on the road. He passed through Thousand Oaks, where he'd once had his house and his BMW and his plum trees, through the hills of Pasadena and along the mountains of the national forest, out through Palm Springs and into the Mojave Desert and Death Valley. He slid over to the fast lane and put the car on cruise control, and he never, not once, allowed himself to look in the rearview mirror. He couldn't bear the thought of watching California slipping away behind him.

He fit in there. When he looked around, he saw others like himself. A few Syrians, even more Muslims, and yet more people like him who had gone wandering, who set off from their original homes in search of something and found it there on the continent's edge. He liked the Lakers and In-N-Out Burger. He spent mornings in spin class and occasional evenings on the beach. California was the place where he had learned that home was portable. It was where he stretched the limits of exactly who and what a *sha'awi* from the desert could be.

He kept driving, all the way through the desert and across the Colorado River and into Arizona, all the way through New Mexico and across a sliver of Texas, through Oklahoma and Arkansas, until finally, a couple of days later, he arrived to Linda and the boys and this place that felt so foreign from either Syria or California, but that he would try to make his new home.

TENNESSEE HAD ONE THING Riyad looked forward to: winter. He loved the winter. Temperatures dropped. Days shortened. The green died, and the world turned gray. In the gray, you could see the truth. Against the bare tendrils of Tennessee's sycamore trees and the pale mass of its early-morning fog, you could take in the full measure of a person, watching them move in color through a world with none. Summer had its joys, of course. But summer could be overwhelming. Everything moving in full brightness. The summer distracted; the fall soothed; the spring energized. But the winter pulled the world into focus.

Riyad spent those first winter months in the only job he could find: stocking shelves at Walmart. Before leaving California, he had fallen out with Sam, in a dispute over the money Riyad believed he was owed when he left the business. Now Riyad felt like he needed to start over. He spent cold nights on the graveyard shift carrying heaping bags of dog food from trucks into the store, stocking the shelves, four or five pallets at a time. He would let his mind drift again to the opportunities that could have awaited him back in Syria. The Ba'ath Party bureaucrats had promised him a government car and driver, the fat life of a regime suit. He knew he couldn't *really* go back there, but still, he wondered, did his life have to bring him here? The hours passed slowly. His muscles ached. He returned home each morning, right around the time the boys were waking up.

He applied for other jobs. Restaurant jobs, delivery jobs. Once he got called back for a position as a janitor at Sammy's school. The pay was decent, the hours more regular.

"*Riyad,*" Linda said. "You can't be Sammy's *janitor.*"

He shrugged. "Why not?"

"His friends will make fun of him!"

He worried that she was right. Winter melted away into spring, and he finally found another job, washing dishes at an Indian restaurant in Green Hills, the area where Linda had once run through forests and chased her dolls through creeks, now one of the wealthiest neighborhoods in Nashville. The work was good, the people were kind, and the pay was a little better than at Walmart.

More months passed. He found meaning in other places, connecting to local activists involved with the Tennessee Immigrant & Refugee Rights Coalition. He lobbied state legislators and took a trip to lobby congressional staffers for refugee rights in Washington, D.C. He joined the coalition's board, working alongside fellow immigrants and white liberal lawyers to advocate on behalf of others like himself. Once while he was in the kitchen at the restaurant, a group of board members came in for dinner. Riyad saw them from the kitchen and immediately asked to take his break, hiding in the back so they would not see that he was a dishwasher, would not begin to think that his occupation disqualified him from a place on their board.

Tennessee's Muslim community was much smaller than that of southern California, but still, he found belonging at the Islamic Center of Nashville. There he connected with a wealthy Palestinian named Ibrahim, who owned a halal meat shop. Ibrahim needed someone honest and hardworking to run the lunch counter during the week, so Riyad took over, splitting his time between his two jobs. Business grew. Riyad and Ibrahim talked for hours about the food business, about strategies for selling Americans on the flavors of the Middle East.

One day he pulled Riyad aside. He wanted to talk.

"You should open a restaurant," he said.

Riyad thought about it. It was true, he loved to cook. For years, he'd searched markets all across southern California for ingredients that reminded him of home. He would make mountains of chicken and rice, lamb korma, and baba ghanoush. Once Linda had a group of friends over, and one of them mentioned how much she loved hummus. Riyad pulled together chickpeas and tahini, olive oil and spices, and soon was moving through their kitchen just as the hummus master Abu Mohamed had moved through that dark room back in Raqqa all those years ago. The recipe Abu Mohamed taught Riyad had never left him. Soon enough Riyad emerged from the kitchen with a plate, the hummus gold and light and kissed by a few drops of olive oil, the plate lined with soft pita bread. By the end of the night, the women were wiping the last remnants off the plate with their fingers, desperate to know when they could come back for Riyad to make them hummus again.

HE COULD COOK. He knew it. But he had no clue if he could run a restaurant. Nor did he know how to translate his skills in the kitchen to suit the palates of Tennessee. But he wanted to try. Ibrahim was offering to lend him the start-up money. He believed in the flavors of their home region, didn't much care that Riyad was Syrian and he was Palestinian. Sure, the flavors changed as you moved across the region, but they were close enough. Besides, ever since 9/11, many Arab Americans had made a silent pact to focus on what linked them. Riyad would feed Americans with Syrian flavors. And maybe, Ibrahim imagined, their taste buds might lead them to appreciate Palestinian culture too.

It took months to find a location. Riyad searched all over Nashville, a liberal city in the heart of a red state, where he imagined he'd find a willing clientele for his food. But the rent was too expensive, the terms of contract too risky. And then one day Riyad drove past a restaurant with a FOR SALE sign, a ladies-who-lunch spot called September's, but it wasn't in Nashville. It was in Hendersonville, the town where Linda had moved as a girl, where Riyad and Linda had lived together early in their marriage, and where her family still remained. It was a small and insular suburb, a place where people spent Friday nights at high school football games and Saturday afternoons fishing on the lake or hunting in the woods. The town was 85 percent white. In 2004, soon after George W. Bush launched a war that killed untold numbers of Muslims in Iraq, 65 percent of Sumner County's residents had voted to reelect him. It was the place where Riyad had been called a "sand nigger," where he'd been rejected for countless low-wage jobs and denied applications for low-rent homes. And it was the place, Riyad now decided, where he would open his restaurant. He would call it Café Raqqa.

No, he decided, something about the letter Q felt too foreign. Maybe he should call it Café Rakka instead.

Café Rakka opened in September 2007. Riyad arrived that morning for his final walk-through with one of the previous owners, a tall and kind white man named Kirk, who showed him the power switches, the buttons to control the ovens and blenders, the refrigerators and freezers, and Riyad convinced Kirk to leave him the nickels and pennies in the register. He told Kirk he didn't have time to go to the bank to get coins. In truth, Riyad had twenty-two dollars in his pocket and absolutely nothing else. Without these nickels and pennies, he had no idea how he'd give his customers change.

Linda came in, and they both took their places: Riyad back in the kitchen, Linda at the register. This was the plan. They stood in their respective spots, quiet, nervous, waiting. And then, maybe forty-five minutes after they opened, Riyad looked up to find Linda running to the back. She was wide-eyed, frantic.

"Riyad!"

"Yes?"

"Someone is here!"

Someone was there. And not just anyone. A customer. Someone to pay money to eat the food that Riyad's grandmother had taught him to make. Riyad looked at Linda. Linda looked at Riyad. This was it. This was the start.

And then he realized, quite quickly, that while they were talking to each other, no one was talking to the customer who'd just walked in. "Go!" he shouted.

And so Linda went. Riyad followed, too jittery to wait by himself in the back. Standing at the front counter, a woman, petite and brunette and brown-skinned, was patiently waiting.

Riyad took charge. "Hi," he said.

"Hi," she said.

"What would you like to eat?"

They had a small menu, with only a few items, written on a chalkboard above him. Chicken and lamb, rice and salad, hummus and bread. Only later would Riyad realize that he'd misspelled hummus ("hummice") and chickpeas ("chick bees"), but right now all he knew was that he was standing before a human who might soon offer him money for food, and he felt so very desperate to make this human happy.

She thought for a moment. "I'm not sure."

"Well," he asked, "what do you like?"

She liked chicken. She liked rice. Back in the kitchen, Riyad set to work. He took a chicken thigh, the bone still in and skin still attached, and he cooked it on a pan over an open flame, the fire flicking up along the edges, in a dance. He mixed it with a blend of ginger and olive oil and saffron, and the pan turned orange and then red, the spices blending and popping and finding their homes inside the meat. Next he grabbed an onion, cut it into a square, and sautéed it until the edges turned dark, until he could practically *see* the crunch he knew she'd taste. Then he tossed the onion and the chicken into a skillet with cilantro and parsley, and he sautéed it until he could tell that it was both smoky and juicy, the skin crunchy but the meat tender. He threw it onto a plate with a serrano pepper and rice and a salad, and he took it out of the kitchen and onto the floor. He placed it before her. He waited. He wanted to see how she liked her first bite.

"Riyad!" Linda called to him, and he turned to see her waving him back. "You can't watch people eat," she said when he returned to the register.

"Why not?"

"It's creepy!"

So he stayed at the register with Linda, watching from afar.

Finally, the woman finished. She stood up, looked at Riyad, and smiled. "That was delicious."

He'd done it. He was a restaurateur. He was on his way. He told the woman that she was his very first customer, and she introduced herself. Her name was Ruby. She was from Costa Rica, but she'd married an American musician and settled here. She missed the spices of her home country, found American food impossibly bland. And even though Central America and the Middle East were thousands of miles apart, Riyad's food, she would later say, offered the faintest hint of home.

"I hope you stick around," she said, and Riyad thanked her and said that he hoped so too.

MORE CUSTOMERS CAME and paid and ate. Some said the food was delicious. A few said little at all. Here and there someone would walk in and realize that this was no longer September's, which was in the process of moving into a bigger space, and they immediately turned and walked out.

"They used to have this turkey sandwich," one woman told Riyad, "that I'm just craving right now."

"What was in it?" he asked her. "I'll make it for you. Free of charge."

She smiled. She thought he was sweet. He thought he was desperate. Either way, she said, only September's would do.

One afternoon a man marched in the door and straight up to Linda. "Who owns this place?"

She studied the man before her. Big belly, a few lumps of muscle, a balding head, and a sense of put-on rage. She knew his kind. She knew why he was here.

"Excuse me?" she asked.

"Who owns this place?"

She looked him in the eye. "I do."

"Oh."

When he walked out the door, Riyad chastened Linda for chasing him away, and she just shook her head. Her husband was so earnest, but he could still be so naïve.

"Honey," she said, "that man didn't want to order anything. He just wanted to find out who was invading his town."

RIYAD SAW HIS RESTAURANT as a kind of bet. On himself, sure, but also on the limits of human openness and curiosity. His strategy was built on a simple idea. Anywhere on this planet, on any street corner or in any strip mall, you can find people who want food to transport them to undiscovered worlds.

He only had to look at himself. When he first arrived in Los Angeles, he had never tasted a cheeseburger. By the time he left, he was stopping multiple times a week at the In-N-Out Burger in Camarillo, ordering a Double-Double, Animal Style, with fries. Los Angeles had introduced him to Chinese and Mexican food; trips to Tennessee with Linda for Thanksgiving had brought him the unknown glories of turkey and mashed potatoes slathered in gravy, kissed by a touch of cranberry sauce on top. So if a *sha'awi* from the desert could learn to love sushi and apple pie, he reasoned, then the people of Tennessee could develop a taste for shawarma and baba ghanoush. By giving people a plate, Riyad believed, he could take them with him to the desert. Here in the American South he'd continue the work of Taha, providing sustenance for strangers as an invitation to build a common home.

Hours passed, and more customers came. Some marched right back out the door, but others stood and studied the chalkboard menu, asking Riyad about his ingredients and his process and even, occasionally, about his native country. After several weeks, he and Linda had earned enough money to hire a small staff, but Riyad still made a point to check on every single table. He learned customers' names. He asked what they liked, what they didn't. If someone told him their meal was "fine," he begged them to tell him how he could do better next time.

Some remained wary. One night a husband and wife came into the restaurant, both dressed sharply—he in a blazer, she in full makeup and a dress. They were in their sixties, perhaps, and carried with them a certain southern sophistication. The man scanned the room, then studied Riyad, who now made a point to hang out in the front of the house when he wasn't cooking.

The man squinted as he read the menu overhead.

"What would you like?" Riyad asked him.

"I don't know," the man said.

Riyad told him to have a seat, that he would make some things for the man to try. This had become his strategy, offering free samples, hoping that by introducing people to his cooking, he would win their business. Minutes later Riyad emerged from the kitchen carrying small plates of falafel and hummus, tabooleh and baba ghanoush.

"Try this," Riyad said, and returned to the kitchen. He'd learned his lesson, from Linda, about standing over people while they ate.

Moments later he returned. "How is everything?"

The man stood. "I'm sorry. We have to leave."

"Okay," Riyad said. "Was the food not good?"

The man shrugged, a little apologetic. "We were just confused."

Riyad felt desperate to win over this couple. "What was confusing?"

"Well," the man said, "we just thought this was American food."

Riyad felt a quick lurch in his gut. Before he had time to process a response, a nearby customer spoke up.

"American food?" the customer asked, raising his voice. "It was made right here! We're in America, aren't we?"

Now the nicely dressed man stiffened. He seemed not to want an argument. He wanted only to leave.

"Well," he said, "I guess I meant we thought it was *Christian* food."

He held no anger, showed little emotion at all. And if anything hurt Riyad, it was *this*. His politeness. He wasn't interested in threatening or intimidating anyone. Riyad knew aggressive bigots; their venom rolled right off his shoulders. This man, though, tried to be as kind as he could be, explaining that he meant no offense when he told Riyad that he wanted nothing to do with whatever was served on those plates. Before Riyad could speak, the other customer got up and made his way toward them.

"You know what?" he said, pointing at the door. "Cracker Barrel is right down the street." He nodded. "Get the hell out of here."

The nicely dressed couple walked out the door, and Riyad turned to his customer, who was still visibly angry as he watched them leave.

"What are you doing?" he asked. "I need every customer I can get!"

AS TIME PASSED, their clientele grew. They even had regulars. The restaurant sat across the street from the offices of the Oak Ridge Boys, a legendary country quartet, and soon their staff, and later the singers themselves, started popping in week after week, curious for the stories behind each dish. Once a young musician came by with his bandmates after closing, and Riyad opened the locked door and invited them in. He fired up the grill and served a massive heaping of lamb korma, then sat with them and talked late into the night about their lives in Tennessee and his in Syria and California.

"I'm going to tell my dad about you," one of them said. And later that week, in walked a white-haired man who would soon become one of the restaurant's most frequent customers and one of Riyad's closest friends: Country Music Hall of Famer Ricky Skaggs.

To all of them, Riyad told stories. He told them how he'd learned to prep cook, sitting on the floor beside his grandmother in the kitchen. He told them the story of the hummus master who'd pulled him into a back room just days before he left for America. After hours, he served them coffee and sat with them, sipping and telling the story of Taha, the man who'd brewed a pot in the desert, inviting the strangers who helped him build the city that became Riyad's home. He told them how he'd gotten his education in the food business right here in America, learning about kitchen management at Raffy's Italian deli, about efficiency while managing a McDonald's, about new flavors while in the kitchen at the Indian restaurant.

The *Tennessean* newspaper sent a critic out to Hendersonville, who gave the café a glowing review. The chef from Margot, a high-end restaurant in East Nashville, included a blurb in her newsletter, distributed to foodies around the city. Riyad built a base of loyal customers, many of whom he knew by name. They knew him by his dishes and his stories. The town's sophisticates came in so they wouldn't have to drive all the way to Nashville for a classy meal. East Nashville's foodies made the trek, because this was the only Syrian restaurant in the region. But as much as anything, Riyad catered to anyone with a curious palate, the contractors who rode in on their pickup trucks, the nurses who got a quick bite before their night shifts, and others from Hendersonville or elsewhere who pulled off the road, eager to be fed.

And yet survival remained a struggle. Riyad knew the statistics: About 60 percent of restaurants fail within the first three years. His environment was casual, but his prices were more expensive than most places in the town. He refused to sell alcohol, which drives so much of restaurant profits, and poured his money into the highest-quality ingredients, including some spices he asked Bashar to ship to him from Raqqa.

A year passed. They were getting by. Another year passed. They were still surviving. But the U.S. economy had begun falling into a recession in 2007, just after he opened, and by 2009 that recession had gotten so deep that economists were talking about the possibility of another Depression. Regulars lost their jobs, then stopped showing up. Potential new customers tightened their spending, cooking at home. This was the worst period for restaurants in modern history, a time when Riyad heard of new closures around town every single day.

The line at his counter shortened. Some days it disappeared. He believed in his food, but he was running out of money. And with that, he was running out of time. One Friday he pulled together his staff after their shifts, to handle the payroll.

"This is the last paycheck I'll be able to give you," he said.

They gathered around him, confused. The dishwashers and cooks were immigrants like him. Some were from Mexico, and he addressed them in kitchen Spanglish, which he considered his second language, more native to him even than proper English. The front-of-house staff were white kids from Hendersonville, teenagers who just picked up a few hours here and there when Linda wasn't available. He'd loved working with both. The immigrants reminded him of himself, the teenagers of his own kids. All had been critical to building the restaurant into what it was, and all seemed to represent, in their own ways, Riyad's vision of what his slice of America could be.

But now he couldn't pay them. "We're running out of money," he said. "I don't know when I'll be able to pay you again."

He apologized. He knew how many of them were counting on the money. Some needed it to support their families. He imagined that without them, he would drop back to just him and Linda, but he thought he would give them a choice.

"If you want to come back to work next week, you're welcome to," he said. "I promise I'll pay you as soon as we get enough money, but I don't know when that will be." One high schooler cut her hours. Another said she didn't mind, that she'd rather be at the restaurant than sitting at home on the couch. A couple of the kitchen staff had to find new jobs to support their families, and a couple of others picked up second jobs and cut their hours at Café Rakka to prioritize the gig where their checks were guaranteed.

That night Riyad and Linda took their dog Krypto for a walk.

The night was cold, the air thick with fog. Winter. Pale and gray and honest. They strolled along the lake where Linda used to ride boats as a teenager. Hendersonville was beautiful, if you knew where to look. Riyad loved running the restaurant, even in its struggles. He'd spent so much of his time in America pouring himself into work for other people, selling products he didn't believe in. Café Rakka felt like an expression of his deepest self. If it failed, he didn't know where he'd turn next.

Linda took his hand. They looked out over the lake, dark and blue, with the gray layer hovering just above it. Krypto was getting old, and as they stopped to stand and look, he lay down, eager for the rest.

"Just remember," Linda told him, "no matter what happens, you are not a failure. You have done something amazing."

Riyad nodded and tried to believe this was true.

A few days later, around noon, the phone rang. It was a producer from the Food Network. He wanted to talk about coming to Tennessee.

- - - - - - - -

The trucks arrived early one morning in April 2010, parking in the lot and unloading cameras and mics. Riyad had never seen anything like it. So many people, each one affixed to his or her own piece of impossibly expensive equipment. So much energy so early in the morning, and there, emerging from a limo, was the man around whom the entire system seemed to orbit. He walked straight toward Riyad and looked him in the eye.

"Hi," he said. He was squat and well-fed, his hair in blond spikes. "I'm Guy Fieri."

Riyad knew who he was. He'd watched his television show *Diners, Drive-Ins and Dives*, using it as a window into other kitchens. Now Guy Fieri was here to take viewers into *Riyad's*.

"Hi," he said, "I'm Chef Rakka."

Riyad extended his hand, but Guy Fieri pulled his back. "Listen," he said, "I'm not feeling good today." He didn't want to shake Riyad's hand, because he had a cold. "So here's what we're gonna do. We're gonna shoot for ninety minutes, maybe two hours, and then we're gonna get out of here."

"Okay," Riyad said. "That's fine."

That was not fine. Riyad had been waiting months for this day. Ever since he'd gotten that very first phone call from the producer, he'd held on to the belief that one visit from Guy Fieri would turn his restaurant around. Yes, things had picked up, slightly, since the day he'd told his staff he couldn't pay them. The recession had ended. The recovery had begun. He'd returned to a regular pay schedule, and even if there were a few close calls, he'd managed to pay the bills every month. But still he knew they were always one slow month away from returning to the brink. He needed whatever boost Fieri and his audience could provide.

BEFORE FIERI ARRIVED, a producer talked with Riyad at length about what they would record. He wanted Riyad to make filet mignon kebabs, cooked on a salt block. And he would need to cook them twice—once with Fieri, once with only the producers, to be used for B-roll. The end product would show the two shots spliced together. A filet, though, would cost Riyad about $120. He had only enough money to buy one. So days before the shoot, he asked his mother-in-law to loan him money, and she did. He needed it. *Linda* needed it. They needed everything to be perfect when Guy Fieri came to town.

And now Guy Fieri was sick. So sick that he wanted to leave after ninety minutes, not the six hours they'd scheduled. The less time they were in the restaurant, Riyad worried, the less time he'd be on the show. Or what if Fieri remained lethargic, and the material they shot came out weak, and Café Rakka didn't make it into the episode at all?

Now Fieri rumbled through the restaurant, eyeing Riyad's setup. "Here's the deal," he said. "We're gonna do a full walk-through. If I see something in here that I don't like, something that makes me think my viewers are gonna be disappointed if they show up, then I'm walking away."

Riyad said he understood. He respected it. Fieri wanted to do right by his audience.

"Don't bring me some dish you cooked yesterday," Fieri said. "Don't bring me some dish you cooked at home. You're gonna cook it right, and you're gonna cook it here."

Riyad nodded.

"Good," Fieri said. He turned around and kept walking through the restaurant, opening cabinets, looking under countertops, taking inventory of knives and produce, ovens and spices and meats.

At one point, while Riyad was talking with a producer, he heard Fieri calling from the back room, "Where's the chef? Bring me the chef!"

Riyad rushed back to find Fieri standing in front of an old freezer. "What is *this*?"

Riyad sidled up to Fieri. Together they looked inside the freezer, where there was no meat, no ice, but instead stacks upon stacks of fine china.

"Well," Riyad said, "we didn't have a china cabinet. But we had a freezer. So we just decided to use that instead." The freezer hadn't been plugged in since the day they opened. It was clean and spacious, so for Riyad, it became a cabinet.

Riyad watched Fieri's cheeks swell, his face opening up into his first smile of the morning.

"All right," he said, looking not at Riyad but at the china. "There's something funky about this place."

He turned back to his producer. "Let's get to work."

RIYAD HAD ANOTHER IDEA. He went digging through his spice rack until he found what he needed: the Euphrates wildflower. He'd

known it since he was a boy. During his childhood, on many Fridays,
his family would spend an afternoon driving deep into the desert.
They would take food and blankets and find a spot for a picnic, sitting under the sun and eating cheese and olives, hummus and bread.
After lunch, they would go exploring, often in the ruins of the ancient village called Resafa.

Resafa had long been abandoned, because as centuries passed
and climate patterns shifted, it came to sit on the wrong side of the
rain line. Now there was no vegetation, nothing but rock and soil
and the bones of a once-mighty fortress. Underneath Resafa, the
Romans had built a network of wells, and now those wells had
turned to caves, and some of the caves sloped gradually, becoming
gentle walkways that ran from the surface deep into the earth, and
there, Riyad found the most gorgeous flowers he'd ever seen. They
were bright red and five-petaled and wide open, their colors a rebuke to the desert's desolation. The grown-ups passed down myths
about the flowers. They said the red color came from the blood of
the warriors who'd once defended the city from foreign invaders,
that the flowers could be found nowhere else but here, that the
strength of the city's protectors now lived in the flowers' petals, re-
born every spring.

Riyad would reach down and yank them from the earth, and late
in the afternoons, they would return to their home in Raqqa. There
they would lay out the flowers, letting them dry for months, so that
in winter, the blood of the martyrs could be used for an elixir. Riyad's grandmother swore it could cure most anything. Sick tea, she
called it. When Riyad got colds as a boy, he would take a few sips of
the drink and feel his body melt. Sweat dripped down his forehead.
He became light, lifted out from underneath his physical fog. As an
adult, he realized that the drink did little more than make him sweat,
expunging toxins from his pores. But still, it felt medicinal. Every
time Riyad got sick in America, he'd wished desperately that he had
a few cups of sick tea. And so he'd called Bashar and asked him if he
could send some of the Euphrates wildflower, so Riyad could make
the tea on his own.

His brother had gone out into the desert and ventured into those same caves they used to explore as boys, and he'd picked the flowers and stuffed them into pillowcases, and then he'd sent the pillowcases from Raqqa to Tennessee.

So now, as Guy Fieri continued walking through the restaurant, Riyad knew what to do. He went digging for the flower. He found a mug and a kettle, and he made the same mix he always had. Euphrates wildflower and hot water. Nothing else.

He approached Fieri. "Here," he said. "Drink this."

Fieri looked at him, curious but questioning. "What's in it?"

"Just flowers."

Fieri shrugged. And then he drank. He roamed the room, studying everything, strategizing with producers, but after a few minutes, his energy seemed to lift. His walk became a bounce, his face fixed with the omnipresent grin Riyad had seen on TV. He looked as if, finally, his body could breathe.

He grabbed Riyad's shirt. "That tea," he said, "is magic."

HE STAYED. NOT NINETY MINUTES, not two hours, but six and a half. He sat at a table out front with the Oak Ridge Boys and with Ricky Skaggs, talking to the country music legends about this desert boy's food. "We kinda like that international flavor," said William Lee Golden, the Oaks' seventy-one-year-old baritone, an Alabama native with long white hair and an even longer white beard.

"This is fine stuff right here," said Skaggs, in his own Kentucky twang, looking up from his dish with his own mop of white hair.

The producers shot his rotating cast of regulars. A middle-aged woman declared it the best falafel she'd ever had. Another said to the camera, "The chef is just amazing." A man wearing a backward cap, a long goatee, and two hoop earrings talked about Café Rakka as his and his wife's Wednesday date night tradition. Both were white, both were Hendersonvillians, and both spoke in thick southern accents as they praised this Arab man's food.

Fieri moved back to the kitchen. Together they made lamb

korma and filet mignon kebab, as well as the ancient recipe Riyad called homemade "farmer's cheese." Fieri even agreed to keep parts of the process secret, the parts that Riyad believed belonged only to the people of the desert.

After taking a bite, sandwiched between a mint leaf and a slice of tomato, Fieri looked up at Riyad. "You're incredible."

Riyad looked back, locked in a nervous and goofy smile. "I'm glad you like it."

Fieri turned to the camera. "What a cool dude."

At the end, when it was finally time to wrap up the shoot and move on to the next dive, Fieri shook Riyad's hand and turned to the camera once more: "You guys are gonna love this place."

They shot in April. The episode aired in October. Days later Riyad looked out from his kitchen and saw a line stretching from the counter to the door.

THE NIGHT HE WATCHED the episode of *Diners, Drive-Ins and Dives,* Riyad felt proud and buoyant, amazed to see his family's recipes beamed over the airwaves all across the United States, even around the world. One thing bothered him, though. His name. The producers insisted on identifying him properly, as Riyad Alkasem. But to everyone who came into the restaurant—and to most everyone he knew here in Hendersonville—he always introduced himself as Chef Rakka. Some people called him "Chef," and others called him "Rakka," but only his wife and family and close friends ever called him Riyad.

Chef Rakka was a character. No matter how much he loved cooking, he still saw this as temporary, an act. He'd started a restaurant because it felt like his only good option, a potential path back to the middle class, but he still saw cooking as frivolous. Even at forty-three years old, he dreamed of finding a way back to law school. He'd taken classes throughout his time in America. He'd never let go of that vision of himself as the man who might revolutionize Syria, even from afar. Chef Rakka, though, thought nothing of politics. He was carefree, didn't worry about what was going on in Syria, barely even cared about the political situation here in the United States. Even if he knew that many of his customers voted for policies that threatened men like Riyad Alkasem, Chef Rakka focused only on delighting them with his food.

And then the Food Network had shown up and identified him as Riyad Alkasem. Barely anyone would notice. His customers and his staff would still greet him as "Chef." But to him, the sight of that name on that screen, a man wearing a chef's jacket and cooking that food, all signified something. This was not a character. This man was not in costume. The man who cooked food for Guy Fieri was the same man who'd spent his life ranting about the evils of Assad. People could call him whatever they wanted. But he was not "Chef." He was Riyad. He was a Syrian and an American. He was a chef and a would-be revolutionary. He was the father of two Tennessee boys and the son of Raqqa's *mukhtar*. He could not split his identities, no matter how much he might want to, or how much the world around him might want him to.

They used to tell a story, back in Syria, about the great poet Al-Mutanabbi. He traveled through the desert region, way back in the tenth century, regaling royalty with his poems, which spoke of battles won and lost, of love and of heartbreak. Mutanabbi's work was so evocative that he was given the nickname Prince of Poets. Beauty poured out of his pen and his mouth, and everywhere he went, he was welcomed as if he belonged to royalty. Eventually, Mutanabbi started wondering: Why *wasn't* he royalty? He'd been called the Prince of Poets, but what if he were an actual prince? The possibility enthralled him. He'd receive even more wealth, even more adulation.

But he never became a prince. He never became anything but a traveling poet, known for the brilliance of his words. And because he was not royalty, because he had no purpose but to write and to speak, to tell the story of the desert in his poems, he gained even more attention and adulation. His words were studied by thousands, remembered for centuries long after he died.

Riyad realized that perhaps he could learn from Mutanabbi. He wanted to be a revolutionary, but he was a chef. He could chase a life that would never be his, or he could embrace the wonders of the life he already had. Business continued building, long after Guy Fieri departed. His restaurant was named among Sumner County's best by readers of the *Nashville Scene* in 2010, and became Restaurant of the Year multiple times in the years that followed. Ricky Skaggs performed at the Grand Ole Opry, and midset, he asked Riyad to stand so he could honor him from the stage.

He didn't need to change Syria with his American ideas. Riyad was changing a small slice of America, simply by being a Syrian who had the gall to live here, exactly as he was. He'd spent so long dreaming of revolutionizing Syria and contorting himself to fit into America. But now he found that by integrating his two identities, by believing that Americans might want what Raqqa had to give, he found a deeper sense of belonging in his new home. He became more American when he became more *sha'awi.*

And it was then, right around the time Riyad let go of his dreams for changing Syria, that he woke up one morning and walked through the living room where Linda had turned on CNN, and he saw on the screen that Syria was now trying to change itself.

It started small, just a dozen or so people on the streets of Damascus. Technically, they weren't even protesting the regime. They marched through the city's market, chanting in support of Libya's uprising against its own dictator, Muammar Gaddafi, the same man whose government had contracted with Linda's airline for flights between there and Saudi Arabia decades ago. But still, the image was striking. Syrians were standing together in the streets, chanting as one, in defiance of the law banning public protests that had been in place since 1963. Now it was 2011.

Linda was flipping channels.

"Wait!" Riyad said. "Go back to CNN."

There he saw about a dozen people, marching through the Al-Hariqah district of Damascus, chanting in protest.

He bolted up from the couch, socks only halfway on his feet. He wanted to jump. He wanted to cry. Instead he just screamed, "The Syrian revolution has begun!"

He couldn't believe it. He'd been obsessively watching the news across the Middle East for months, as demonstrations spread from Tunisia to Libya, Egypt to Bahrain. They were calling it the Arab Spring. Never, though, did most observers believe the unrest would spread to Syria. Assad was too shrewd, had too many allies. Most of the country's Shi'a, as well as most of its Christians and Alawites and a sizable minority of Sunnis, supported Assad. Most of the country, regardless of faith or class, supported his foreign policy, which talked tough on Israel and demonized the United States.

And yet here they were, just a few of them, chanting in support of revolutionary ideas. Riyad called Bashar, breathless. Had his brother heard anything?

"No," Bashar said, "there is nothing like that going on here."

In Syria, the government controlled all news stations. He'd heard no news of protests elsewhere, and Raqqa remained as quiet as before.

Besides, Bashar didn't much care for the glee he heard in his brother's voice. Riyad didn't live there. He hadn't lived there in decades. What did he care about the possibility of a revolution that would have no impact on his daily life?

"Whatever is going on in Damascus," Bashar said, "it's not going to happen here. We don't want that."

"Whether you want it or not," Riyad said, "get ready. It's coming."

IT TOOK TWO YEARS. The protests spread to Dera'a in the south, to Aleppo in the north, and to Homs, right there in between. It took some time, but eventually they reached Deir ez-Zor, a desert city like Raqqa, all the way in the country's far east. Across Syria, the regime responded to unrest with violence. Protesters were jailed and tortured, demonstrations met with gunfire. Bashar continued disbelieving until early 2012, when people from Homs showed up in Raqqa, seeking shelter. Their houses had been destroyed, their family members killed. The whole world was watching—Riyad could see it on the news every single day on CNN—but in Raqqa, the war didn't feel real until its victims arrived in the city, desperate and afraid.

For almost a year, Raqqa remained quiet. The city cared nothing for politics. The town was built on tribal order, on the structure set up by Taha. The people had lived through the rule of the Ottomans, of the French, of the Assads. They would live through this revolution, most believed, and they would do so by keeping to themselves.

But then a few young men started getting other ideas. They'd heard from friends in other cities, who spoke with passion about the future of their country, about the need to stand up, to fight. And so they started marching. They would walk through the square, right in front of the storefront that was once the Alkasem family's shop, and chant, "God! Syria! Freedom and nothing else!"

"The people want to topple the regime! The people want to topple the regime!"

Riyad heard the news and felt wonder and jealousy. He ached to be among them, drunk on revolutionary fervor, screaming for death to President Assad.

He called Bashar. "Did you protest?"

"Of course not."

Why protest? Bashar thought. Protesting invited chaos. Raqqa had been just fine before.

Bashar's curiosity pulled him from home, and he stood on the edges of the streets and watched, but he never marched. He never raised his voice. He couldn't imagine such a thing, couldn't believe so many people he thought he knew were practically begging their government to bring them a war. The protests grew as months passed. He saw faces young and old, some he considered friends, some he knew from his legal duties, people who worked as informants on behalf of the regime.

He didn't know what to think. He only knew that he wanted to return to a life of simplicity and order. He'd gotten married in 2008. By the time the revolution started in 2011, he had two daughters under two years old, Jenan and Wajid. He wanted to practice law and raise his family and read his books. He clung to that hope, even as the demonstrations turned into battles, even as the revolutionaries turned into an army, even as their country spiraled into war.

He clung to it for years, all the way up until the day in 2013 when Raqqa fell to the rebels, until his big brother showed up at his family's front door.

CHAPTER

10

Riyad knocked. The streets around him were quiet, no people shuffling past. The sun had crept toward the desert's edges, bathing the city in gold. On his journey to this doorstep, Riyad had found his neighborhood changed but recognizable. Now he wondered what he'd find inside the house.

The door opened, and he barely recognized the woman who came to answer. His baby sister was grown now, her cheeks fuller and features sharper than the last time he'd seen her, seven years before.

"Riyad!" she screamed as she threw her arms around him. He laughed, giddy and nervous, his brain processing the reality of her arms around his neck. The fact that she was hugging him meant that she was, in fact, still alive. He said it was good to see her and asked how she was, but before she could answer, they both heard another voice, their mother's, shouting from inside the house.

"Is that real?!" she said. "That cannot be real."

She rushed into the courtyard, her head uncovered and her gray hair a mess, the fabric of her gown scraping the tiles of the floor. She looked at her son and wept, and he looked at her and wept, too, and their arms wrapped around each other's bodies, kissing cheeks and wiping tears and taking each other in.

Now Bashar appeared, and he hugged and kissed his brother, too, and introduced him to Aisha, whom he'd married two years after Riyad had last seen him, and his daughters, three-year-old Jenan and two-year-old Wajid.

Everyone was here. Everyone was safe. Riyad felt relief wash over him as his *mama* prepared a pot of tea. She handed Riyad a small glass cup, and he dropped in a pinch of sugar, then stirred. How quickly he fell into the rituals of a previous life, a time when afternoons and evenings could have been spent anywhere in this city, talking over tea.

Now, though, his mother had no patience for small talk. She did not comment on the weather. She did not ask him about his ride. She asked, first, if his wife and children were healthy. He said yes, and she nodded, satisfied.

Then she fixed her eyes on his and moved to the only question that mattered: "Why are you here?"

Her directness startled him. "Well," he said, and as he tried to answer, he found himself stumbling over his own thoughts.

Why was he here? Well, he was here because their phones were dead, and so he couldn't reach them, and that had sent him into a panic, leaving him barely functional at his restaurant and emotionally absent in his home. He was here because there was a revolution under way, an uprising of Syria's people, the kind he'd long dreamed of now unfolding right here in the land he'd left behind. Up until now, he'd been able to follow it only from the farthest distance, watching videos on YouTube and leaving comments on Facebook, never getting to march or chant or rip down images of Assad. He was here because he was jealous of Syria's youth, the generation who had actually done it, who had built the collective will to call for a change that so many imagined would never come.

And he was here because he missed *this*—this city, this house, this tea; because no matter how many years he'd spent in the United States, and no matter how much he loved his American family and his American business and his peaceful home in his small American town, some part of him still ached with longing for Raqqa.

But when faced with the question from his mother, he found himself at a loss for words. *Why was he here?*

"Well," he said, "I came here to see if maybe we could all get out."

That was the easiest answer. He came because they had to go.

His *mama* tilted her head, curious. "Get out where?"

Riyad had thought this through. He'd already spoken to an immigration lawyer, back in the States. The lawyer had told him they would need to register as refugees in a neighboring country, and then they could begin the process of applying for asylum, eventually settling somewhere in the West. With his U.S. citizen status, Riyad imagined he could bring them to Tennessee. But first, they had to get across the border and out of Syria.

"We can go to Turkey," he said.

"Oh, son," his mother said, her face melting, almost pitying. "No. If you came here for this, you have wasted your time. We will not go to Turkey."

Riyad went quiet for a moment, a little stunned.

Bashar sat across the room, saying nothing, aware that there would be time for the two of them to talk things over later on. He listened with one ear, tending to the girls as they played.

Riyad stirred his tea, unsure what to say next. "Well," he finally offered, trying to measure out his words, "why don't we just go to the border and see?"

Right now the border was wide open. Syrians didn't even need passports. Turkey was letting them enter the country and seek refuge, and thousands were arriving every day. Riyad's family could walk right in, then find a home in southern Turkey, perhaps in the city of Şanlıurfa, just a forty-five-minute drive from the border. The language would be different and the culture unfamiliar, but the more Syrians poured into Turkey, the more those differences would fade. Entire neighborhoods in cities across southern Turkey now had storefront signs in Arabic and restaurants serving Syrian food. He could find them a nice house in one of those neighborhoods, their expenses paid by himself and his brother Kasem, who was still in the Gulf. They'd already been sending money to the family. This new life would cost the exact same. "The only difference," Riyad said, "would be that we would be able to sleep at night, knowing you're safe."

She shook her head. This was not acceptable. This was not reason enough for him to have traveled all this way. "Why would you leave Linda and the boys to come here for *this*?"

"I had to," Riyad said.

Didn't she know that they needed him? Sitting at home in Tennessee, he'd read news far different from what they'd heard here in Raqqa. He had access to international journalistic reporting, whereas here in the thick of the war, they would hear only regime propaganda and local gossip. Riyad knew that the rebels were fractured but ferocious. He knew that once the regime lost Raqqa, it would take many months, even years, to get it back. And he knew that some splinter groups of rebels were extremists, determined to change the very fabric of Syrian society, that they could turn Raqqa into a city unrecognizable from the one their ancestors had built.

The rest of the world, Riyad explained, looked at the chaos in Syria and stood with open arms. Syrians were settling all over Europe, in Germany and Sweden and Iceland. Many, he said, would even find their way to the United States. Yes, these places might be foreign and strange, and yes, the journeys were long. But Riyad knew more than most that a life could be built anywhere. Besides, what good was your native country if you were just buried in its ground?

"*Yuoma*," Riyad said, using his tribe's ancient word for mother. "Don't you know what is coming to you?"

She stood and returned to the kitchen, getting Riyad more sugar for his tea. "Whatever it is, we can take it."

Riyad shook his head. They couldn't. He knew it.

But before he could respond, his mother continued. "For me"—and she held up two fingers, index and middle, touching each other with no space in between—"death and leaving home are like *this*."

She held Riyad's gaze and kept her fingers up, pressed tight together, unmoving.

She spoke again, as if to make sure he understood. "Death and leaving home are the same. There is no difference."

RIYAD FELT THE ADRENALINE of his travels recede. It began to register that he'd flown more than six thousand miles, had ridden twelve hours through a war zone, for nothing. His family was in denial, he thought, blind to the horrors at their doorstep. He could always exercise his rights as the family patriarch, demanding that they leave. If he did, they would obey him. It didn't matter that he lived thousands of miles away, that he hadn't been a part of daily family life for decades. He was the oldest male; his word reigned. If he demanded they leave, they would leave.

And yet he knew, leaving Raqqa didn't guarantee an escape from danger. Death awaited on the road through the war zone and even at the border. It awaited in refugee camps in Turkey and in the journey across Europe. Wherever they went, violence could find them. And if, after leaving at Riyad's insistence, they were killed, he would never forgive himself.

He decided to rest and collect his thoughts. He settled into a spare bedroom, grabbing a blanket of goat hair and wrapping himself in its thin fibers. Hours passed, and he lay awake, captive to adrenaline and jet lag and his restless mind. How, he wondered, could he come all this way only to have his family refuse to leave? They'd been brainwashed—that was how he saw it. The regime's propaganda machine was finely honed. State-sponsored media had told the people that the revolution was a conspiracy, hatched by Syria's enemies, led by Israel, Saudi Arabia, and the United States.

For their part, his family thought Riyad had been compromised by the American media, telling him lies about the reality on the ground.

Riyad felt helpless. Maybe, he thought, he'd convince them to leave in the morning. A little tea, a little breakfast, and a lot of straightforward talk regarding the dangers in their midst. Perhaps then they'd see his point. Perhaps they'd decide to go. But now, finally, he closed his eyes and let himself drift.

———

THE FIRST BOMB DROPPED at three A.M. Its sound boomed through the city, one blast as it hit a building and another a split second later as it exploded inside, the noise loud but somewhat distant, pulling Riyad from his sleep. He sat up, afraid and confused, hands gripping the bed, and his heartbeat quickened as his breaths grew short. His eyes darted across the room, as if he might find safety somewhere in the dark. He jumped out of bed and ran into the den, where he found his mother, emerging from her own bedroom.

"Don't worry, my son," she told him. "The bombing is not around the city."

As she spoke, the house shook with another blast, louder now. Windows vibrated. Little Jenan and Wajid ran from their own bedroom in tears. Aisha rushed to them, unable to quell her own yelps of fear. The earth underneath Riyad seemed to move, ever so slightly. Surely, he thought, the bombs were getting closer. The next one could fall right on top of them. These minutes could be his last.

"What do we do?" he asked his mother, panicked. "That one was close."

She smiled gently. "No, that was about three or four kilometers away."

Bashar had emerged from his own room and now held his daughters close, trying to comfort them. He looked up, and Riyad saw the faintest smile on his face. "Are you okay?" Bashar asked his brother.

Riyad took deep breaths, working to place himself there in the room. "Yes, I'm fine." If he was afraid, Bashar said he could go across the street, to the bomb shelter.

"Do you want to go?"

Riyad thought for a moment. "Are you going?"

"No. It's easier for us to stay here."

"Then I will stay."

Another bomb dropped. Then another.

"Okay," Bashar said after the fourth one. "We're okay."

Typically, the regime dropped four bombs per plane. So if Bashar heard one plane, he knew to expect four bombs. If he heard two or three, he knew to expect eight or twelve. Tonight he'd only heard one.

"That should be all."

They returned to sleep.

RIYAD WOKE HOURS LATER. Light had crept into the bedroom through a window, and now he could hear footsteps through the house, moving at an easy pace, unattached to panic. He rose and stretched and felt—*how is it possible?*—relaxed. Sometime after the bombings, in between spells of sleep, he had arrived at a certain peace. He would not, could not, make his family leave Raqqa. All he could do was give them his very best pitch. If he stated his case, at least he would know he'd done all he could.

He joined his mother as she worked to prepare breakfast. The rest of the household rustled in their own corners, then made their way, one by one, to the kitchen. His *mama* set the table, and Riyad tore through his plate—eyes ravenous and mouth full—eating eggs with tomato and relish, seasoned with salt and vinegar and oil. He added a few olives, all pickled right there in their home, and a little cheese, stuffing himself while the family looked on in wonder.

Maybe *this* was why he'd come here. Not to be a hero, not to convince his family of something to which they'd never agree, but simply to sit at this table.

"Are you okay?" Bashar asked him.

Riyad swallowed another bite, then grinned. "No!" He pointed at Bashar. "You get to eat *mama*'s cooking every day! I never get this!"

After breakfast, he sat while his *mama* cleared the table, washed dishes, and began her morning chores.

"Okay," she said finally, sounding more upbeat now. "You came here. You saw us. You see that we're okay. When are you going back?"

Riyad was struck dumb. He'd been here only a night. He wasn't sure when he'd return, but he'd imagined he'd stay for at least a few weeks. His family here needed him. Surely they understood that they needed him.

His mother waited for a response, but he only shrugged, arrested by his own thoughts. Then she spoke again, softer now but no less direct: "My son, you have to leave."

"What?"

Leave? He'd come all this way to convince them to flee the war, and now his own mother was trying to kick him out of his home?

"Why?" he asked.

"The longer you stay here, the more you put us in danger."

He didn't understand. They needed another man, someone strong and healthy, to help them in this time of crisis. His presence brought greater security, he thought. How could he bring them danger?

"People will know who you are," she said.

He nodded. Of course they would know who he was. He was the descendant of Ibrahim and Taha, the grandson of Muhammad, the son of Abdul-Rahman the *mukhtar*. His plot of the city's community land sat just north of the table where they now ate, marking him as belonging to the founding members of this town. Of course people would know who he was. He was an *Alkasem*.

His *mama* shook her head—it was more complicated than that. She came closer and fixed her eyes on his and spoke slowly, making sure he understood.

"I love you," she said. "I want you to stay here." She wanted him in her kitchen and at her table. She wanted her kisses on his cheeks and her arms around his back. She wanted these things more than she could begin to explain.

"If I could," she said, and she pointed to a closet, "I would put you in there and keep you there forever."

He nodded. The tears creeping toward the edges of her eyes let him know she was telling the truth.

"But you have to go," she said.

She held his eyes a moment longer.

"You're an American now."

CHAPTER

11

Riyad understood the danger, of course he did. Buried under his clothes, he still had his American passport. Militants coveted that document, a ticket to the West. What they would covet even more was Riyad's body. An American hostage could command the world's attention and invite a six-figure ransom. Of the forces who roamed Syria's deserts, a few would capture Riyad and kill his family without giving it a second thought.

Now that he was in Syria, he saw that the revolution was becoming something altogether different from what he had imagined. When demonstrations turned into battles, and protesters turned into warriors, a once-beautiful uprising morphed into something messy and ugly, endlessly complex. Riyad could see it, even in just a few days in his homeland. So many foreigners. *Why are they fighting for Syria?* He was afraid he knew the answer. They weren't. They were fighting just to fight. Fighting because they'd given themselves over to the nihilism of extremists. Chaos had created a vacuum, and it was being filled by *mahabil*, as the old man on the bus had said, "crazies." Riyad's *mama* couldn't bear to think of what the *mahabil* would do with her oldest son.

But Riyad couldn't bear the thought of leaving. Not now. Not yet. So he begged for a couple more days. He'd come all this way. Maybe it had been stupid, but still, he was here. Let him spend more time sipping tea with his mother and talking politics with his brother. Let him gather up his nieces in his arms. He wanted to memorize the shapes of their smiles and the texture of their laughs. He wanted just a little more time in this city he knew he might never see again.

"Fine," his *mama* said, with a wave and a shrug. "A couple more days."

THAT NIGHT RIYAD AND BASHAR ventured out together, the streets quiet, the city not yet sure of itself. Bashar was happy to see Riyad, even if he thought his brother was crazy for coming back here. As they walked, he spoke for a few moments as if there were no war around them, as if he were merely taking his big brother on a tour of the city he'd long ago left, showing him the ways Raqqa had transformed. Even before the war, the city had begun to change, with high-rise buildings looming over centuries-old squares. Office buildings stood where Riyad remembered camel stables. A forest of iron and concrete stretched across what used to be empty land. There were new restaurants, even hotels. Before the war halted progress, Raqqa had been growing into a modern city.

As they walked, they could avoid the war's damage for only so long. Even though there had been only a few days of bombings, they occasionally walked past a building cratered in, rubble spilling into the streets. All across the city, Riyad sensed unease. No matter what his family said about the regime returning, the energy betrayed deep confusion and fear. No one knew what might come next. No one knew whether to weep or cheer, to leave or stay. Should they resume life as usual? In the midst of a war, what did that even mean?

Bashar, meanwhile, took delight in his brother's presence and the city's calm. He'd missed Riyad—the vastness of his wisdom and the fierceness of his love, but as much as anything, the wildness of his dreams. *Of course* Riyad wanted the family to flee to Turkey. For

Riyad, home was impermanent, transient. Bashar was different. His only home was the one their ancestors had built centuries ago, the structure that housed their boyhood games and adolescent schemes, the place where they'd studied during law school and where they'd wept after they buried their *yahba,* where Bashar was working to raise his children with the knowledge of all the people in their family who had come before.

So finally, after letting Riyad ramble on for a while, Bashar placed a hand on his brother's shoulder. "Riyad, I don't want to go to Turkey."

He agreed with his mother. Riyad had been duped by the foreign media.

"All this," he said, "will pass."

THEY WALKED ON, both of them eager to enjoy the evening. The city was quiet. Shops remained empty, restaurants closed. Passersby avoided eye contact. Every few blocks, they encountered a soldier, wandering the streets. A few of the soldiers wore masks.

"Those guys are the worst," Bashar whispered to Riyad. "If you get stopped by one of them, you're not going to see tomorrow."

One part of town, though, still teemed with life. As they approached Al Moujammah Street downtown, they found themselves at the complex of government offices. The governor's mansion, a sprawling compound, had once housed the most powerful of Assad's local cronies. Inside, green chandeliers hung above marble floors. Art remained on walls, glassware in cabinets, expensive furniture in its place. The regime had moved out, and new powers had moved in, but they'd kept most of the décor intact. There was one change, however. The golden bust of Hafez al-Assad, which had long resided in the mansion's foyer, now lay just outside the black and gold gate, the word *tyrant* scrawled across its head.

After the regime's workers had fled, other organizations had moved into the abandoned buildings. Brigades and militias, mostly. No sense in a war causing prime office space to go unused. So they set up their own headquarters. Each office had a desk, a chair, a flag, and a middle-aged man, twice the age of most soldiers.

When they saw Riyad, they beckoned to him, offering trays of tea. "Come, my brother," the men said, and Riyad smiled and stepped inside, Bashar shaking his head and trailing behind.

They talked about the war. They bragged about their battles. *Do you see how the city has been liberated? Aren't you hopeful about how we will build a new Syria after Assad is dead?* They wanted him to see it. *Do you see it?* The people were on the rise; the regime was a thing of the past.

Riyad nodded, enthralled. Here in Raqqa, he felt a bit like he was experiencing a uniquely American tradition, one he'd seen in movies and heard about from American friends: *This is exactly like rush week on frat row.* And just like the fraternities that lure pledges with access to booze and women, the brigades showed off their connections to high-powered weaponry and deep-pocketed Saudis.

And eventually, in every single office, they finally made it around to their point: "Will you join us, brother?"

Riyad's family wanted him to leave, but listen to these men! They wanted Riyad to join them. He found himself intoxicated by their hopes for revolution. Even as Syria had become a chaotic mess, Riyad still believed this war could end with a democratic government, a country freed from the shackles of Assad. Also, they called him "brother." Riyad loved it when strangers called him "brother." That didn't happen nearly enough back home in Tennessee.

But still, he wasn't going to join any army. He just wanted to linger for a while, to hear more stories from the war.

"Let's go," Bashar urged, and finally Riyad agreed to leave.

As they reached the street, the brothers began to argue.

"What are you doing?" Riyad asked Bashar, awash in delight from his conversations. "These are our people. They're from our tribe."

Bashar shook his head.

"We're just talking," Riyad continued. "That's all."

Bashar stopped. "These people do not care about you," he said. "They want you to fight with them or to give them money. They're not your friends. If you're not going to do one of those two things, they don't have any use for you."

Riyad brushed him off and kept walking. At another storefront, he dipped inside and made small talk with a thin and gray-haired wisp of a man, an artist. It was here, finally, that Riyad let it slip: "I'm from America."

The artist leaned in, eyes gleaming. "America?"

"America."

"Can you take me back with you?"

Riyad laughed lightly, just enough to invite the man to keep talking.

"You know," the artist said, "in America, they respect art. It's not like here."

Art was his passion, not his living. Before the revolution, he'd worked odd jobs around town. Now, two years into the war, a man who felt most at home in front of a canvas found himself in a makeshift office, trying to convince strangers to take up arms.

So yes, the artist had to admit, it would be wonderful if Riyad committed time or money to his brigade. But while they were here, just the two of them chatting, he mostly wanted to fantasize about another life, in another place, a country where his art would command the respect and the cash that he knew it so richly deserved.

Riyad smiled, sympathetic. He knew what it was like to project fantasies onto foreign nations. He knew, too, that sometimes it was best to let reality tarnish misplaced dreams.

"You have to understand something," Riyad said. "Even in America, most artists don't make very much money."

"Really?"

"Really. Only the famous artists actually make a living."

In his eyes, Riyad saw a flash of disappointment.

"So look at it this way," he said. "You're not missing out on anything. Everywhere in the world, artists are poor."

They laughed together, and Riyad saw the artist's face turn bright. He was ravenous for any scrap of insight into a country he knew he'd never see.

"Come have dinner with us," he said. "I want to hear more about America."

"Wonderful," said Riyad.

"No," said Bashar.

They turned to each other. "Our mother is making dinner," Bashar said. "We have to go."

The man slumped, just a little, and his eyes tightened, as if confused. "Well," he said, "what about a cup of tea?"

In Riyad's Syria, an invitation declined was an insult upon a family. In Bashar's Syria, *wartime* Syria, any man who offered hospitality one moment could offer death the next.

"Come on," Riyad said, "we can't turn him down."

Bashar stood. "We're leaving." He turned to Riyad. "Let's go."

Riyad still didn't understand. He didn't know the artist, but he knew his family. These were people with generations of ties to the Alkasems. Why would they mistrust them now?

"I've been trying to tell you," Bashar said. "Everyone is dangerous now. Respectable people have become thugs."

"If it's so dangerous," Riyad said, "then why won't you leave?"

Bashar walked quickly, eyes straight ahead. "It's safe for me," he said. Then he looked at Riyad.

"*You're* different."

A COUPLE OF DAYS later, the two brothers went on a road trip. They packed into a passenger van and headed north to Tal Abyad, a small town that straddles the Turkish border. The border itself stretched along the edge of the town, a porous and haphazard thing. In some places, a fence divided Turkey from Syria. In others, all that divided the two countries was a cluster of trees. Right now the border was completely open; anyone could walk across. Some did and stayed. Others, like Bashar, crossed for just a few minutes, to go shopping.

He needed medicine. He'd been having sporadic, unexplained seizures, dating back to his time in America, and the medication he took was no longer available in Raqqa. Riyad and Bashar walked into the woods, nearing the border. It struck Riyad how casual this all seemed, how easy it was to come and go. On one side, a war zone. On the other, peace. So little seemed to separate danger from safety.

They waited. The forest was thick, the day cool. Soon a teenage boy approached them, wearing jeans and a T-shirt and hair gel. He asked casually, "What do you need?"

"Keppra," Bashar said.

"Got it," said the boy, and he was off. This was how Bashar got his medication. He didn't want to cross into Turkish territory if he could help it. At any moment the border might close, he imagined, and he'd be stuck in another country. The moment they had approached the border, Riyad noticed, his brother's breath grew short.

Twenty minutes later the boy returned, medicine in hand. This was the new pharmacy. A single teenager, unafraid to run back and forth across a border.

They returned to the Tal Abyad market, firmly on the Syrian side. There Riyad noticed that for the first time since arriving in the country, he had cellphone service. His phone was connecting to Turkish towers. He hadn't spoken to Linda since his flight departed Nashville, three days ago. He dialed and listened as the phone rang, standing in the middle of the market, a whir of activity all around him.

To his left, Riyad saw a massive man, his prodigious belly stretching the fabric of his robes, a Bedouin headscarf perched atop his beach ball of a head. The man glared at everyone who passed him, but Riyad knew that customers would approach him all the same, because down at his waist, he wore a belt upon which hung four black, shiny pistols.

Linda answered. "Hello?"

"Hi!" said Riyad. "It's me!"

Through the phone, he could hear her breath collapse: "Oh, *finally.*" She exhaled, and then in an instant, her tone snapped from relief to agitation. "Why haven't you called me? I haven't slept for three days!"

Riyad apologized and grinned, sorry that he'd worried Linda but thrilled to be standing in a Syrian market, listening to his wife's

Middle Tennessee drawl. He explained that he hadn't had service, and he told her that his family was doing just fine.

"I'm not going anywhere dangerous," he told her. "Where I am, everything is peaceful."

He listened to updates from home as he watched a small and fidgety twig of a man approach the gun dealer. He was no soldier, just some guy in need of a weapon. Merchant and customer haggled, the ancient dance of the Middle Eastern market. A price was quoted and then countered. They argued over who was taking advantage of whom. They whittled away at the gaps between their two figures, coming close to a deal. Finally, in one of Riyad's ears, Linda was explaining that their boys were both doing well if a little worried, while in the other, the customer shouted, "How do I even know this gun works?"

The merchant grabbed the pistol from his belt and pointed it skyward. "Look!" He fired off a few rounds, quick blasts echoing around the market and into the phone.

"Riyad!" Linda yelled. "Where are you?"

He laughed. "I'm just in the market! Just buying medicine."

They talked for several minutes, Riyad explaining that he'd been unable to convince his family to leave but he was still working on it—he just needed a little time. Moments later another gun began firing, pointed once again benignly toward the sky. These were the sounds and rhythms of Syria now, blasts of gunfire melting into the soundscape of daily life.

"Are you sure you're not in the middle of a gunfight or something?"

Riyad smiled. "Yes, yes, I swear," he assured her. He promised he was safe. He promised the dangers of the war lay many miles away.

RIYAD HAD PLANS FOR their time in Tal Abyad: He wanted to meet with their distant cousin Ismail. Still intent on getting his mother and brother out of the country, he had a hunch that maybe Ismail could help. So they wandered to a small village just outside the city's center, where they found their cousin sitting in a folding chair behind a makeshift desk, square in the middle of a field. Ismail had no office, just this lone desk in an open expanse. It looked, to Riyad, like something out of a movie.

He stood. "My cousins!" he said. "Welcome, welcome." He hugged and kissed them both, his taut muscles wrapping around their backs. He was young, perhaps thirty, and wore Western clothes and a brilliant smile, face chiseled and eyes gleaming.

Ismail was in charge of his own brigade. At this point in Syria, if you were young and handsome and charismatic, if you had some midlevel military experience and could sell yourself as a leader of men, then chances were you had your own brigade. All you needed was a few dozen willing soldiers to follow you, along with enough charm to coax money out of foreign donors, the rich Arab oilmen who had a stake—whether financial or religious—in the outcome of Syria's war. At this point, as many as one thousand brigades were roaming throughout Syria, each with its own sliver of power and land. Ismail's brigade had just seized control of this neighborhood in Tal Abyad.

Surely, Riyad thought, Ismail could convince Bashar that Raqqa was in danger. Here was a man soaked in the brutal realities of this war, who would agree with Riyad that Raqqa was no place for a family.

They sat down in low-slung Turkish-style chairs, situated around the table in the middle of the field. Ismail put his nine-millimeter handgun on the table before him and stretched out his legs. He looked relaxed. His smile shone. A few feet away, a soldier wearing military fatigues, a big black beard, and a loosely wound kaffiyeh carried an AK-47 and a look of bland menace on his face. Riyad suspected the beard and the kaffiyeh were largely for show, symbols of retrograde faux-piety meant to impress the brigade's conservative Saudi donors. The gun, though, was likely there for its proper purpose.

Ismail motioned to the bodyguard, then to the table before him. "Tea."

The soldier came over and poured them cups of black tea in tiny glasses, each with a couple spoonfuls of sugar, all while managing an assault rifle slung over his shoulder. They took it and sipped and talked, Riyad's face aglow, Bashar's eyes darting.

Finally, Ismail leaned forward and asked Riyad, "So. Why did you come here?" He shrugged his massive shoulders. "Why would you come all the way from America?" He gestured around him, pointing vaguely at rubble. "You know we're in a war, right?" He laughed. Big and hearty, delighted by himself.

Riyad explained that he'd come to get his family out of Raqqa and into Turkey. They just needed a little more convincing. "Can you help us?"

Ismail's head tilted. "Really?"

"Well, yeah."

He laughed, as if considering the request of a child, and shrugged. "Everything is going to be just fine." The FSA, the moderates, would soon drive Jabhat al-Nusra, the Al Qaeda–linked extremists, out of Raqqa, he said. No problem.

Even though it was called the Free Syrian Army, the FSA wasn't an army as much as a coalition of loosely linked brigades, including Ismail's.

"We're doing great," he said. The Assad regime would keep bombing in Raqqa, he said, but that would be it. No ground troops would arrive. No snipers. The rebels would keep control of the city. They would deliver to Bashar and his family a new Syria, a Syria of which they could be proud.

This wasn't what either brother wanted to hear. Riyad wanted Ismail to scare Bashar into leaving. Bashar wanted to believe that the regime would soon return. But Bashar didn't much care what Ismail had to say. He was an idiot with a gun, like so many people running around Syria these days, having power only because he was tall and handsome and could convince the Saudis or the Kuwaitis or whoever else that he would help bring down Assad.

Nonetheless, Riyad kept listening, smiling. Several soldiers had been drifting in their direction, all with identical beards and head coverings and shoulder-slung assault rifles. Bodyguards, probably.

"What about these new people?" Riyad asked. On the roads between Turkey and Raqqa, he'd seen their black flags flying, their faces covered in masks. He'd seen their recruits pouring in from all over the world—Europeans, North Africans, even Chinese Uighurs. They were already in Manbij. Wouldn't they try to take over Raqqa too?

Ismail found this absurd and flicked his wrist. "We're going to crush them right away." Then he leaned forward, his eyes flickering. "Tell me, how is America?"

Riyad had been reckless, telling Ismail he lived in the United States moments after they sat down. "It's a beautiful country," he said. "Maybe the greatest country in the world."

He told them about his restaurant, about selling Syrian food to Americans. He told them about Los Angeles, with its endless sprawl and omnipresent sun, about Santa Barbara, with its dramatic coast and violent sea.

Ismail smiled and nodded, and soon the other men who had gathered around him were smiling and nodding too. To Riyad, these were not soldiers. They were an audience, a group of strangely familiar men who were indulging his need, whether he was sitting under this tree in a war zone or was back at a table in his restaurant, to tell a good story.

Ismail's smile remained. "An amazing place," he said. "I wish I could go."

They went quiet for a moment, and Ismail reached for his Sig Sauer pistol.

"Isn't this the most beautiful gun?" Ismail asked, turning it over in his hands.

It was a muscular thing, all angles and fine etching.

"It's very nice," Riyad said.

"It's gorgeous!" Ismail said. "Just gorgeous." He shot his eyes from the gun back to Riyad.

"You know where it's from, right?"

Riyad did. He'd bought one like it years ago in Los Angeles, after one of the first stores he managed had been robbed.

"America," Ismail said, not waiting for his cousin's answer. Even though his teeth were yellow, his smile shone.

He tapped Riyad's knee. "I bet you have so many of these in America, don't you?"

Now he leaned back and looked at his bodyguards.

"Hey, boys!" he said. "We just need some American weapons, right?"

They nodded and grinned.

"Let me tell you something," Ismail continued. "If we had just ten million pounds to buy some more American weapons—two tanks, maybe some more guns—then we could take all of Tal Abyad for ourselves."

Riyad smiled at this. "I believe it."

Bashar had remained silent the entire time, unsmiling. To him, Ismail was not family, and his soldiers were not friends. They were like almost everyone else outside his own household—they were threats. So while Riyad regaled Ismail with stories, Bashar scanned faces and escape routes. He was listening, yes, as Riyad and Ismail discussed rebel strategy, but he was also noticing a particular long-silent soldier, now standing just over his shoulder, clutching his own gun.

Bashar looked up at him.

For the first time since they all first exchanged pleasantries, Bashar spoke. "What are you doing here?"

All went quiet. Riyad paused, midsentence.

Bashar held the young man's gaze. His beard and his put-on menace gave him the look of an impostor. Where the soldier tried to project strength, Bashar saw insecurity.

Ismail looked over from his chair. He tilted his head in the direction of the village—a quick flick of the neck—and just like that, the young man left.

Ismail leaned forward again, smiling. They were back among friends now. "You know something funny?"

"What?" Riyad asked, still smiling.

"Someone like you could be worth a lot of money around here."

Riyad laughed, but inside he felt the faintest rumbling of nerves. "Yeah, I guess so."

Ismail's smile grew. "Wouldn't it be funny," he said, "if we"— he gestured to the men around him—"kidnapped you?"

He looked to Riyad and Bashar for their approval. This, he believed, was just hilarious. Didn't they think it was hilarious too?

He bobbed his head, as if reconsidering. "I mean, not *really* kidnapped you. But what if we just *pretended* to kidnap you? What if we sold you to the new guys"—meaning the foreigners quickly setting up residence and flying their black flags all over the region—"and then we came up with a plan to get you back?"

He clapped, rocking now, thrilled with himself. "Then we could split the money!"

The ransom would be hefty, for sure. American hostages were going for tens of thousands of dollars on the open market. The hostage economy was simple. Local militias—or even just fixers or runners who moonlighted as thugs—would kidnap Americans and then sell them to larger extremist groups, who then demanded ransom from families and governments. Peter Theo Curtis, a journalist from Atlanta, had been kidnapped by his own fixers and then sold to Jabhat al-Nusra. The extremists were now demanding a ransom of at least $3 million if his family wanted him back.

"What a plan, right?" Ismail said.

Riyad laughed along with him, and then they sat, letting their laughter die down. For a moment they heard nothing but the cawing of crows, flying around nearby trees, and the faint sound of car engines, humming on their way into town. Riyad looked at Ismail and willed himself to smile. This *was* a joke, right?

Ismail's eyes shifted from Riyad, up to his bodyguard, then down to his phone. "Excuse me," he said, shaking his head. "This guy has been texting me all day. I guess I finally need to call him." He stood and shrugged. "Business."

Riyad nodded. *Business.* He let himself exhale.

Ismail pointed to his guards. "They'll take care of you. Just wait here." He smiled. "I hope you're hungry! When I come back, we'll have a feast."

Riyad relaxed, but Bashar went into high alert. He shot up from his seat and called out to Ismail as he walked away.

"We need to pray," he said. "Is there somewhere we can go to wash ourselves?"

If you ever needed to manipulate a jihadi, Bashar thought, all you had to do was appeal to his fake piety.

"Yes, of course," Ismail said.

He pointed to a house, maybe twenty yards away. "Go in there. Wash, pray, and then come back, and we'll eat."

BASHAR AND RIYAD WALKED into the house. Riyad went straight to the bathroom to begin the *wudhu*—the Muslim ritual of washing before prayer, cleansing the mouth, the nose, the arms and hands and feet, all meant to purify the body before the body encounters God. But as Riyad turned on the faucet, Bashar stopped him.

"What are you doing?" he said.

Riyad looked at the faucet. He looked at his hands. He looked at his brother. Wasn't it clear?

Bashar shook his head. "We're not praying now. Let's go."

They left the bathroom and slipped out of the house through a back door. They climbed over a short wall, walking quickly but not so fast as to draw attention.

"Where are we going?" Riyad asked.

"Just walk," said Bashar under his breath.

They crossed a street and melted into a crowd.

BACK IN THE MAIN SQUARE, Riyad stepped in front of his little brother and blocked him.

"Why did we do that?"

Bashar met Riyad's stare, and his eyes went big. "Don't you see what was going on? He was going to kidnap you!"

This, Riyad thought, was preposterous. They had been joking over tea. Nothing more. Besides, Riyad said, "He's our cousin! Our blood!"

Bashar rolled his eyes. "Our *cousin*." His voice dripped with sarcasm. "Right."

Technically, this was true. But the definition of *cousin* had always been stretched thin in the tribal regions of Syria. Riyad barely knew who Ismail's parents were; they could be cousins, but probably five or six times removed. He wasn't exactly the kind of man their *yahba* had in mind when he told Riyad to cross the river only with blood.

"Listen to me," Bashar said. "Right now there are no cousins." War had made strangers out of relatives and enemies out of friends. They could trust each other, Bashar insisted. No one else.

"Leave."

Sitting down to dinner that evening, their mother was no longer polite. Her patience had eroded. She'd heard about the encounter with Ismail and his brigade (though the brothers spared her the details), and now she was more certain than ever: Riyad brought danger. As long as he remained in Raqqa, no one under their roof would be safe.

Bashar agreed. "The problem," he said, "is that you are still thinking of yourself as a Syrian. But here no one else thinks of you that way. You can't hide. You can't pretend. People know who you are."

Riyad found this absurd. He'd melted so easily back into the rhythms of Syrian life, had found himself at home while browsing the markets and walking the streets. He missed Linda, yes, and of course he missed his boys, but this place still offered him something America never had. There was an ease here, even in wartime, a sense that Syria's very oxygen was meant for Riyad's lungs.

And yet on his way through the desert, soldiers had noticed his American shoes. When he rode a taxi through the city, everyone he encountered sensed that he had not lived in Raqqa for some time. In the kitchen of his childhood home, his own mother declared that his presence brought her danger. From his chair in the camp, his cousin Ismail had lusted over the ransom Riyad would command— and maybe he wasn't joking.

It didn't matter how brown his skin or flawless his Arabic, how well he could cook lamb *yakhney* or how many generations back he could trace his family. All that mattered was the oath he'd taken that day in Los Angeles back in 1996, pledging loyalty to another nation and love for another flag. He'd worked at McDonald's and Walmart. He loved cable news, and he grilled burgers on the Fourth of July. The passport buried in his suitcase told the truth. Riyad had only one home, and that home was many thousands of miles away.

"I understand," he said. "I will go."

SO A COUPLE OF DAYS later he climbed into a van, alone, and rode north toward the border. His mother had wept as she packed his suitcase, and Bashar's arms quivered as he hugged Riyad goodbye. Even though they feared the risk he brought to their doorstep, they ached as they watched him leave. He crossed into southern Turkey, then continued to Istanbul and onto a plane that took him back across Europe and the Atlantic, back to the United States. He didn't know if he'd ever see his family again, but he had to believe that he would.

CHAPTER

12

Bashar had loved seeing his brother, but he felt relief the moment he left. Riyad had been reckless to come here, but the rest of them would be foolish to leave. They would survive. The war would pass. Didn't his brother understand that you don't leave home unless you feel the call of someplace else? Riyad had felt called by wild fantasies of America. And while Bashar once felt called to America by the duty of caring for his father, here he had a life. Anywhere else, he would only be sitting and waiting for this life to resume.

Winter receded, and the spring of 2013 crawled toward summer. In the evenings, Bashar would bring his daughters into the courtyard with their pillows and blankets, and they would lie on their backs and stare up at the stars. He and Riyad had slept outside on summer nights as children, and he and Aisha slept out there with their daughters in summers before the war. Bashar felt desperate to maintain any connection to old traditions, so every few nights he brought out pillows and sheets, and they all looked, together, at the heavens. The sky was gorgeous in the desert. When the city went dark, the world above them shone. Bashar hadn't realized just how beautiful Raqqa's sky was until he'd gone away to Aleppo and Damascus and California. In those places, city lights obscured the heavens. Here in the desert, he saw layers of outer space that so many around the world must never have seen. There were places up there, farther from this life than he could imagine. Places people could see but never reach, not even as astronauts, not even if they traveled all their lives. It was an amazing thing, to be able to lie down amid bombings and to look up, just above you, and see something so utterly indifferent to the realities of your world.

"I see the Big Dipper!" Jenan said. She was already learning constellations.

"Yes," Bashar said. "There it is."

"Look, *baba*!" said Wajid. "There's a shooting star!"

"Yes. I see it too."

He allowed a few moments of wonder. He wanted them to think about faraway galaxies and sink into their own sense of awe. But he also wanted them to know the important lessons of the skies.

He asked them to listen closely while he explained, "Our people have been studying the stars since ancient times."

It was true. All the way back in the eighth and ninth centuries, while Europe was locked in its Dark Ages, Arab astronomers had spent evenings just like this one, staring up from this very same desert at these very same stars.

Arabs did not invent astronomy, Bashar said, "but we excelled in it."

"How?" Jenan asked.

"We mapped the sky," said Bashar.

To this day, he explained, astronomers all over the world refer to stars by their Arabic names: Deneb, Algol, Altair.

The girls looked at the sky in silent awe. The night was hot, the air light, the only sound an occasional car rolling past.

"You know what?" Bashar said. "You girls can do the same thing. You can be just like them. You can do something in your life that people will remember for years and years."

His daughters remained quiet, but he hoped that they were listening. He hoped they understood. He leaned over, kissed them both, and told them to get some sleep. Soon they drifted off, and he let them lie there awhile longer while he watched them breathe, until he decided it was time to scoop them up in his arms and carry them back to bed. Before the city fell, they'd spent entire nights in that courtyard, sleeping under the stars. But no longer. They needed shelter. It was getting late. The bombs would be dropping soon.

SUMMER DEEPENED, and the city fell further into chaos. The regime had not returned; the rebels had instilled no order. And a corrupt government, Raqqa soon found, functioned far better than no government at all. The energy surrounding the city's fall had given way to an endless lethargy, punctured only by moments of horror in the daily bombings.

Bashar agonized over whether to continue pursuing a judgeship. The city belonged to the rebels. Ascending to the bench meant working for the regime, and working for the regime meant making his family a target.

He called Riyad. "Forget it," his brother said. That dream, Riyad insisted, had to be put on hold. Riyad did not urge his younger brother once again to leave Syria. He'd decided to lay off that argument—for now at least—and instead help his family in Syria however he was able. He sent regular money transfers. He kept in touch by phone. He supported them from afar as best he could. And right now, supporting his brother meant speaking up when Bashar talked about pursuing a doomed judgeship.

But Bashar knew that if he formally rejected the post, he'd draw regime suspicion. Either way, he would be a target. So he came up with a simple idea. He intentionally failed his oral exam in Damascus. He returned from there to Raqqa, resolved to focus only on survival until the war passed.

ONE AFTERNOON BASHAR WAS walking to the bakery—it was early 2014—when he came upon a man, sitting on the ground with his back against a building's wall. In his lap was a plate, topped with a mountain of chicken and rice. This was a Saudi dish called *kabsa*. Next to him lay a Kalashnikov rifle, and next to the rifle, a rocket-propelled grenade, one of those over-the-shoulder warheads that could be fired off with a quick jolt. Most armies used them to fire at tanks. In a pinch, though, RPGs could be used to blow up most anything.

The man looked up at Bashar, calm but serious. "My brother," he said, patting the ground next to him. "Join me."

Bashar smiled, trying to be polite, but shook his head. He felt no fear. He'd learned how to bury it, moments after the very first bombs fell. If he died, he would die because God had willed it. In the meantime, he just wanted to go about his day.

"No, thank you."

He turned to keep walking, but as he took a step, the man grabbed his leg. "Wait!"

Bashar looked down.

The man shook his head. "Don't cross," he said. He pointed up to a building across the street. "Sniper." He patted the ground beside him again, then held up his plate. *"Kabsa?"*

Bashar shook his head again. He did not want *kabsa*.

The man nodded, understanding. He gestured to his weapon. "Kalashnikov?"

Bashar shook his head again. He did not want a rifle. He wanted to go to the bakery. And then he wanted to go home. He decided to take his chances. He crossed the street. He was clearly not a soldier; surely, he thought, no sniper would gun him down. He moved, slowly, carefully, down the block until he reached the bakery, then stood in line and bought his bread.

When he returned, he reached the same block and saw men scattered across the street, guns drawn and firing. The man who'd offered him *kabsa* was standing, shooting, a look of wild hunger on his face. He finished off his bullets, dropped his rifle to the ground, then picked up the RPG and fired that too.

This, Bashar decided, was not the best route. He turned around and hurried the other way, and he thought to himself that something in Raqqa had shifted. These were not rebels fighting regime

soldiers. This wasn't even a battle between the terrorists and democratic rebels. Everyone on the street, as far as he could tell, belonged
to the *mahabil.*

He called Riyad. "The crazies are fighting each other."

He saw them in the streets, glaring at pedestrians, and wondered
if ever in their lives these men had cracked smiles. He saw them in
the breadlines, cutting in front of everyone just as Assad's soldiers
had always done, the same corruption under a different flag. And he
saw them in the mosques. Their sermons unnerved him. They
preached that men should shave their mustaches and grow their
beards, that women should cover every inch of their bodies every
time they left the home.

But it was more than that. They didn't just want to impose strict
laws here in Raqqa; they preached about the coming formation of a
new caliphate, an Islamic kingdom that would stretch beyond Syria
and into Europe, eventually across the entire world. They called
themselves the Islamic State. Soon the world would know them as
ISIS. To Bashar and most everyone else in Raqqa, they were called
Daesh.

SOMETIMES THEY FELT NUMB to the violence. More gunshots, more
bombs, a new soundtrack to their lives—it was amazing how quickly
the horrific became mundane. But other things, smaller things,
began to insidiously change their lives. The women in his family
could walk nowhere without Bashar or another male relative beside
them. The hard-line rebels shut down the local schools. In the square
near their home, the severed heads of Daesh's now-executed prison-
ers sometimes sat on spikes. When taking a taxi, Aisha would often
ask the driver, "Are there any heads today?" If the answer was yes, she
would request another route.

One morning Aisha took her neighbor to the doctor. The neighbor's family was poor and her son was sick, and so Aisha and Bashar
decided to pay for whatever medical care he needed. This was the
Alkasems' place in their neighborhood; so many of their friends
didn't have relatives earning steady incomes in stable countries, as

they did. Islam taught to care for the poor, so they helped in whatever ways they could. Aisha put on her burqa and walked outside
into the heat. She was pregnant—hoping this third time for a son—
and the burqa covered her face and her neck while the abaya covered
the rest of her skin. She felt the desert sun's violence the moment
she walked out the door, the sun soaking into the fabric, heating
every inch of her body. This was her biggest problem with the burqa.
It was just so very hot. She couldn't even find the relief of the river's
breeze.

Daesh had demanded this. The burqa (which covers the entire
face and chest, with only a mesh window for the eyes to look
through) or the niqab (which looks similar, but with a slit for the
eyes) was now mandatory for all women anytime they left home.
Aisha had been wearing a hijab since she was thirteen; she loved
wrapping it around her head each morning, and she made a ritual of
covering her hair before she left the home. Some parts of her body
were reserved only for her husband, she believed. She'd been proud
to wear the hijab when she was single, and she still felt proud, now
that she was married to Bashar. But she hated the burqa. Her girls
had cried the first time they saw her in it. Once she and Bashar arrived home from separate errands at the same time. He walked into
the house and nearly closed the door on her, until she yelled at him,
"Bashar! It's me!"

How did it serve marital purity that she vanished from even her
husband's view? Until recently, she'd never even seen a burqa in
Raqqa, or anywhere else in Syria for that matter. She knew women
in other parts of the world liked to wear them, and that was fine. If
one of them came to her with an argument for it, rooted in the
scriptures, then who knew, maybe she would even decide that she
wanted to wear the burqa too. But that's not what Daesh did. They
made no arguments. They allowed no discussion about the teachings
of Islam. They just arrived in town and told every woman to buy a
burqa and wear it. If they didn't, they'd be punished. So would their
families.

Aisha and her neighbor began walking. The streets were busy

enough. They saw merchants walking to their shops, Daesh police out on patrol. She recognized a few of the men, but of course, none of the women; all were completely covered. She did know, however, when she passed a Daesh wife. Those women stood out because around their shoulders many carried AK-47s.

Suddenly, Aisha and her neighbor heard a voice behind them: "Stop!"

She pretended she did not hear.

"You two! Stop right there!"

She felt her breath leave her. The dialect was not from Raqqa, not even from Syria. The men who were calling to her, she thought, must be from Saudi Arabia, or perhaps Qatar or another one of the rich countries on the Arab Gulf. *Of course,* she thought. *Daesh.*

She and her neighbor did as they were told.

The men approached. "There is a problem," one said.

"What is it?" Aisha asked.

He pointed at her neighbor's feet. "This is not Islamic."

Aisha looked down. All she saw was the fabric of the abaya grazing her neighbor's feet, then a pair of thin socks underneath slip-on shoes. But then she looked to the back of the feet and saw the issue. One sock had a hole. She was showing, on her heel, a two-inch sliver of uncovered skin.

"Come with me," the man said.

Aisha's insides twisted. Where would they go? She knew too many terrifying stories. Women raped, and jailed for years without anyone telling their families. Her pulse quickened as panic rose. She turned to a crowd of men, standing nearby. As she scanned their faces, she felt a flash of recognition. *Her cousins!* A couple of them were standing and watching, right there.

"Will you help us?" she asked.

They looked away, pretending not to hear. They did not want to argue against Daesh, would not risk their own safety in order to protect hers. She couldn't believe it. She had told herself so many stories about the way tribal culture elevated the place of women, about the lengths men would go to protect any woman in need. This had been their way since long before her birth. But now she saw that fear of Daesh had stripped her people of tribal honor. That would haunt her for years to come, make her want to scream whenever she thought back to that day. Not the evils of Daesh itself but the ways it warped the world around it. A Raqqa without honor was a Raqqa she did not know.

Hours later Aisha and her neighbor were released. They'd been lucky; they'd suffered no more than a few minutes of intimidation and passed most of the time in a cell with other "immodest women." Bashar showed up and paid for their bail—and brought a new pair of socks with no holes.

BASHAR DEALT WITH DAESH most directly every Friday, when he went to the mosque. The Prophet Muhammad had said that no Muslim should miss Friday prayers, so no matter who controlled the city, Bashar went every single week. He felt his body turn cold when Daesh soldiers knelt to pray beside him, AK-47s on their shoulders, raptly watching an imam preach about the expansion of the caliphate and the deaths of infidels. These men had transformed the mosque beyond recognition. Bashar had long adhered to Sufism, a strand of Islamic belief that celebrated God's mystery. These men, though, carried a false certainty that repelled him. They called themselves pious, but Bashar knew that while many were educated, many more had been trained by sitting in front of their laptops back at home, watching terrorist recruitment videos on dark corners of the internet.

He hated listening to them claim the religion he so loved. He heard that they'd imprisoned his grandfather, the grand mufti of Raqqa. The man who had taught Bashar to love Islam, who had told Riyad to teach Americans about their religion while serving their food, now sat in a Daesh prison, deemed an infidel.

In the West, people liked to divide Muslims up into "moderates" and "extremists." Bashar never cared much for this distinction. There was nothing *moderate* about his own faith. He felt more committed to Islam than to anything else on this planet; he went through every single day thinking of how he could best live a life pleasing to God. His friends called him "Sheikh." In his devotion to his faith, Bashar figured, he was the very definition of "extreme."

But Daesh was something altogether different. Bashar saw the world as a place filled with the wonders of God's creation. Daesh saw it only as a place full of things to burn.

SOON IT BECAME CLEAR that Daesh had little interest in the actual country, in Syria, at all. Its aim seemed simply to recruit members and terrorize enemies—and eventually to extend its reach into other Middle Eastern countries, then beyond that to the entire world. And at the heart of its power was violence. A man was caught stealing: Daesh cut off his hand, then paraded him around the city in a pickup truck, wearing his own appendage as a necklace. Others were deemed apostates, and Daesh cut off their heads. It controlled land that stretched across Iraq and Syria, and it declared that those countries' borders had been erased, at least in parts, that all of their land now belonged to a new country, the Islamic State. On June 29, 2014, their leader Abu Bakr al-Baghdadi delivered a sermon in a mosque in Mosul, where he declared that their caliphate had been established. He called upon all Muslims to come and join them, to take up arms and kill apostates, to fight to spread their theocratic nation across the world.

SIX DAYS BEFORE THAT SPEECH, Aisha gave birth to a beautiful baby boy in Raqqa's lone remaining hospital. They named him Abdul-Rahman, after Bashar and Riyad's father, and called him Abood. Like the *mukhtar,* he had dark hair and big eyes and cheeks that sloped like dunes of sand. He latched on to Aisha, ravenous, and slept and cried, and together they cried, too. Amid so much death, here was a new life. Someone to be a brother to their two little girls. Someone to carry on the Alkasem name. For one night, they did not care that their city had succumbed to terror. They did not care about the bombs that would soon fall. They barely worried when the generator that powered the hospital went down, turning the room dark. They just went home to be with their family and praised God and sipped tea, never taking their eyes off of baby Abdul-Rahman, a perfect creature in an unrecognizable world.

The baby ate constantly. Aisha knew it wasn't every hour, but it seemed that way. He would cry and crane his head, and she would feed him until he turned happy and sleepy. He woke her several times each night, Bashar and the girls still sleeping, the world dark. During these moments with just the two of them, Aisha wondered who her son would be. Maybe he'd have his father's tough but gentle spirit; maybe he'd inherit her passion, her will to fight. They would teach him to be a great leader in his city and his tribe, a man of bravery when so many in Raqqa had turned into cowards, a man of goodness when so much of the world around him had gone bad.

Those wishes would have to wait, though. Right now she just sat and nourished her child in the dark. She held him close, feeling peace and wonder, until, in an instant, she heard a shattering, as if the entire universe were a delicate vase, now split into a million pieces on the floor.

That's what she would remember most. Not the way the entire room lit up bright red. Not the blast of the explosions, louder than any she'd ever heard. But rather that first moment, before she even knew it was a bombing, when all was silent but for the breaking of Raqqa's windows, the sound of glass shards falling to the floor in homes all over town.

She jumped up. She did not yet know that the Americans had just attacked Raqqa. But she realized immediately: *This is not the regime.* This was someone new. More bombs fell, each with the same force, and she took little Abood and ran to the bathroom. The walls were thicker there, and they'd long ago decided it was the safest room in the house. She clutched her baby, feeling every cell in her body shaking, and she hoped that as he clung to her, he would not feel her shaking too.

The girls woke and came running, huddling close to her, clinging to her body.

Wajid looked up. Her eyes were planets. "Why are you afraid?" she asked her mother. "God is with us."

Aisha tried to believe it was true.

THESE NEW BOMBINGS BECAME routine, all so much more terrifying than what the regime had long delivered. Sure, the regime had dropped barrel bombs, which sent shrapnel in a million directions, killing or maiming anyone around. But even those hadn't compared to *this*. Whatever artillery the regime had, the Americans seemed to have it times a thousand. And yes, technically, Raqqa's residents would soon find out that it wasn't just the Americans, that it was rather the "American-led coalition," but still, everyone knew which country was most powerful. And they knew that the most powerful countries in the world feared Daesh.

Raqqa had tolerated the terrorists, who brought order amid chaos. They ended the petty lawlessness and kept the water and electricity running. They even transported people to hospitals in Iraq if they needed specialized care. The Islamic State planned to build an empire. So even as they terrorized the people they deemed apostates, they worked hard to help others, to build support for their side.

And so it didn't matter what anyone in this household believed, didn't matter that Bashar and Aisha had told their daughters Daesh was the worst *ashrar,* the worst bad guys of them all. Now the world's most powerful countries were dropping bombs to destroy Daesh. And that meant they were dropping bombs by the Euphrates, by the Eastern Market, by the place Taha had founded and the Alkasems had called home.

"We need to leave," Aisha told her husband. Riyad had been right. Their home invited death.

Bashar, though, couldn't imagine a life outside his city. It wasn't just because of simple loyalty. It was as if he could not picture the steps that would lead to leaving, as if his mind could not transport to any other place. Later he would wonder if the bombs had altered the chemistry inside him, as if the regime or the Americans or

Daesh had reached into his skull and covered his brain with thick layers of fog.

So he shook his head when Aisha argued for them to leave. He told himself she was irrational. She was a mother; she was protective; she didn't know what *leaving* entailed.

"Look at your parents," he said. "Look at your siblings. *They're* still here. Don't you trust them? We're doing the same thing they are."

Aisha didn't relent. She couldn't bear the bombings. She wanted to go.

So they moved to the regime-controlled city of Latakia. But once there, they could not make it work. The displaced were gouged and mistreated, the opportunities even fewer than back at home. Apartments were too expensive, even with money coming in from Riyad and Kasem. They knew no one. They had nothing. This was not a home. This was not a life. After a couple months they returned to Raqqa and hoped the chaos would pass.

The following year Abdul-Rahman started walking. The girls learned reading and writing from a tutor each morning, a junior attorney who risked his life to teach them, and they learned math from their *baba* each afternoon. It was 2015, and Daesh kept up its act of menace in the streets, all while the coalition's bombs kept dropping. Whenever Bashar talked to his brother, the stories of American bombs dropping over Raqqa gutted Riyad. He always imagined his new country might intervene to help Syria's people. Now he saw a bleak irony in the way enemy factions seemed to unite against the citizens of Raqqa: Daesh terrorized them in the daytime; the American-led coalition rained down horrors at night.

It wore on them. One night the coalition's bombs lit up the sky, and they all woke and bolted to their respective places; Aisha and the children to the bathroom, Bashar running around the house opening windows, out of some hope that relieving atmospheric pressure would keep them safe. The bombs fell in succession, but then, eventually, they stopped.

The real terror came afterward, in the quiet moments, when they realized they couldn't find their little boy.

"Abdul-Rahman!" Bashar shouted. He darted from room to room and out into the courtyard and back again. His body raced while his mind stalled. He ducked under tables. He flung open doors. His city was slowly turning to rubble. His son could be stuck under any of it, anywhere, whether in this house or outside. His daughters and wife and mother all rushed alongside him; every few seconds a new voice shouted, "Abood!"

They opened closets. They opened cabinets. And then, hiding in a kitchen cupboard, grinning—there he was.

WAJID WAS FOUR when she started to stutter. They barely noticed at first. They could pretend she was just stuck on certain words. But soon it felt like every sentence had a hitch, like her brain could never interact properly with her mouth. She worried, constantly, about her *m-m-mama*. She heard stories about other people's mothers dying, and she assumed that this must mean Aisha would be next. She became fixated, obsessed, unworried about anything or anyone but Aisha. When the bombs fell, she asked for her *m-m-mama*. When they sat down to lunch, she asked for her *m-m-mama*. In the middle of the night, she would come running, awake from a nightmare, desperate to make sure that her mother was safe.

One day she came to Aisha, her face serious. "I have an idea," she said.

"What is it, my girl?"

Wajid explained. Their family had a generator. They'd used it throughout the war, to power the house when the city's electricity went down. Bashar and Aisha both had told her never to touch it, that if she did, the electric current would be so strong that she would die.

"We can hold hands," Wajid said, "and then we can all touch the generator together."

Aisha felt the words prick her skin. "What? *No!* Why would we do that?"

Wajid shrugged, her face resolute but calm.

"Then you won't die without me," she said. "We can all be buried together."

MAYBE IT WAS TIME. Maybe they should go. Bashar couldn't believe he was thinking it, but he also couldn't believe that his family would remain safe in Raqqa. Their fear ate at them all from the inside. Throughout the war, Bashar had tried to steal moments of peace, often just after the bombings finished. He would count the blasts and listen for the sound of planes flying away, then walk into his kitchen to find a pot and a few cups and a little sugar, then sit out in the courtyard, in the post-bomb quiet, sipping tea. He would look across the street and see neighbors through their windows, and moments later they would walk outside with their pots of tea too. Soon the entire block would be dotted with people in their courtyards, sipping tea. They would look at each other and say things like "not so bad today" or "that was close." Mostly, though, they sat and sipped, and if they were lucky they caught the river's breeze.

But all that had now ended. The regime bombings allowed for windows of relaxation, but the coalition bombs were far too powerful, the fear they inspired too great. Many residents had begun fleeing the city. Some for Turkey, as Riyad had now so long ago suggested. Others for the regime-held areas of Latakia or Damascus, or the Kurdish cities of Qamishli or Afrin. A few ventured into the refugee camps of Jordan and Lebanon.

One day Bashar was doing a favor for his friend Rahad, manning his pharmacy while Rahad left on an errand. A man walked in, wearing the familiar black clothes and full beard.

"Are you in charge?" the man asked.

"Yes," Bashar said. "You could say that."

The man said nothing.

Bashar clarified, "Well, it's not my pharmacy, but I'm here right now."

The man shook his head. "So you lied. You are not in charge. Why would you lie?"

"Well," Bashar stammered, "I thought you needed help. I can help you find medicine, if that's what you need."

The man did not need medicine. "I think I've seen you before. What's your name?"

Bashar told him.

"Okay," he said. "Goodbye."

When Rahad returned, Bashar told him what had happened.

"Go home," his friend said. "Now."

Rahad told Bashar that he had heard that Daesh had recently put together a list of local attorneys, practitioners of secular law. If the man knew who Bashar was, that was why.

"Go," he said again, nodding toward the door.

Bashar left. Later, Rahad told him the man from Daesh had returned with several companions, all of them looking for Bashar. Rahad had said that he did not know who they were talking about, that it must have been some petty thug pretending to run his shop, but did they need to buy any medicine, and they said no, they did not.

For weeks after the encounter, Aisha could barely sleep. Every time Bashar left the house, she wondered if it was the last time she'd see him. And every night when she lay down to sleep, she wondered if she'd wake up in one piece or in a million. She wanted to leave. *Desperately.* She didn't care how bad it had been in Latakia, didn't care that her parents and siblings were remaining in town. She craved safety.

"Wait," Bashar told her. "Give me time. Let me think."

Bashar knew she was right, but he still did not have a plan. Days later he went out shopping, eyes newly opened to how the city's crumbling had quickened. Rubble now spilled into most every street. The shops' shelves had thinned. Roads had closed, shipments now had to pass through untold numbers of checkpoints, and many never arrived. Still, though, they could find food.

Bashar stopped at a little stand selling produce. The bombs hadn't destroyed the soil on the banks of the Euphrates. Behind the stand stood a small farmer who'd been selling to Bashar for years, his skin dark from days in the sun, selling his harvest to whoever remained in town.

"Why are you still here?" he asked Bashar.

He didn't get it. So many people remained in Raqqa only because they couldn't afford to pay a smuggler. Bashar was a lawyer. Not only that, a lawyer with brothers working stable jobs abroad.

"Why don't you leave?"

Bashar shrugged. "Where are we going to go? This is our home."

Bashar had long ago made his peace with death. He felt firm in his standing with God, felt the same about his children. His girls had already begun memorizing passages of the Quran. They prayed together as a family. If one of the coalition's bombs landed directly on their house, Bashar imagined, they would feel brief moments of pain just before an eternity of joy, returning as a family to their Creator in paradise, together. Death might bring comfort. Life, right now, brought mostly fear and pain.

Bashar explained his thinking, but the farmer mentioned another possibility. "Okay, but what if you die and your daughters survive?"

Bashar had thought of this, of course, but he'd always kept it tucked away in some barely accessible corner of his mind.

"Or," the farmer continued, "what if you survive, but your bodies are deformed for the rest of your lives?"

In the months after Abood's birth, the hospital had been destroyed. Most doctors had fled the city. If anyone lost a limb, no one could treat them as they'd require.

"What if something happens to your daughters' faces? What if no one will marry them?"

Bashar had never considered this. But it was true—women who suffered catastrophic injuries rarely found husbands in Raqqa. And if Bashar's daughters never found husbands, their culture dictated they would spend their entire lives with him and Aisha at home. A whole world of possibility would be closed off to them, all because of one fire from one bombing, one injury that left them disfigured forever.

Years later he still wouldn't know why this was the conversation that did it. Until now, his mind seemed only to process two possibilities: They would all die together, or they would be just fine. It seemed so simple, the realization that so much else could go wrong, but only now, standing at that farmer's stand on that early fall morning, did Bashar begin to see the various permutations of his family's future. War held possibilities he'd never let himself fathom. It could destroy them all in so many creatively vicious ways.

BASHAR TALKED WITH an old neighbor, who put him in touch with a smuggler. He didn't know where they would go, but he knew they had to leave. The smuggler would make plans. He would find the safest checkpoints and bribe soldiers where he knew he could. He would find safe houses scattered along their route, places where they could rest while he went ahead, scouting checkpoints farther down the road. He couldn't say when they would go, only that they should be ready, that as soon as he thought the road was safe enough, he would let them know.

One morning, around four A.M., the phone rang. Bashar answered.

"It's time."

Bashar awoke his family and told them, "We are leaving Raqqa today."

CHAPTER
13

The moment she heard from Bashar that they were leaving Raqqa, Aisha couldn't help herself. She turned giddy. She let a thought linger. Sometime soon she and her family would sleep—where, she didn't know—and dream for an entire night without waking up to the sound of bombings overhead. She could barely imagine it. She'd never understood how Bashar and his mother could remain so calm during bombings. To Aisha, they seemed like soldiers, both of them, winning hourly battles against their own fear. She felt desperate to escape the blasts and rumblings they had long ago learned to endure. Now the thought of a night without bombs seemed like a luxury, almost decadent. In her mind, this would be a journey not to Damascus or to Turkey or to Lebanon or to any other city or country. For her, it would be a journey to a quiet bed.

She made food. Potatoes, a little meat, a few boiled eggs. They had leftovers in the refrigerator, and Aisha took them over to the neighbor who'd been arrested by Daesh for the hole in her sock. Aisha did not tell her that they were leaving, only that she thought she might need something to eat. Still, the neighbor hugged her, and Aisha could feel her clinging tight. Tears rushed to Aisha's eyes, so she let go, to step back, to say goodbye.

When she got home, her mother-in-law stood at the door, watching her wipe her eyes. "Now is not the time for emotion," she said. "Now is the time for survival."

Aisha nodded and walked back inside. She couldn't say why, would never be able to say why, but when faced with a quiet house and a few hours before she had to leave it, she suddenly felt the urgent desire to clean. So she did. They all did. All together, as a family, they moved through their home, room by room. The whir of the vacuum filled the silence, rolling over every inch of every room's floor, sucking up the mess of the life they were leaving behind.

She made her bed, and the girls made theirs. She walked in to find them hugging their favorite stuffed animal, a multicolored worm their grandmother had given them. Its name was Duda, Arabic for "worm." All through the war, they would both hug Duda close during bombings, and together they would rub it softly, would tell Duda not to be afraid, that God would protect them. Now they begged to take Duda with them, but Aisha told them no, they had to leave it behind.

Next they picked up their Barbie dolls and walked through the house, sitting them upright in chairs and on couches, around the dining room table and in the den. The dolls would look after the house while they were gone, the girls decided. They laughed at this just a little, even though they were crying, too.

When it was time to go, Aisha took one last look at her bedroom. She still did not know where they were going, if they were staying in Syria or leaving the country altogether, if they would be gone for weeks or months or years or even, the faintest of possibilities, for the rest of their lives. She knew, though, that if ever she returned, she would not find her room like this, bed made and floors cleaned, every single thing in its exact right place. Someone would come here. Something would change it. Maybe there would be looters; maybe the house would turn to rubble; or maybe a neighbor would just walk in one day and dirty up the floors. No matter what, though, she'd never find her home this perfect.

Bashar made sure they packed just a couple of bags with one or two changes of clothes for every member of the family, then a small

sack with important documents: passports, birth certificates, a marriage certificate, both Bashar's and Aisha's law degrees. Even though
they did not know exactly where they were going, maybe they'd find
a place where Bashar could work, where his brothers could send
money, where they could wait out the war. He did know, though,
that they would never settle in a refugee camp. Their stubborn tribal
pride would not allow even the thought.

Bashar thought the most dangerous leg of their journey might be
the ten yards between their front door and the car that would carry
them away. He was wrong about that, would be proven wrong time
and again in the days and weeks that followed, but still, in the moment, it held a certain logic. Daesh was everywhere. So, too, were
their informants. People all across the city took money from the
foreign fighters to spy on their own neighbors. One look at Bashar
and his family rushing to a car carrying suitcases, and someone
nearby could place a phone call that would put them in jail or in
their graves.

So he left his suitcase just outside his doorstep, and he called the
smuggler and told him to come pick it up. Then he went and made
small talk with the shop owners on his block. He would treat today
as if it were any other. They discussed the morning's weather and the
last night's bombings. Bashar did not turn around when the smuggler pulled up in a van to fetch his bags.

"What is that guy doing?" one of the shopkeepers asked.

Bashar looked over his shoulder. "Oh," he said. "We're just do-
nating some clothes. He's taking them away."

It was a lie, of course, but not wholly unbelievable. Relief organizations continued their work all over Syria, drawing support even
from those in decimated cities, *especially* from families like the Alkasems, whose position in the city compelled them to continue giving aid, never receiving it.

Aisha took the girls in a taxi to say a brief goodbye to her family,
then returned to join Bashar's mother in the smuggler's van. Bashar
did not want to draw suspicion by leaving at the same time as the
rest of his family, so he returned home and sat outside in the courtyard one last time, sipping tea. The morning was cool, but the tea

warmed him. It was November 2015, a month when rains stir the soil and the winds off the Euphrates turn the air sweet. Bashar felt anxious but resigned. He sat and sipped and wondered if he'd ever return here, or if these were the last moments an Alkasem would ever spend in this courtyard, the last tea a member of his family would ever sip in the city their ancestors built.

He heard the phone ringing and ran inside. The smuggler was ready. He gave Bashar a location a few blocks away, and Bashar headed out, walking at a casual pace, doing his best to hide the nerves that buzzed inside him, until he reached the van and jumped in.

They drove through town. It was difficult now to imagine Raqqa as it had been when Bashar and Riyad were boys. Back then there had been only a handful of cars in the entire city. Any time a new vehicle showed up, everyone started talking. *What rich person is that? Where are they from?* Now new trucks and vans rolled through every minute. At a few intersections, they actually had traffic, something Bashar had grown to loathe in Los Angeles. Out the window they saw Toyota Tacomas and Chevy Astro vans. Some carried soldiers and *doshka* weapons; others just rolled along curiously, leaving everyone to wonder who was inside.

Bashar hoped no one would give a second thought to who was in their white van. He wanted to draw no eyes. He'd told no one they were leaving—not even Riyad. They all packed in together, Bashar and his *mama*, Aisha and Abood and the girls; their former neighbor Ahmed, then his entire family as well. They rode south across the Euphrates, then down a dirt road that stretched deep into the desert, a road left abandoned by daily traffic for some fifty or sixty years.

EVEN NOW, they did not know their final destination. The smuggler had bribed a Daesh soldier to forge traveling papers that would get them to Manbij, and there they would slip out of Daesh territory and decide what to do next. For now, they continued away from the city and into the desert, bodies vibrating with every inch of the dirt road, no cars ahead or behind them, nothing around them but rock and sand. And then, finally, after nearly an hour, they saw something up ahead. The familiar black flag, planted in the ground, flanked by a couple of soldiers in chairs, holding guns. The van slowed, then stopped. They'd reached their first Daesh checkpoint.

Bashar sat in the very back, against the window. Ahmed was up front, next to the smuggler. Their families sat in between.

"Hello," said the soldier. He reached out his hand. "Papers."

Ahmed handed him their documents, which said they were all traveling together to a family wedding in Manbij.

The soldier took them and read. He looked back at Ahmed.

"A wedding?"

"Yes."

He tilted his head with suspicion, as if to say, *Give me a break.* The smuggler sat in the driver's seat, silent. They all knew the deal. The smuggler had made it clear before they ever got on the road. If Daesh questioned him, he would say he was no more than a driver, that he knew nothing about these people, and that if they'd broken the law, the soldiers should do whatever they felt was needed. He would leave them behind, heading back to Raqqa to smuggle another family, cutting the exact same deal.

This soldier looked up, back at Ahmed. "I don't buy that bullshit," he said.

Ahmed said nothing. Sitting in the back, Bashar wondered if their trip was about to end, here and now, only an hour after leaving town.

The soldier shrugged. "Whatever," he said. "I don't care." He handed the papers back.

"Just go."

THEY SPENT THE NIGHT in a safe house, out in the countryside. This land was something of a neutral territory, uncontrolled by Daesh and untended to by the regime. A small piece of untouched Syria, too remote for anyone's bombs or guns. The home was arranged by the smuggler, owned by a family who wanted to help their compatriots escape the war.

The house was massive, and they shared it with other families, all on the road from their homes scattered across the country. Some were fleeing Daesh, others the regime. All had their own stories of the moment they decided to leave. Now they gathered around a large table, laid out by the hosts, where they dug into a dinner of bread, olive oil, farm eggs, and olives.

In the morning they made plans. The smuggler returned to Raqqa, leaving them to decide where they'd go next and which new smuggler would take them. Should they go to a regime-controlled city? They'd already tried that, with their brief move to Latakia. They could go into Kurdish territory, but there they knew they'd remain in the war zone. The Kurds were in good standing with the Americans, but still there could be bombings and gunfights; their nightly terrors might well resume. They had already ruled out the refugee camps of Lebanon and Jordan—they were a family who helped others, not one who sought aid. But now they were sitting in the far north of the Syrian desert, just a few miles from a country that promised some measure of safety, if little else: Turkey.

IT WOULD BE DIFFICULT. Back when Riyad had tried to convince them to leave two years ago, Turkey's border was wide open. But by now, in November 2015, the war had escalated and so many foreigners had poured into Syria to fight in Daesh's army that the European Union had pressured Turkey to tighten its borders. They could not vet every person who came across, did not know if they were Syrian families fleeing carnage or Daesh soldiers on their way back to Europe to spread the terror they'd learned from the front lines. The Turkish government now had bases with border police, complete with watchtowers and spotlights, designed to catch anyone who tried to sneak into their country. They had even begun building a border wall.

But still, Turkey seemed their best option. Bashar needed to find somewhere that might promise long-term stability, somewhere he and his family could rebuild their life. Perhaps they could do that in Turkey. Or maybe they could use Turkey as an entry point to the

United Nations' refugee program, taking them on to Europe or the United States. Either way, the first step was to make their way over the border that Riyad had begged them to cross years ago.

THEY WOULD WAIT in Azaz, a town of about thirty thousand just north of Aleppo, four miles from the border. Control of Azaz had shifted throughout the war. Rebels had taken it from the regime all the way back in the summer of 2012, when Raqqa was still at peace. Daesh had moved in the next fall, a few months after Riyad's visit, but gave it up only a few months later. Now the extremists still controlled land just outside the town, and to get in, Bashar and his family would have to pass through one last Daesh checkpoint.

At the checkpoint, Bashar handed over their travel documents to a guard, who looked them over, mild disgust taking hold of his face. "This is bullshit," he said.

Bashar did his best to look confused, head tilting, eyes narrowing, and face opening. He was a terrible liar, but he knew that any good lie began with the eyes, so he did his best to seem shocked, to will his face to say, *Bullshit? No!*

The guard nodded to himself, then looked back down at the documents. This was the last Daesh checkpoint on this road to Turkey. He saw travelers like them every hour of every day. He knew there couldn't possibly be so many "family weddings" in Azaz. He knew exactly why people passed through town.

"You're leaving, aren't you?"

Bashar told his best lie. "We're going to see my relatives."

Now the guard wanted to poke holes. Who were these relatives? Where did they live? What street? What kind of house? Why was he visiting them now?

Bashar couldn't answer. His brain couldn't work fast enough. So he repeated the same sentence. "We're going to see my relatives."

The soldier laughed. "You've said that."

He scanned the faces in the back of the van. "Now tell me. Who are your relatives?"

"This is the only answer I have," Bashar said. "We are going to see my relatives. You can believe me or not. Do whatever you want."

He took a breath, then said it again. "We're going to see my relatives."

The soldier rolled his eyes. *"Fine."*

He let them through.

THREE DAYS LATER, first thing in the morning, they left for the border, walking out of the village to the sounds of the call to morning prayer. A new smuggler led them, alongside other families, all shivering as they walked. They could take no vehicles, so they were traveling on foot. Bashar carried one suitcase and walked alongside his *mama*, helping her up and over the jagged rocks of the hills they climbed. Aisha walked beside him. With one hand, she clung to the hands of both girls. In the other, she carried a duffel bag. And there, nestled among the family's clothing, with the bag zipped all the way up except for a small opening for his head to peek out, was little Abood. His eyes were big and searching, staring at the sky as he bobbed up and down with Aisha's every step.

The walk was long, dark, and cold. They struggled to find solid earth with every step on the rocky hills. They came down to a flat clearing, and that was when the smuggler stopped them.

"We're here."

Now it was time to wait. They sat beneath bushes; they did not know how long it would take. The smuggler had gone ahead of them, presumably to pay bribes, but he warned them that he would not be able to pay off everyone, that still some Turkish border police might be waiting to grab them and bring them back across the border to the Syrian side.

They rested, slumped on the ground all together, breath barely visible before them in the cold. They could see one another by the moonlight, and the shape of the hills they'd just crossed. And then, up ahead at the border, they saw a tower looming over everything, a light on inside it, and on the tower's exterior they saw a spotlight, scanning the earth below. The light moved across the surface of the land, lighting up grass and rock, roots and bushes. And then, as the light continued crawling, that's when they saw the *people*. So many people scattered all across the land before them, most huddled together underneath bushes of their own. There must have been hundreds of them, men and women, young and old, every single one trying to cross the same border. After days of traveling and years of war, they'd all arrived here together, where they would fight for position, all trying to squeeze across thin barbed wire, a sharp and flimsy coil of metal that separated likely death from new hope.

The smuggler returned. "Let's go."

They rose and walked. Now was the time. The border was open. Bashar was not entirely certain what had happened or how. He knew only that some of the guards were "sleeping," likely because they'd been paid to close their eyes. And now, one way or another, every single person who had been waiting for their moment moved as one, pouring in the direction of the barbed wire. Bodies pushed together. Bashar clung to his mother, holding her upright. Behind him Aisha and the children followed, and behind them came their neighbor Ahmed and his family.

They moved through a quiet and suffocating chaos. Shoulders rubbed against shoulders. Feet tripped over roots and rocks. They made their way through the crowd, pressed up against the flesh of strangers. They pushed and pushed until, all of a sudden, they were standing face-to-face with a man who held down the barbed wire, allowing them to step over it. Bashar stepped over. He turned around and grabbed his mother's hand, and she stepped over too.

They waited on the other side for Aisha and the children, and here they came, Jenan and Wajid each taking their own steps over the border, then Aisha walking across carrying Abood. They were here. Turkey. A democracy. A country at peace.

That was when the guns started firing. A few blasts, sporadic, coming from somewhere near the watchtower.

"Run!" the smuggler shouted, and they did.

His *mama* moved quickly for her age, and so they ran together, across the open land and into a thicket of forest. They waded through a small creek, the water frigid, then rushed up the other side of the bank and continued up a small hill. It was there, after several minutes of running, with their legs numb from the water's cold, that Bashar's *mama* fell. She let out a light yelp as her shoulder crashed into a rock, and then she whimpered, just for a moment, as Bashar lifted her to her feet. They kept running, lungs ripped open, insides screaming, until they reached a small olive orchard, the trees short and thick and visible in the moonlight, and there they stopped, surely safe now, and Bashar looked around them, searching, and he realized.

Aisha. The children. They were gone.

CHAPTER

14

A isha did not make it far. With gunfire all around her, she ran as
fast as she could, but just a few feet into Turkey, the border
police stopped her, along with the children and Ahmed and his
family. Bashar and his mother were somewhere up ahead, lost in the
mass of bodies, but now she and the rest of their group were stuck.
The police took them back across the border into Syria, while Bashar
and his mother kept running. Her adrenaline vanished, replaced by
a dull and heavy fear.

The police let them go, and soon they reconnected with their
smuggler, who took her and the children back to his own house to
wait. Aisha's phone did not work along the border, so she could not
call Bashar, but the smuggler told her he'd been in touch with his
colleague on the other side, and that Bashar and his mother were
fine, they were safe, not to worry. They knew they were coming.
They'd see them soon enough.

Aisha wanted to believe him. Panic rose, but she tried to ignore
it. She'd spent years giving in to her own terror. Now she pushed her
panic down someplace hidden, somewhere her children could not
see. She huddled together with them, waiting out the night. The
smuggler did not feed them or even let them inside; he told them to

sleep on the roof, and so they sat up there together, the girls weak and lethargic, not having eaten for days, Abood babbling *ma-ma-ma-ma-ma* and drifting in and out of sleep. In the morning, the smuggler's wife came up onto the roof, carrying a full breakfast, which the children devoured. It was the women, Aisha thought, always the women. Without this simple decency, Aisha did not know how they would have lasted another day.

They waited most of the day, still up on the roof, and then, in the afternoon, they returned to the border. It looked so different in the daytime. Now she could clearly see all the people fanned out across the land. And she could see the point of crossing, where smugglers were taking turns with their own groups, trading off, like a dance. So little seemed to separate the Turkish from the Syrian side, no more than grass and dirt and stone. Both sides looked desolate. She knew that both felt equally cold. And yet she felt desperate to reach the other side and to stay there. She would find Bashar. She knew he'd be waiting.

In the early evening, the sun began to set. They still had not crossed. The smuggler told them to wait; their turn would come soon. She overheard a boy say he was going into town, and so she gave him two hundred Syrian pounds and asked him to buy her children cookies.

"What if you're gone when I come back?"

"Then keep the cookies."

If they were gone, she figured, then they'd be in Turkey. They'd be closer to that bed. They would not need cookies. They would be just fine. But when the boy returned, they were still there. He gave her the cookies, and the children ate. An hour passed. Then two. Three. Darkness fell, the land around them lit only by the moon and by the tower's spotlight, crawling across the earth once again. The cold set in, and she and the children held one another, shivering together as one.

She looked up and saw a gray-haired man, a little older, wearing a coat, and he was walking around into the woods and back out to the clearing, carrying wood. He piled logs and branches together.

"I don't care if they see us," he said. "They already know we're here anyway."

So he built a fire. It started slow, flame attaching itself to kindling, and soon it grew, big enough for about a dozen people to gather around and feel its warmth. He went and grabbed still more pieces of wood, and he stacked them even higher, until the fire grew so big that it lit everything around them. When the old man felt satisfied, he stood up in front of the fire and began to recite passages from the Quran.

"'We will surely test you,'" he said, quoting the words of God, "'with fear and hunger, and a loss of wealth and lives and fruits.'"

He was strong and seemed kind, his voice loud and deep, carrying across the fire.

"'But give good tidings to the patient,'" he continued, "'who when disaster strikes them say, "Indeed we belong to Allah, and indeed to Him we will return."'"

He reminded Aisha of her father. And it was only then, days after they'd left Raqqa, that she began to think back on the morning they left. She'd taken a taxi with the children over to her parents' home to say goodbye to her mother and brother. She'd felt no sadness when she hugged them, only the exhilaration that they were finally leaving.

But now, as she watched the old man recite scripture in front of the fire, she thought of her father. He had not been home when she went to say goodbye. She'd arrived without warning, so she saw only those who happened to be there. But now she could see her *baba* in this man's face and in his spirit. Her father was a good, kind man, a man who raised her to work hard in school and to nurture those around her, who taught her from the time she was small to memorize the Quran. She looked at this man and thought he was good and kind, too, and she felt something crack open inside her, and for the first time since they left home, she cried.

After the man finished reciting scripture, he went quiet for a moment, and his eyes bored into the flames. He let a few seconds pass, quiet, and he spoke again.

"The war is like this fire," he said, and looked up.

Aisha did not know who among them belonged to his family. For all she knew, he'd never met anyone in this crowd until today.

"This war has burned all of us," he continued.

He scanned their faces. There were older women and men; an Iraqi mother Aisha had befriended during the day, bonding over their shared hatred of Daesh and of the red-sky bombs; the boy who had gone to buy Aisha cookies from the market; and then her daughters, sitting right beside her, and little Abdul-Rahman, resting in her lap. They all listened.

"This war is so ugly. It has no mercy. Not on anyone."

Aisha felt her tears growing, and she no longer knew if she was crying about her father or about something else.

"All over the world," he continued, "people are watching us. They see our pain. They write about our pain. They talk about our pain on television. On the radio. On Facebook."

He collected himself, then looked back up at them once again.

"But no one else is *living* this pain. *We* are living this pain. Only us."

This was true. When she thought back on it, Aisha felt staggered by the memories of her own pain. She had lived decades on this earth, building a career and then a family, enjoying so many of life's pleasures. And then in a matter of months so much of that life had crumbled, replaced by a series of unrelenting terrors. It astonished her, the way she could know such joy and such agony, all held within the span of a single life.

"They report the news," the man continued. "They talk about us everywhere." The fire was big now, bright and hot. "But the minute they finish, we are forgotten names."

SOMETIME LATER—MAYBE IT WAS minutes, maybe hours—the smuggler finally came for them. Aisha picked up Abood and walked with the girls to another spot, closer to the border. Away from the fire, the dark and the cold felt heavy. She pulled her children close. On their feet each wore a second layer of socks, but still they shivered. She told them not to talk, not to cry, and they obeyed.

They walked behind the smuggler, in the dark.

"It's time," he said.

The spotlight crawled toward them, and up ahead, barely visible, was another smuggler holding the barbed wire just as before, allowing people to pass through. Aisha waited as the light drew closer, and then it reached her, and she looked up at the tower and saw a guard looking down, directly at her, and yet she knew that she would run across the border anyway, no matter what he might do. It was only then, in that moment, as she watched the guard watch her while she prepared to run across, that Aisha realized that she was brave.

She held Abdul-Rahman to her chest in one hand and the hands of the girls in the other, but she also had the sack with every single paper of importance that would document for the world that she and her family were humans with names. She asked around, to see if anyone would carry the bag for her while she helped her children across, but no one could. Their hands were just as full. Finally a smuggler said he'd toss it over the barbed wire if she paid him, and so she gave him every cent she had.

She crossed. The smuggler tossed her the bag and she caught it, and then she ran. They all did, Jenan and Wajid beside her, Abdul-Rahman bobbing up and down in her arms. Next to them, there ran an old man. Not the man who had recited the Quran by the fire, but one even a bit older, a man who carried a giant sack on top of his head. The terrain was rough, the wind biting, the world around them covered in dark.

"*Mama!*" Jenan shouted, and she slowed.

"Keep running!" Aisha told her, and Jenan did as told.

But seconds later she shouted again. "*Mama!* My shoe!"

Aisha paused and looked down. One of Jenan's shoes had fallen off, and now she was running over rocks and thorns in only the double layer of socks, and soon her feet would be bleeding, but Aisha could only tell her not to worry, just to run.

Then Aisha tripped. She fell, and Abood fell with her. She lost her breath for a moment. As she tried to find her footing, she felt two arms around her, holding her shoulders, lifting her up. She looked. It was the old man. He'd set his sack down on the ground to help her.

Now he picked it back up. "Go," he said.

They resumed running, and soon she fell again. It occurred to her at this moment that perhaps, if you thought about it really, life was a frivolous and pathetic thing. She and her children were enduring all this, pushing themselves beyond her imagination, for what? Just to keep living? That seemed absurd. Their muscles ached, and their lungs screamed. Fear rocketed through their bodies, infecting even their toenails and hair. If she could slow down, she might vomit. If she had enough energy, she would scream. If she could bear the shame, she would lie down. Every piece of her wanted to do anything but the exact thing that she was doing, and she was doing it for what? To keep breathing? Was the simple act of drawing breath worth all *this*?

She felt the arms around her once more, lifting her up. She had no more time to think, only to run, and she fell and was lifted again, and then again a fourth and final time. They crossed a garden, and the people around them all ran in separate directions, and then they were in an olive orchard, and they ran among the trees, and somewhere in all this the old man left her, and she realized that if she ran into him somewhere, someday, whether in a Turkish border town or back in Raqqa, or maybe even in Damascus or Stockholm or Berlin, she would never be able to stop him and thank him. In truth, she wasn't sure she'd ever seen his face.

THEY KEPT RUNNING AND RUNNING, and then they saw it. The light. Cars. They stepped out of the woods, onto the pavement, and there, finally, she collapsed. She held her children close and wept, even as they told her not to, even as Jenan and Wajid wiped her tears and said not to worry, that everything was okay. They saw a van, waiting, with the smuggler inside it, and he drove toward them and helped them all inside. They were here. Turkey. It looked so much like Syria. The same hills, the same light trees, the same arid land.

They pulled up to a quiet office building. This was where the smuggler had taken Bashar and his mother, where they'd been waiting. Once inside, tired and hungry and filthy, they saw Bashar. He ran to them, wrapped his arms around his girls and his son.

They were together. Safe for now. When the smugglers said the road was clear, they got into a car and drove from Kilis to Şanlıurfa, where they checked in to a hotel. Aisha was too tired to think of whether the hotel bed matched her visions. But she had a blanket and pillows. She heard no bombs. And so she slept.

CHAPTER

15

They were refugees now, even if they'd never live in a camp. That felt strange. The word evoked images of the poor and the underfed, the kind of people the Alkasem family was used to helping, never the kind of people they would become. And yet here they were.

Southern Turkey was dotted with camps, massive tent cities packed with Syrians and Iraqis, alongside others from Afghanistan or Yemen or anywhere else where time was measured by bombings. Turkey held more Syrian refugees than the rest of the world combined, and it showed. The country felt like a giant waiting room. Many storefront signs all across the city of Şanlıurfa, where they first arrived, were written in Arabic, not Turkish. Public parks and squares were filled with Syrian teenage boys, smoking and flirting, or playing soccer, with little else to do.

But the country had grown tired of playing host. This was apparent in the gunshots that had greeted Bashar's family at the border. *The Times* of London reported that sixteen Syrians had been killed by Turkish border guards over the previous four months. It continued when they went to apply for refugee identification cards, called *kimliks*. Everyone in the family received one except Bashar, who had a visa in his passport from a previous visit to Lebanon. He'd been there once before, authorities told him, so he should try going there again. For Syrians, the *kimlik* was the only ticket to a life—even a meager one—in Turkey. Without it, Bashar could not work or receive health care. If he ever encountered police, he'd be arrested and deported on the spot.

They saw the country's exasperation most clearly, though, in their interactions with the Turkish people. They'd heard that when the war began, the people had welcomed Syrians with empathy and hospitality, stopping them in the streets to let them know they were praying for their safety, greeting new neighbors with freshly cooked meals. But in the years since, so many visitors had poured into their country that they had changed its texture. The Turks did not necessarily like the new signs in a foreign language. They did not like Syrian youth with too much time on their hands, hanging out in parks. They did not like the fact that no one else was offering much help in shouldering the burden, that richer countries from Saudi Arabia to France to the United States were not welcoming enough refugees. Bashar and Aisha felt a coldness in almost every interaction, from the shops to the street corners, where the tones of voices and the looks in eyes all carried the same message: *Leave.*

SO THEY DID. Or at least they left Şanlıurfa. They moved four and a half hours away, to the coastal city of Mersin. Overlooking the Mediterranean Sea, Mersin was beautiful, but here Bashar saw that beauty and misery could coexist. He rarely stepped outside the apartment that Riyad and their younger brother Kasem, the doctor in the Gulf, had rented for them, afraid to be confronted by someone who might demand his *kimlik*. He'd dedicated his life to the law in Syria, felt shamed to be breaking it in Turkey. Aisha did her best to keep the family running, going out on her own to do all the shopping, finding a Syrian doctor to treat the children when they got sick, as children do. And Bashar's *mama* took it upon herself to reintroduce the girls to the joys of a world in peacetime. She took them for walks on the beach, where they ran through shallow waters, feeling the sun on their necks, no shoes on their feet. They started going to school, their first time in an actual classroom since before Raqqa fell.

Within a matter of weeks, Jenan grabbed her *mama*. "Did you notice?" she asked. "Wajid doesn't stutter anymore!"

It was true, at least much of the time. Here in Turkey, Wajid had begun to find the space and air she needed to speak.

So one day Wajid sat with her mother and asked her, "Why aren't you happy?"

The question pulled Aisha's posture upright. She worked to move the muscles around her mouth into something approximating a smile. "What do you mean? I *am* happy."

Wajid shook her head. "No, you're not. Why not?"

Aisha couldn't say. She couldn't tell her daughters that their father could not work, that he risked arrest here in Turkey just as he had living under Daesh. She couldn't tell them that they might someday run out of money, that it was expensive for Bashar's brothers to support them. She couldn't tell them that even though the girls were enjoying their time here, she knew they had no real future in this country. She couldn't say what she felt: that they'd fled a war zone for a prison.

AISHA SAW A WAY OUT. On YouTube she watched videos of Syrians filming themselves going through daily life in Europe. Some were in Germany, others in Scandinavia, and still others in Belgium or France. She followed them on tours of their apartments—modest but safe, tucked away in quiet neighborhoods on the outskirts of big cities, with windows that opened up to views of streets where their children ran and rode bikes and called out to their neighbors, asking them to come and play. Their neighbors always seemed so welcoming, happy to have these displaced families in their midst. The European countries offered homes to refugees while they settled into their new lives, with job training and language classes and schools for the children.

She ached to go there. She watched other YouTube videos of refugees making the journey, traveling to the western edge of Turkey and setting off on motorized rafts across the Aegean Sea. Then they showed themselves again on arrival, wet and shivering and standing on a Greek beach, finally on the land of a country that belonged to the European Union. She knew the dangers. She knew the statistics. The seas were filled with Syrian corpses. Nearly four thousand people had died trying to cross the Mediterranean and Aegean seas in 2015. She didn't care. The YouTubers had made it. So could they.

No one, she thought, would take that journey because they wanted so badly to live in Europe. They took it only because their home countries would kill them, and Turkey would let them sit idly until they died. You did not step into that sea because you wanted a nice apartment. You did it because it felt like your only chance at reclaiming an actual *life*. Turkey was free of bombings, yes, but the precariousness of their status hung over them. This country was exactly as Bashar had predicted it would be, years ago when Riyad came on his visit: a place for them to sit and do nothing but wait for their real lives to resume.

That's what Bashar wanted—but he still seemed to think their lives could resume in Syria. He kept telling himself that soon Daesh would be defeated, and the Americans would stop dropping their bombs. Maybe the regime would return. Maybe this war would reach its end. Maybe Bashar could go back to being a lawyer. Maybe he would even contact the Ministry of Justice to see if he could still become a judge.

His *mama*, though, decided she'd had enough. Her son Kasem was living in one of those rich countries on the Arabian Gulf, and she had secured a visa to go live with him there. The day she left, she pulled Bashar aside to talk, alone.

"You need to admit something to yourself," she said. "You"—she pointed at him—"don't have a future. This war has destroyed it. You need to let it go." He would never resume his old law practice. He would never ascend to the bench as a judge. She pointed to the other room, where they could hear the children's voices.

"But just because your future is ruined, that doesn't mean your children's future is ruined. They can still have a life."

Bashar nodded.

"But if you want them to have a future, then the very first step is to cross that sea."

FOR SEVERAL NIGHTS in early 2016, just a few months after they'd arrived in Turkey, they stayed in a hotel in the town of Didim, right on the Aegean Sea. There they waited for yet another smuggler to tell them it was time to go. On the fourth night, Bashar got the call. Just before midnight, they would set off for the sea. They put the children to bed early, but they did not let them wear pajamas, instead making them crawl under the covers fully dressed, even in jackets, even wearing shoes.

Around eleven P.M., Bashar got another call. It was time. They woke the children and lifted them into their arms and carried them out into the parking lot, where they knew they'd find a waiting car. Abdul-Rahman fell back to sleep the moment they lifted him out of bed, while the girls wiped their eyes, not quite sure why they weren't asleep or where they were going.

"It's not very fair to them," Aisha said to Bashar as they walked outside. That night five lives could be lost to the sea, but only two had consented to the journey.

"I know," he said.

"No one asked *them* if they wanted to go to Europe."

They rode through the night in the direction of a remote beach, one car in a caravan of many, and it was then, while staring out the window into darkness, that Aisha finally let herself think about the fact that she didn't know how to swim. When she was a little girl, her father had taught her brothers to swim in the Euphrates, but she had never joined their lessons. She had been afraid, probably, but also she was a girl, and girls were not encouraged to learn these things in the way of boys. She'd never really regretted it; she could still enjoy a lazy afternoon in the river's shallows. Someday, she'd always imagined, when the war ended, she would go out there and watch Bashar teach their children how to swim. That day had never arrived, of course. Raqqa's people stopped swimming in the Euphrates during the years of Daesh and endless bombings. And now they were here, hundreds of miles away and heading toward a far bigger and deadlier mass of water. *Are we crazy?* Aisha wondered, too, if they were paying a smuggler to deliver them to their deaths.

They arrived and gave the smuggler his money. A chill descended on the beach, the temperature hovering around forty degrees Fahrenheit, and they scooped the children into their arms and walked down to the water, where they saw a motorized rubber raft. They all had life jackets, but as they walked to the water, another smuggler stopped them. "The jackets are too heavy," he said. "You need to give them back."

What?

The smugglers did not wait for a response. They walked down the beach, and person by person, they grabbed the jackets. Bashar knew they were not too heavy. They weighed barely anything at all. The men were taking them only because they did not want to buy new ones, wanted to give them to the next boatful of people, only to take them away at the last minute again, repeating over and over the exact same charade.

Seconds later the smuggler all but confirmed this. "If you want," he said, "you can buy the jackets from us."

Bashar gave them whatever they wanted to get the life jackets for Aisha and the children, and then together they began walking into the water, the shock of cold running up their toes to the tops of their heads. He wondered, *Have we made a mistake?* but at this point it made no difference. He would not turn back. When the water hit their thighs, they put the children in the boat while the adults continued walking. The water hit their waists, and their upper bodies shivered. The water hit Bashar's chest, and he looked to make sure his children were safe, and he saw them, sitting in the middle of the raft with a few other children, all their parents out in the water pushing, just like him.

As for Aisha, when the water hit her neck, she felt something she'd never expected: *peace*. Panic had followed her into the sea, but now it dissolved beneath the surface. Her body had given itself over to the water, and the water had delivered calm. If they died, they would die. They would enter paradise and meet their Creator. That thought soothed her. If they lived, they would live. They would enter Europe and start over there. That thought soothed her too. Either way, she knew that the fear she had been living with would soon vanish. Dead or alive, she would never make this journey again.

They hauled themselves up into the raft. Aisha moved to the middle, the safest spot, with the children. Bashar sat on the edge, along with the rest of the men. The raft was about twelve feet long, and there were perhaps forty-five of them inside it, arms against arms, thighs touching thighs. Aisha and Bashar could see each other, but just barely. The sky was clear, but it held only a sliver of a moon, and when they looked up, they saw infinite stars, fanning out in every direction, so many with Arabic names.

They sat in the boat, shivering, waiting. The smuggler stood at the back, near the motor. He shouted, "Okay!"

He pointed into the distance. "Go that way!"

Then he jumped off the boat and swam back to shore.

What?

This was the man they'd paid to take them across the sea. And now, after he'd led them out about a hundred yards into the water, he was leaving?

Passengers shouted, "Wait!" "Where are you going?" "Who's going to drive us?"

From the water, the smuggler yelled back, "Not me!"

He'd left them several hundred feet out in the water, shivering, well after midnight, all alone. Bashar felt a new panic, something writhing and terrible. His breath dropped through him; his insides revolted. Fear spread across the raft in a matter of seconds, until the adults were all yelling and the children all crying, everyone equally confused. They were floating between countries and lives, stuck. They'd approached the door and found it open, but they could not enter.

Bashar heard a voice: "Be quiet!"

He looked across the boat. Another man was standing.

"Settle down!"

The man crawled across the boat, climbing over other passengers. He reached the back and stood again. He was young and handsome, carrying a confidence that, in this moment, felt obscene.

"My father is a sailor," he said. "In Algeria."

He pointed down to the motor. "I know how to steer these boats. I think I can get us there." He sat down and tended to the motor. It hummed.

Bashar felt his breath return. The others around him went quiet. They rode up and over waves, deeper into the dark.

Light chatter ricocheted across the raft, mothers tending to children's jackets, men speculating about how long the journey would take. Near the center of the boat, one conversation caught Aisha's attention:

"Would you move?"

"You move! This is my spot!"

Aisha looked up. Just ahead of her, she saw a husband and wife bickering.

"I sat here first!" the wife said. She was on the inside of the raft, farther from the edge.

"I don't care who sat there first! It makes more sense for me to be on the inside!"

Aisha stifled her own laughter, and she looked down and made eye contact with both Jenan and Wajid, who were giggling too. *Is this real?* On a rubber raft in the middle of the Aegean Sea, with everyone around them soaked and shivering, were these two really fighting over who got the best seat?

"Move!"

"No!"

Aisha kept trying to hold her laughter until she couldn't, and soon the others around her were laughing too. And she thought right then that maybe God had done this, had put this ornery couple on this flimsy raft as a gift to them all, just to let them feel, for a few brief minutes out here in the water, something other than cold and fear. She laughed until she grew tired, and even when she stopped laughing, her smile lingered, there on her face where barely anyone could see it, her white teeth gleaming in the dark.

They hit a wave. Water splashed up into the air and then down onto the raft, spraying everyone aboard. All went quiet. Children who'd been crying swallowed their tears. The squabbling couple shut up. Water was in the raft, and more waves would come soon. Ahead they still saw only darkness. Behind, the Turkish shore had vanished, and there they saw only darkness too. They just needed to cross over into Greek waters. If they came across the Turkish coast guard, with a red stripe down the boat's hull, they would be returned to Turkey. If they reached a boat from the Greek coast guard, with a blue stripe down *its* hull, they would be welcomed into Greece.

Bashar gripped the strap that wrapped around the edge of the raft and held it tightly. He sat so close to the edge that he could reach down and touch the water if he wanted. As the waves grew, the edges of the raft rocked the most, bouncing up into the air, then slapping the surface of the sea on the way down.

Bounce, *slap*.

More water sprayed him. Wind whipped across his face.

Bounce, *slap*.

Bashar was getting nervous. He looked to the middle of the raft and saw Jenan and Wajid, and they were looking at him.

Bounce, *slap*.

They dropped back to the water's surface, bodies rocking on impact. Bashar did his best to keep his face calm. This was the one lie he could tell with confidence. He had told it that day years ago when they were scattered around the dining room table, when dust filled their home after the first regime bombing. He'd told it from his chair, where he sat and read books while the rebels took over Raqqa, pretending that day was no different from any other. He'd told it when the Americans turned the sky red with their bombings and when Daesh put out the call for his capture, told it on the way up to the border and again as they approached the sea. He could tell this lie so masterfully because it required no words; he told it only with his face, again and again.

Everything is going to be okay. The lie was simple and gorgeous. He told it so well because he tricked himself into believing it was true.

Bounce, *slap.*

The waves feasted on the wind that blew through them, growing until they looked like mountains, and the raft sloped upward, tilting so far that Bashar had to cling to the strap on the raft's edge to keep from falling in. He kept his face calm, but he let something terrible grab ahold of his mind. What would he do if they flipped? He looked at all four of them. Aisha sat up straight. She was his love and his partner, the woman with whom he'd built everything he had. Jenan clung to one side of her mother. His older daughter was so much like him. Observant and studious and sensitive, hyperattuned to the world around her, desperate to make everyone else feel okay. Wajid held on to Aisha from the other side. She was more like her mother. Passionate and brilliant, led through the world by curious eyes. And then there, in Aisha's lap, sat little Abdul-Rahman. The boy who'd been born into a world of carnage and still found it worth exploring. The one who carried on the name of Bashar's *baba,* the *mukhtar.*

Bounce, *slap.*

None of them knew how to swim. If the raft flipped, they would all scatter, bodies flung across the sea. Bashar wondered: *Who would I go to? Who would I save?*

Bounce, *slap.*

And that was it. That was the moment. In the end, his lie was exposed not by a bullet or a bombing but by the contortions of his own mind. *Who would I save?* He didn't know. *Why don't I know?*

The raft rocked, and his mouth opened and quivered. It smacked the water's surface, and his eyes tried to jump from his skull. Water sprayed him from the sky, and he knew, finally, that his face was no longer lying, that it finally told the truth of his fear. He looked across the boat and locked eyes with both his daughters, and he watched them watch him submit to his own terror. He knew right then that they knew he'd been lying, that they would not be okay, that they were right to be afraid. The waves rose. The water poured in. Bashar didn't know if he could save a single one.

Bounce, *slap.*

Then somewhere in the distance, he saw a light.

THE LIGHT BLINKED and then drew closer. It moved fast. Bashar knew immediately. *A boat.* The waters calmed. They sat and waited, and soon they saw it. A stripe, painted on the boat's hull.

Red. *Turkey.*

Now they felt no panic. They were much too tired for fear. Only resignation. The Algerian son of a sailor stopped the motor, and they waited as the boat drew closer. It shone a spotlight upon them, and all of a sudden they were bathed in brightness, able to see themselves in full color, soaking wet. Bodies slumped against each other. Maybe Syria would get better soon. Maybe they would find their home just as they left it. Maybe the girls' stuffed worm was still on their bed, patiently awaiting their return.

The light was blinding, but soon it swung around, aimed at the water just ahead of them. It crawled across the surface of the sea, then returned to them and crawled along the same path once again.

In the back, the Algerian reached down and restarted the motor. The raft started moving toward the light. The Turkish boat came no closer, just remained at a comfortable distance, shining its light on the sea before them. It had not come to capture them. It had come to light their way.

The vessel kept moving, keeping the light just ahead of their raft, and they followed. The waters were calm now. They still saw no shore, just the boat and its spotlight and the stars. They kept riding, up and over gentle waves, until the Turkish boat stopped.

And then, up ahead, they saw another light. Another boat. On its hull, another stripe.

Blue. *Greece.*

—————

THE BEACH WAS LIT by yet more lights, these strapped to the heads of soldiers, and they came to the raft and pulled it ashore, and they wrapped the children in blankets and held them to keep them warm. Water dripped from their bodies, but they did not feel wet; they continued to shiver but did not feel cold.

It was about five A.M., and soon the sun rose. Locals came to the beach carrying toys for the children, and they sat together there, bodies drying, and they laughed and played. Soon another boat arrived, a massive one, bigger than any they'd ever seen. The coast guard explained that this boat brought workers and volunteers who would process them as refugees, who would enter them into the United Nations system and help them. They would be resettled elsewhere, not in Greece, most likely, but somewhere they could begin again.

As they walked back to the water, the girls began to cry. Not another boat. Not more time in water. *Please.*

Bashar and Aisha held them close. "It's okay," they said. "We are safe now."

The girls looked up and saw that this time their parents' faces held the truth. They would be okay.

EPILOGUE

Airports still make Riyad nervous.

In 1990, LAX: *What is your legal residence?*

In 2006, in Amsterdam: the angry woman who refused to check on his father's casket.

In 2013, in Gaziantep: stepping off the plane alongside men he knew were arriving to fight in his country's war.

And now he has a new reason. Today, in March 2018, as he walks toward the security line at Nashville International Airport, three hours before his flight, Riyad will fly for the first time since the election of President Donald Trump.

The morning after Trump's election, he woke up, put on his clothes, and drove into work, as if it were any other day. He knew that many of the people he served in his restaurant would be happy. Seventy percent of Sumner County voters cast their ballots for Trump. Riyad had long leaned to the left in American politics. "You go where you feel welcomed," he liked to say. But he also tried to say little publicly about his views. Back in Syria, he'd been a would-be revolutionary railing against the government daily. Now he was a grown man with a family and a business, in a country that sometimes still made him feel like a visitor. He thought of the perhaps-apocryphal Michael Jordan quote, "Republicans buy sneakers too."

And so he went to work and cooked the best he knew how, serving a steady stream of customers, barely any talk of politics filling his day. But sometimes he asked himself: *Did I spend the last twenty-six years of my life living a dream? Or living a lie?*

RIYAD HAS ALWAYS BUDGETED time for random baggage checks and intensive screenings. Now he inches his way forward, watching other passengers step up to the agent and scan passports and boarding passes, then continue on their way to remove shoes from feet and laptops from bags, to step through scanners and onto waiting planes.

Riyad reaches the front of the line. The guard is tall, thick-bodied and bespectacled and white. He takes Riyad's American passport. He looks at the document, then at Riyad's face. Riyad has grown fleshier since the photo was taken, spending a few too many nights working late hours at the restaurant and not making it to the gym, but it is unmistakably him.

"Okay," the agent says. "Go ahead."

HE WASN'T CRAZY ABOUT President Obama. That's the thing Riyad feels like he always has to say, anytime he enters conversations about Trump. He wanted to like Obama. Really. He looked at the president and thought he saw a good man, a principled man, with deep compassion for his country's people and a desire to do good. But he could never forgive him.

Back in 2013, before he crossed the border from Turkey into Syria, he had met a little girl who was young, maybe eight. She had wandered to the border from a nearby refugee camp. She approached Riyad with curiosity, so he had spoken to her. He asked about her life, and she told him she was Syrian—from where, he couldn't remember—but now her parents were dead, her home destroyed. She lived in a tent at the refugee camp, where she'd been for more than a year. She had a sister, who was a few years older, and she was getting worried because she thought that soon her sister might die. Her reason for thinking this was simple: Her sister said she wanted to die. She wanted to die because they had no home and no family, yes, and also because sometimes strange men came into her tent in the night and climbed in her bed and made her do things that she did not want to do, and now, the little girl explained, her big sister was considering suicide.

Riyad nodded and listened as the little girl said all this so very matter-of-factly, as if she were describing the weather or what she'd eaten for lunch. She'd been thinking about it, she said, and if her sister killed herself, then she'd be sad but probably okay. She'd lived without parents. Surely, she could survive without a big sister too.

She asked Riyad where he was from.

"America," he said.

"America?" she asked.

"Yes," he said.

Now she smiled. "You can help us!"

She asked him to sit, and he did. She had something she needed to explain. She pointed to a nearby radio tower. "See that?"

He nodded.

"I think that is blocking the news."

Riyad understood. He'd heard this when he was younger, that Syrians could get no outside news because the radio towers were designed to block the signal, that the regime had set up a system to keep all foreign radio and broadcast networks from reaching its people. He nodded and the girl continued.

"No one knows what is happening to us," she said, "because the tower is blocking the news."

She pulled on Riyad's shirt. "When you go back to America, will you tell them what is happening? Will you tell them about the war?"

Before he could answer, she nodded to herself.

"I think they will help us then. If they know what is happening, then they will come here, and they will help."

Riyad sat, stunned into silence for a moment, unable to explain the gulf between the world she hoped for and the world that was.

"I will tell them," he said. "Then maybe they will come."

He did not have the heart to tell the girl from the camp that the United States already knew all about Syria's violence and had not come yet. But back then, he still believed that they would. He thought the solution could be so simple: Set up a no-fly zone, running along the Turkish border. That would give Syrians a place inside their own country to settle, waiting out the violence. Then no one would have to flee to Turkey or Lebanon, or to attempt to cross the sea into Europe.

American political leaders didn't see it as simple, though. Some advocated staying out of Syria altogether. Others argued for American boots on the ground, fighting alongside the democratic rebel groups to help them topple Assad. Riyad couldn't bear the thought of American soldiers fighting inside Syria, even to defeat the president he loathed. The possibility of even one American dying in that fight pained him. He'd moved all the way across the world to get away from Assad's evils. The thought of watching soldiers from his new country get slaughtered by the same regime filled him with a deep and terrible dread.

But still, he believed, the Americans would come. They didn't need boots on the ground. They could provide support from the air, launching attacks from their base in Turkey. At the time Riyad met the little girl, in March 2013, President Obama was still noncommittal about America's involvement in Syria. The president had made one comment, though, that Riyad could never forget. He discussed the possibility of Assad's regime using chemical weapons against its own people. This, Obama said, would constitute a "red line," perhaps prompting a U.S. military response. And then Assad did it. In August 2013, the regime launched attacks on residential neighborhoods in the town of Ghouta, just outside Damascus, dropping warheads filled with sarin gas, a chemical with no odor or taste that attacks the nervous system, causing convulsions, then paralysis. The attack killed fourteen hundred people.

But Obama did not respond with military action. He later said that he worried that a single attack would pull the United States into prolonged involvement in another country's messy and complicated civil war. Instead, he and Secretary of State John Kerry brokered a deal with the Russians to remove—at least in theory—chemical weapons from Syria. Meanwhile, in the five years after that deal, the Syrian government launched dozens more chemical attacks against its own people.

In all, more than 400,000 people were killed in Syria's war. When Riyad talked to that little girl, he'd believed what he said. But he had been wrong; the Americans did not come. At least not to support the Syrians against Assad, only to drop their own bombs on Daesh.

As the years passed, he thought about the girl often. He wondered if she was still alive, still waiting. He wondered if she'd learned that the whole world actually knew what had happened in Syria. That they'd known all along and had just chosen to stay away.

HE FLIES FROM NASHVILLE to Detroit for a short layover before catching his next flight. He looks down at his boarding pass and notices that he's not been assigned a seat. He approaches the gate agent, a polite woman, about forty years old, and she takes his boarding pass and scans it. She studies her computer screen, for just a second, and looks a little confused.

Riyad hands her his passport. She inputs his information into the computer. She scans his boarding pass again, then picks up her phone and dials a number.

"Hi," she says. "I'm getting an error message I've never seen before."

She goes back and forth with the voice on the other end, then hangs up.

"Can you step over there and wait for a few minutes?" she asks him.

Riyad does as told. He walks to the side of the desk, letting other passengers get the help they need. He shakes his head, just a little.

"Here we go," he says. His face curls into an exasperated grin.

———

IT WAS FUNNY, which things about Trump bothered Riyad and which ones didn't. People expected him to get worked up over Trump's declaration that the United States would accept no Syrian refugees. But at first Riyad didn't want refugees. He only wanted the United States to help Syria become a place people didn't have to flee.

Then there was the so-called Muslim ban. When Trump's election platform included a promise to bar Muslims from entering the country, this bothered Riyad, yes. But he found himself even more annoyed by the nation's shock. So many, he thought, seemed to think Trump was proposing something out of step with American norms. But in Riyad's mind, a "Muslim ban" had already been in place. It had taken him five years to get visas approved for his parents, so they could come meet their grandchildren. After 9/11, Bashar had entered the deportation process as a result of the special registration. If the towers had never fallen, Riyad believed, his brother would be an American citizen, just like him. He thought back to his own meeting at the American embassy in 1990. The man who interviewed him had looked positively delighted when he stamped Riyad's passport and told him, "Welcome to the United States." He couldn't imagine that kind of interaction between an American diplomat and a young Syrian visa applicant today.

Back in his American government class in college, Riyad had been assigned to read the text of Ronald Reagan's last speech as president. "You can go to Japan to live," Reagan had said, "but you cannot become Japanese. You can go to France to live and not become a Frenchman. You can go to live in Germany or Turkey, but you won't become a German or a Turk. Anybody from any corner of the world can come to America to live and become American.

"This, I believe, is one of the most important sources of America's greatness. We lead the world because, unique among nations, we draw our people, our strength, from every country and every corner of the world.

"And by doing so we continuously renew and enrich our nation. While other countries cling to the stale past, here in America we breathe life into dreams. We create the future. And the world follows us into tomorrow."

Riyad believed, truly, that America had breathed life into his dreams. Those dreams had shifted over time, of course. His more radical edges had softened; his desire to build a family had grown. He had struggled at times to find where he fit into this vast and often-mysterious country, but he felt that he became more American when he most fully embraced his identity as a Syrian desert boy.

He believed, too, that he had helped to create America's future. He had injected it with energy and new ideas. He had created jobs, some for teenagers working part time or during summers; some for newly arrived immigrants, for men and women from Egypt or Mexico or Guatemala who reminded him so very much of his former self. His cooking had connected him to business leaders and cultural icons. He believed his food had shaped, in the smallest of ways, the way that people in his sliver of America interacted with the world.

But now he wondered whether stories like his would continue to be told here. After 9/11, so many Americans had allowed themselves to be driven by fear. In terms of policies, Riyad believed, President Trump would continue much of the work done by President Obama and President George W. Bush before him. No matter what so many liberals liked to tell themselves, Riyad believed that Trump's proposals were not anomalous, that this country had long ago shifted into governance by fear.

It was Trump's tone, though, that scared him. The president emboldened the worst of America. White supremacists saw him as their hero. Crowds at his rallies chanted for immigrants to go back to the places from which they came. Riyad used to think most Americans were ashamed by their government's more discriminatory policies. Now so many seemed to celebrate them, to crave even more.

This was not the country he had thought it was when he arrived. Its constitution was not the flawless and omnipotent document he had once imagined it to be. America was still a great nation, though. He believed that. He'd tell his children there was nowhere he'd rather live. Besides, he'd say, "Where else am I going to go? America is the only home I have."

THE AGENT CALLS HIM back to the desk. "Here you go, sir. I apologize for the delay."

She hands him his passport and his boarding pass. There will be no further questions. There will be no extra screening. He doesn't know why she couldn't print his boarding pass at first. Perhaps it was a clerical error. Perhaps it had something to do with the fact that his passport marks him as an American citizen but lists Syria as his place of birth. This is the confusion he carries through a world that often views him with suspicion. It can be hard to tell the difference between coincidence and malice, between an act of discrimination and a simple mistake.

He boards the plane. In his seat, awaiting takeoff, he prays, his fourth of the five for today. Soon the engine rumbles, and the plane soars over the eastern United States, over the Atlantic Ocean, over Britain, into France. He lands in Paris. He exits the plane, into the gorgeous and byzantine terminals of Charles de Gaulle International Airport, then boards another, smaller plane.

Riyad is tired. His black hair is matted, greasy, and flat. He's been in transit for about fifteen hours, excited about this trip for several days. But when he walks off the plane and through the terminal, through the baggage claim, then out the door into the waiting area, there he sees them: two little girls, their hair black and eyes big, both holding bouquets of flowers. They rush to Riyad, hand him their bouquets, then throw their arms around him. He leans down and hugs them and kisses their cheeks, and he laughs, and they laugh too. He stands back up and takes a couple more steps, then wraps his arms around a man whose body is sturdier and hair grayer than Riyad's own, whose smile is more subdued but carries the same joy.

"Salaam alaikum."

"Alaikum salaam."

It is so very good to see Bashar.

After they arrived on the beach in Greece, after they convinced Jenan and Wajid that the large boat that came for them was far safer than the small raft they had taken from Turkey, Bashar and his family rode to Athens. On the boat, they were fingerprinted, photographed, and registered with the UN High Commissioner for Refugees, the organization that works with governments to place refugees in new homes.

In Athens, they found a hotel. They planned to stay there for a few days, checking in with UNHCR before continuing their journey. For months now refugees had been following the same path—from Turkey across the sea into Greece, and then by land from Greece toward northern Europe, passing through Macedonia, Serbia, Hungary, Austria, and then into Germany and perhaps on to Scandinavia or France. Refugees traveled alongside migrants, people from the Middle East and Africa who were not fleeing war but rather traveling to Europe in search of economic opportunity. More than a million migrants and refugees sought asylum in Europe in 2015. By March 2016, when Bashar's family arrived in Greece, European political leaders and news media had become consumed by debate over how best to approach the continent's so-called migrant crisis. Some countries—Germany, Austria, Sweden—opened their arms and their borders, granting asylum by the hundreds of thousands. Others— Italy, Ireland, the United Kingdom—granted asylum to relatively few applicants. In all European countries, debate raged for months; some argued that it was Europe's responsibility to offer shelter to those fleeing war, while others insisted that the refugees and migrants were changing the fabric of European society, bringing a culture that didn't belong in their own neighborhoods and schools.

Three days after they arrived in Greece, the border to Macedonia closed completely. Refugees who tried to cross were rounded up and returned. So instead of continuing their journey, Bashar and Aisha had no choice but to remain in Athens. They could not afford to stay any longer in a hotel, and so they moved to an abandoned school building where a nongovernmental organization was housing people like themselves. They stayed there for weeks, sleeping on the floor of a classroom alongside several other families. Aisha kept her head covered, all day and all night, maintaining modesty in a place with no privacy. Bashar talked with agency workers and volunteers, telling their story, showing their documents that proved they were not lying when they said they came from Raqqa, now one of the most dangerous places on earth.

"Come," Bashar says, and Riyad follows.

He hands Riyad a train ticket. One of Bashar's first tasks upon arrival in Germany was to master the public transit system. Now he has their hour-long journey to his home completely mapped. They ride together from Hannover Flughafen to Hannover-Nordstadt, where they switch to another train, which takes them to the town of Seelze, where they wait for a bus, which takes them to the neighborhood of Lohnde, where they get out and begin to walk.

They head down a busy street, passed by Volkswagens and BMWs and Audis, row after row of small cottage homes lining either side. They turn left, off the main drag, then right, deeper into a quiet neighborhood, and then they see a little boy, and he sees them and he starts running.

"Abdul-Rahman!"

He is giggling as he runs, all the way down the block, Aisha walking close behind him. He runs all the way to Riyad, then stops and stares upward. He's never met his uncle before. He is three years old, born more than a year after Riyad's visit to Raqqa. But he's heard the stories. He knows exactly who this is. Riyad scoops him up into his arms, and Abdul-Rahman buries his face in Riyad's chest, laughing. Riyad puts him back down and studies him for a minute. He has exuberant brown eyes and long dark hair, so long that he can be mistaken at times for a little girl. But Riyad sees something different.

"Abood!" he says. "Abood the surfer dude!"

Riyad greets Aisha, and she is beaming. "Welcome," she says.

All together, they walk down the street, then stop at a small house. They open a side door and go up the stairs to the apartment they've made their home.

It has been two years since they crossed the sea. The wait in Greece was long, but it had its moments. The girls ran around the schoolhouse where their family slept, playing with children from all across the world, a joy in their faces that Bashar and Aisha had rarely seen. One day a volunteer who had taken a liking to Jenan asked to meet her parents, and the woman gave Aisha and Bashar a key to her house so they could come over to take a hot shower anytime they liked.

Another afternoon Aisha walked down the street in Athens with all three children, and a Greek woman stopped her and grabbed her by the arm. She took Aisha's hand and put five euros in her palm, and then she kept walking, saying nothing.

Aisha felt tears well. Was it possible to feel staggering gratitude and embarrassment at the same time? She couldn't believe that her life had brought her here, that she and her family were now accepting assistance from others. There remained a sense of tribal shame in taking on the role of the receiver, and yet at the same time, here she was, crying at the gift of five euros. She called to the woman, thanking her as she walked away.

They had stayed in Greece for eight months, waiting to be processed, and then one day they were told they'd be resettled in Portugal. They moved to a small town there in November 2016, where they were housed in a church. The Portuguese government had a policy of giving each refugee a stipend of 150 euros a month, as well as regular language classes, but the program was rife with mismanagement, and Bashar and Aisha felt cut off from Portuguese society, with no idea how to begin to build a life there. They decided to try somewhere else. They heard that they could arrive in Germany and go to any police station, and when they showed the officers their IDs, they would be taken directly to a refugee camp.

It was there, in that refugee camp in the town of Bad Fallingbostel, that Aisha felt for the first time that she was being treated as a full human being. She had received compassion in other places—on the beach in Greece, among the volunteers in Athens, even by neighbors in Portugal—but in all these places, she had also felt like an object of pity. To the German workers, she was more than her suffering. She was her ideas and her emotions, her ambitions and even her flaws. She knew right then that she wanted to stay there. This is where they would begin again. They would learn a new language and delight in a new culture; they would raise their children and call this country home.

THE APARTMENT IS SMALL. Three bedrooms, one bathroom, a cozy kitchen, and a living room with a dining area off to the side. The whole thing could fit inside one wing of their family home back in Raqqa. But it is clean, quiet, and safe. Bashar asks if Riyad wants some tea, and yes, of course he wants some tea, and so Bashar pours them cups, each with a pinch of sugar, and they stir and they sip and they talk.

Riyad is here just to visit, to play with his nephew and nieces, to take a tour through his brother's new life. It is so much unlike the last time he saw his brother, five years ago, when he showed up unannounced to beg his family to leave Raqqa. And so much unlike the time before that, when he brought his *yahba*'s body home, or before that, when Bashar left the apartment they shared in California, soon to be deported by the United States. Now there is no pressing matter, no weight hanging over them both. The time feels decadent.

"What should we do?" Riyad asks his brother the next morning, after sleeping off his jet lag.

Bashar thinks for a moment. "Do you want to see the city?"

Riyad does. They head back to the bus and then to the train, and soon they are in Hannover's Old Town, walking past its opera house and its modern art museum, its beer halls and cafés. Sitting among the shops and squares are a few storefronts with signs in Arabic, restaurants selling falafel and hummus next to markets selling Syrian spices. The streets are dotted with brown faces, and as Riyad and Bashar walk past strangers, they pick out a range of Arabic dialects, from Saudi to Tunisian, Damascene and Aleppan, and every once in a while, they hear the accent of the desert, the voice of their home.

A country of 83 million, Germany now hosts 1.4 million refugees, three times more than the European country with the second-highest number, France. The sudden influx has spurred a rise in far-right politics, with the anti-immigrant Alternative for Germany Party entering parliament for the first time in 2017.

Bashar, though, will not hear a single negative word about Germany. "I don't care," he says when Riyad brings up the far-right politicians. "It doesn't matter what a few people say or think. This country has welcomed us."

Bashar's family has only provisional status here in Germany. While the country debates refugees' place in its society, their family's case remains in the courts for review. Bashar and Aisha spend much of each day in German-language classes. They receive a stipend from the government, enough to cover their living expenses, and their girls, now eight and seven years old, are already practically fluent in German, spending all day in German schools. Bashar and Aisha are proud, but they get jealous, sometimes, of how quickly their daughters have learned the language. What a gift, to still have such a young and malleable mind.

Abdul-Rahman can't wait to join them. At three and a half years old, he's still more than a year from kindergarten, and he spends all day speaking Arabic in their home. Sometimes he asks his sisters to translate for him when he's running around outside. Can they go knock on the neighbor boy's door? Can they tell him in German that Abdul-Rahman wants to play?

When they speak to one another at home, most of the family still carries the desert dialect.

"Never lose it," Riyad tells his nieces. "It's the most beautiful dialect in the world."

Abdul-Rahman, though, sounds different from the rest of his family. He's spent most of his life in Greece and Portugal and Germany. He's learned to speak not only from his parents and sisters but also from the cartoons he watches, where all of the voices are in Classical Arabic, the formal dialect used on television so it can be understood by people from Morocco to Qatar and all places in between.

Riyad has to stifle laughter every time he hears Abdul-Rahman asking for juice boxes and for cartoons and for a few more minutes to play before bedtime. It is, he says, as if a toddler born to rural Tennessee parents with thick country accents marched around the house speaking with the accent of the queen.

AFTER A DAY EXPLORING the city, they return home in the evening. The air is cool, the evening quiet. A few children ride bicycles past them, and they wave. Riyad is happy to see his brother here, comfortable and safe, but something has been gnawing at him.

"You should come to America," he says.

Bashar laughs. "I already tried that."

If Bashar had stayed in America, he wouldn't be married to Aisha, and Jenan, Wajid, and Abdul-Rahman would not exist in this world. Today, though, Riyad aches to bring their whole family back to Tennessee with him. His restaurant is thriving. New opportunities are arising. He's been talking with investors about opening a second location in the heart of Nashville. He's just purchased a food truck and is ready to spend the spring and summer serving some of the restaurant's lighter dishes all over Middle Tennessee. He's going to call it Rakka & Roll.

"I'll put you to work right away," Riyad says. "Aisha too."

Bashar smiles.

"And as soon as those kids are old enough, we'll put them in food trucks too."

Bashar puts his hand on his brother's shoulder. "We're not leaving Germany," he says.

Bashar still carries a fondness for the United States. He harbors little resentment toward the country for how it responded to 9/11; no country on earth, he believes, is immune to the ugliness of its own fears. As of right now, though, the U.S. government isn't exactly inviting Bashar and his family to come. The year 2018 will end with the United States admitting the fewest number of refugees in forty years, about twenty-two thousand overall but only *sixty-two* from Syria, owing largely to the Trump administration's efforts to ban arrivals from that and several other Muslim-majority countries.

Besides, for Bashar, Germany will always be the country that offered his family acceptance when they were at their most desperate. It will always be the place he remembers extending welcome when they could find none. Now he delights in listening to his daughters go back and forth with each other in their new language. He can't wait until he's able to speak it as well as they do. He can't wait to start working, to participate more fully in the life of his new country. He remains anxious about his provisional status, fearful that the political climate might push judges to refuse his family full asylum. But he is hopeful. For him, Germany is what Riyad has long believed the United States to be: the kind of place Ronald Reagan once called the "shining city upon a hill."

THERE IS, OF COURSE, another place they could go. Raqqa. Wajid has said she's jealous of her parents because they can remember their country. The older she gets, the more her memories of Raqqa slip away. She and Jenan both still ask about the stuffed worm their grandmother gave them, Duda. They ask if it's still in their house. They ask if it's okay. They scroll through photos of their old life and say they wish they could step inside the screen, imagining their parents' phones as portals, taking them back to a life they left behind.

"I like Germany," Wajid told her mother once. "But it's not my home. Someday I want to go back to my home."

Aisha didn't have the heart to tell her that most of Raqqa is no longer standing. Germany is the only home she has.

The battle to take Raqqa from Daesh began on June 6, 2017, more than eighteen months after Bashar and Aisha left. It started with a heavy round of air strikes by the American air force, then continued with the deployment of ground troops from the Syrian Democratic Forces—a mostly Kurdish and Arab group that the Americans supported in fighting Daesh, though not in fighting the Assad regime. That fight continued for four months with the same rhythm, the Americans bombing from the air, the SDF gaining further control on the ground. By September 1, the SDF had captured most of Raqqa's old city, including the neighborhood where the Alkasem family lived.

In October, Raqqa fell. Again. This time, though, it was Daesh that relinquished control. The terrorists were gone, but so was much of Raqqa itself. At least fifteen hundred civilians were killed in the fight, though most of Raqqa's residents had long ago left the city. The UN estimated that 80 percent of Raqqa was now uninhabitable.

Bashar received a text from an old neighbor several months after the fight ended. The neighbor had filmed a walk through the Alkasem home. In the video, the front door where Riyad had knocked the night he returned was now blown completely open. The courtyard where Bashar had sipped tea after bombings was now littered with detritus—doors off their hinges, furniture blown to pieces, pots and pans scattered around outside. The kitchen where Riyad had devoured his mother's cooking had imploded into itself, floor tiles dislodged, the sink on the ground. The cabinets where Abood had hidden during bombings had spilled their guts all over the room.

Bashar's library was ravaged. The bedroom that Aisha had tidied the morning she left was strewn with debris. A building next door, seen through a window, had completely collapsed. Inside the bedrooms, there was no sign of Jenan and Wajid's dolls or their stuffed worm.

It had been easy, for a long time after they left, to imagine a day when they would return to Raqqa. Perhaps the rest of their family would filter back from their various corners of the world. Perhaps Riyad would bring Linda and even his boys, Kasem and Sammy. Riyad and his *mama* would work together in their family's kitchen, preparing an afternoon feast. Linda and her sons would dote on Aisha and Bashar's children, burying them in toys they'd brought, filling their bellies with American candies they'd never tasted. Aisha would move from room to room, making certain the house was in order. Bashar would check in on every single member of the family until he knew that everyone was well and content.

Maybe they would eat in the kitchen all packed together, or maybe they would spread out across the den. Afterward they would make coffee, and of course tea, and they'd move outside to the courtyard, dropping pinches of sugar into every cup. Maybe when their food settled, they would walk down the street, down the hill toward the river. They would cross the Old Bridge and pass the French military outpost. They would descend the banks of the Euphrates, then swim out to the point where their feet no longer touched the bottom, and for a few seconds just beyond. They would return and would not worry about how late it had gotten. Their *baba* would not be there to scold them. And besides, they would only cross the river with blood.

Afternoon would turn to evening, evening would bleed into night. Maybe they would return to the courtyard to stare at the stars, to see the work of their ancestors who'd mapped the sky; and sometime late, knowing that no bombing would wake them, they would drift away to sleep.

That's what they used to be able to imagine. But now that they had seen what became of Raqqa, they could imagine it no more.

———

ONE EVENING BASHAR AND RIYAD come home, the lights off and the apartment quiet. They continue down the hallway, where they see light coming from the den, and they walk in.

"Surprise!"

Abdul-Rahman has his arms in the air, shouting. Jenan and Wajid are both wearing party hats, jumping up and down. Aisha is standing at the far end of the room, standing over a table full of bread and salad and rice, silverware and paper napkins set in front of every chair. In the center, there sits a chocolate cake, with two candles, one a five, the other a zero.

"Happy birthday!"

Riyad turned fifty almost a year ago. But now they are together, and so they will celebrate today. Riyad scans the room. He wears a black Under Armour hoodie and jeans, his curly hair buzzed, his smile bursting. Party decorations hang from the ceiling, a red-and-white-tissue-paper garland with the number 50 hanging below.

"Why did you do this?" he asks.

"Happy birthday, brother," Bashar says.

They sit. They eat. At the center of the table is a card, written in German, and Wajid picks it up and reads it aloud, her big sister helping over her shoulder. Then Riyad stands to blow out the candles, and soon they are cutting and passing around cake, the girls devouring the pieces before them, Abood smearing chocolate all over his face. They do not know when or where they will next see one another. But the room fills with the clinking of dishes and the sounds of excited chatter. Riyad and Bashar sit on opposite sides of the table, and both are laughing, Bashar calmly and gently, Riyad big and loud. Tonight the others will go to bed, and the two of them will sit and sip tea and talk around this table in this tiny German apartment for hours and hours until sleep calls them, and then Riyad will wake and rise and fly across the ocean to his home.

They say there is something different about the wind in Raqqa. That it starts on the river and lifts across the desert, pouring down the streets of the Old City, into squares and private courtyards, always carrying the season's scent. In the spring, it holds the smell of the desert's wildflowers, sweet and pungent and warning of the heat to come. In summer, when the sun threatens to obliterate the world beneath it, the wind carries only the odor of sweat and perhaps the faintest smell of sand. But then the fall arrives with the first rain of the season, and that's when you really smell the soil, when the raindrops pelt the earth and send it whipping through the city on the breeze, and that is when the wind most seems to dance, as if celebrating that summer has ended and relief has arrived.

Without that wind from the Euphrates, maybe no one ever would have smelled the coffee brewed by Taha, all those centuries ago. Maybe if he'd picked another campsite in another stretch of desert, the smell of his coffee would have traveled nowhere and called to no one, and it would have been enjoyed by Taha alone.

The Alkasems' home was rubble. It became clearer every day that soon Assad would win the war. Their mosques and schools and tribe houses had collapsed. The work that began the moment Taha brewed that coffee was now, centuries later, almost completely undone. There remained, though, that patch of land, the community land, sitting just north of the Old City. It was the land owned by every male descendant of the original subtribes of Raqqa. Riyad still owned a piece. So did Bashar. So did Riyad's boys, Kasem and Sammy, even though they'd never been there, and so, too, did little Abood. The bombs could destroy whatever sat atop that land, the crops and the flowers that grew on those plots, but the earth itself would remain.

Raqqa's people were scattered, but not by the Euphrates wind. Riyad had been called by the fraught promise of another country. Bashar had been pushed by the brutal realities of his own. Now, though, they all hoped to further the traditions of their homeland in far-off places. In a strip mall in Tennessee, Riyad would continue to stand in a kitchen or a food truck and piece together the tastes of the desert. In a tiny apartment in Germany, Bashar hoped to open his door to those around him, to learn their language so he could invite them inside.

In both places, there would be coffee, thick and hot and bitter. This, Taha seemed to know, was how you built a new home. You found a place, and you settled there, and you made something that called to strangers, inviting them to join you. And so Riyad and Bashar would sit at their own tables, in their new countries, so many miles from the desert, both hoping that they held within them some of Raqqa's wind.

ACKNOWLEDGMENTS

In the fall of 2015, I was working as a staff writer at *Grantland* when my editor Rafe Bartholomew asked if I wanted to write about the Syrian refugee crisis. Over four years of editing my work, Rafe had become a dear friend and the person who understood my tics and tendencies and strengths and weaknesses as a writer better than anyone else on Earth. He knew that I liked to use sports as an excuse to write about the wider world, and so he pushed me to find a story on the Syria-Turkey border. In early 2016, after I'd made that initial trip and after *Grantland* was shuttered, Paul Kix, my editor at *ESPN: The Magazine,* encouraged me to return to the border and continue reporting, eventually giving a home to that piece on a Syrian refugee soccer team.

Those two trips served as my entry points into writing about Syria, its people, and its conflict. On them, so many people shared their stories, hospitality, and insights with me. Those people do not appear in this book, but without them, it would not exist. Thanks to Jassem al-Nuweiji, Jamil Abdullah, Omar Alkhani, Anas Ammo, Mohamad Ajouz, Ahmad Alshikhouni, and Erin Trieb. And special thanks to Ahmad Ajouz, who served as my translator and guide, and who remained a friend in the years to follow, reading and offering feedback on a draft of this book before its publication.

Back home in Tennessee, Rashed Fakhruddin of the Islamic Center of Nashville first encouraged me to contact Riyad, leading to the conversations mentioned in the author's note of this book. In November 2016, months after I had begun getting to know Riyad and his story, I asked my editors at *The Ringer*, Mallory Rubin and Sean Fennessey, if I could write a story about Riyad, tied to his experience of the 2016 presidential election. They responded the way they have so many times before and since, by encouraging and trusting me to pursue a story that they knew I was burning to tell, and by providing incisive and probing edits as they shepherded that story from its first draft to its final form. I owe them, along with Bill Simmons and so many others at *The Ringer*, deep gratitude for empowering me to do work that I love and for treating that work with so much respect and care.

My agent, William LoTurco, believed in this story from the first moment I mentioned it, and he championed it to publishers. I had two editors at Ballantine, both of whom provided the kind of guidance and direction of which writers dream. Brendan Vaughan helped me find the initial shape of the story, and Andra Miller helped me refine it. I can't imagine a version of this book that lacks the careful work they each brought to the page. Thanks to them, and to cover designer Robbin Schiff, production editor Loren Noveck, copy editor Janet Biehl, and the whole team at Ballantine.

Several books played a particularly critical role in helping to shape my understanding of Syria's history and its conflict. In particular: *No Turning Back: Life, Loss, and Hope in Wartime Syria* by Rania Abouzeid; *My House in Damascus: An Inside View of the Syrian Revolution* by Diana Darke; *The Master Plan: ISIS, al-Qaeda, and the Jihadi Strategy for Final Victory* by Brian H. Fishman; *From Beirut to Jerusalem* by Thomas Friedman; *The Home That Was Our Country: A Memoir of Syria* by Alia Malek; and *Black Flags: The Rise of ISIS* by Joby Warrick. Additionally, the work of a number of journalists informed my understanding of the situations in Syria and Turkey, including Thanassis Cambanis, Rukmini Callimachi, Medyan Dairieh, Mike Giglio, Ben Hubbard, Gabriel Mac, Liz Sly, Sonia Smith, and Robin Wright.

Over the three years I was working on this book, the staff at Café Rakka welcomed and fed me, night after night, as I sat in the back of the restaurant, talking with Riyad and calling Bashar.

So many teachers and mentors have helped to mold me as a writer and reporter, but none more so than three faculty members at the UC Berkeley Graduate School of Journalism: Lydia Chavez, Jennifer Kahn, and Chris Ballard. Throughout the process of this book, I relied on the encouragement and friendship of Elise Craig, Adam Garner, Ben Howard, and Jill and Drew Zimmer. My parents, Jeff and Anita Conn, fostered my love for reading and writing, and, much more important, taught me to have empathy and curiosity. My siblings, Elizabeth and Nathan Conn, have offered love and friendship and have broadened the way I see the world. My wife, Beth Ritter Conn, has loved me and supported me in more ways than I can express here. Among them: reading a draft of this book before anyone else laid eyes on it. Her storytelling instincts, her moral conviction, and her wells of religious expertise inform the texture of the book, from start to finish.

I owe Riyad and Bashar's families more gratitude than I can express. Linda, for her exuberant hospitality and her passion for telling her and her husband's story. Kasem and Sammy, for their kindness and warmth. Aisha, for welcoming me into her home on a trip to Germany, and for telling her family's story with a courage and fierceness that can be felt in every word she speaks. Jenan, Wajid, and Abood, for sharing their toys, their desserts, and their laughter. Those children are brilliant and fearless. It fills me with incredible joy to imagine the lives they will live.

And finally, I owe the deepest gratitude to Riyad and Bashar: for the untold hours they spent answering my questions, and for the many more hours they spent offering friendship and laughter. For their bravery, in living the lives that they've lived, and for their vulnerability, in sharing the pieces of themselves that they've shared. Telling their story has been among the great honors of my life.

ABOUT THE AUTHOR

JORDAN RITTER CONN is a staff writer for *The Ringer*. He previously worked at *Grantland* and *ESPN: The Magazine*, and he has written for *The New York Times* and *Sports Illustrated*. His work has been cited or recognized by *The New Yorker, The Atlantic, The New York Times, The Wall Street Journal*, and *Slate*.

jordanritterconn.com
Twitter: @jordanconn

ABOUT THE TYPE

This book was set in Caslon, a typeface first designed in 1722 by William Caslon (1692–1766). Its widespread use by most English printers in the early eighteenth century soon supplanted the Dutch typefaces that had formerly prevailed. The roman is considered a "workhorse" typeface due to its pleasant, open appearance, while the italic is exceedingly decorative.